RiskGrade® Your Investments

Measure Your Risk and Create Wealth

Gregory Elmiger
Steve S. Kim

John Wiley & Sons, Inc.

Library of Congress Cataloging-in-Publication Data:
Elmiger, Gregory.
    RiskGrade your investments : measure your risk and create wealth / Gregory Elmiger.
       p.   cm.
    Includes index.
    ISBN 0-471-41861-7 (cloth : alk. paper)
       1. Investments.   2. Risk management.   I. Title: Risk grade your investments.   II.
Title.

HG4521 .B4393   2001
658.15'5—dc21   2001026959

Printed in the United States of America.

10 9 8 7 6 5 4 3 2 1

RiskGrade® Your Investments

Acknowledgments

Thanks to everyone at RiskMetrics for the valuable feedback and contributions, in particular, Ethan Berman, Alan Laubsch, Alvin Lee, Chris Carey, Nitzan Melamed, Alan Fang, Theresa Galli, and Marty Nemeth. And special thanks to Melanie Elmiger and the efforts of our editor, Bill Falloon, who helped us to develop and shape the book from its beginning.

Contents

RiskGrade® Your Investments

Introduction

Ethan Berman
CEO, RiskMetrics Group

The question started only weeks after I got my first job on Wall Street. Family, friends, anyone I met in a social gathering, all asked the same thing: "So, Ethan, what should I do with my money?"

At first I laughed and shrugged it off as a way to congratulate me for finally finding a job. But the question continued. "Seriously, Ethan, I have a little cash around and could use a hot tip or two."

I had worked on the trading floor of J.P. Morgan for all of three weeks, armed only with a college degree in theater arts and psychology, and the whole world it seemed was looking for me to tell them how they could convert their small savings into vast riches. Everyone was looking for an edge, a way to get into the financial game. And I had Wall Street on my business card.

Over the next decade, I spent my days investing literally trillions of J.P. Morgan dollars in various assets all over the world. I was fortunate to work with some of the world's best and most famous traders. And in 1998 I founded a company, RiskMetrics, that today provides investment tools to hundreds of leading financial institutions, asset managers, and hedge funds throughout the world.

Although you might think these experiences would change my answer to these questions, it hasn't. Even today, I answer the question the same way I did three weeks after I started at J.P. Morgan: "I don't know."

That is not to say that I didn't learn anything about investing in my years on Wall Street. Or that I can't help you or anyone else looking to invest your money. In fact, quite the contrary. My 15 years on Wall Street have taught me valuable lessons about the markets and what it takes to be a successful investor. I learned about bids and offers, technical retracements, momentum investing, and "bear traps." I learned how to create an intelligent portfolio, to choose among assets, to rebalance, and to ride my profits and cut my losses. However, what it didn't teach me about is *you*.

You see, despite what you might be led to believe, there is no investment or series of investments that is right for everybody. There is no fund, no stock, no tax-deferred annuity that is perfect for every investor. That's what makes markets and drives the creation of new products and services. Optimal investments and portfolios have to be tailored to each of us, reflecting our own financial situation, our own expectations, and our own risk tolerance. It is only with a full understanding of an individual's needs that can one give sound financial advice.

The point of this book, the product RiskGrades, and in fact the company RiskMetrics, is to help *you* to decide what you should do with your money. We don't prescribe the answer. As they say on Wall Street, "If I knew a surefire way to make money, I wouldn't be here talking to you." We don't believe in trading strategies or complex mathematical models that guarantee superior returns. We have watched the Nobel laureates fall and the Internet bubble burst. Instead, we believe in a few basic principles that we have found in every successful investor, trader, financial advisor, and asset manager. These same five principles will be crucial in helping you be successful.

1. *Defining your objectives.* Different people have different financial objectives. Day traders are trying to make short-term profits while limiting their losses. Recent college graduates are often saving for their future. Young couples are planning for a first home or their children's education. Retirees are trying to maintain their standard of living. Understanding why you are investing and what you are trying to get out of it ("becoming rich" is not a good objective) is crucial to becoming successful at it.

2. *Discipline.* Several years after I started trading at J.P. Morgan, a friend of mine asked me what it took to be a successful investor. He was getting his Ph.D. at the time, and I'm sure that he was expecting me to comment on how smart and intelligent the top traders on Wall Street were. After all, they were making decisions on vast amounts of

other people's money. Although many very smart people work on Wall Street, the distinguishing characteristic of great investors is not their intelligence but their discipline. Markets become volatile, people become emotional, new stories come out every day, but the great investors remain disciplined and focused throughout. The more you are able to keep a disciplined approach to your investing, to stay calm through emotional times, and to avoid the fad of the moment, the more successful you will be in the long run.

3. *Understanding.* This works in two ways. The more you understand about the investments you are making, the more successful those investments will be over time. Everyone has heard a story about some hot tip received by a friend who then bought a stock or fund he or she knew nothing about that immediately skyrocketed, but it is rare that those tips don't eventually fall back to earth. Investing is a serious business. If you don't understand it, invest the time to learn. Or get help from a professional who does understand it. And make sure that the professional has a credible track record as well as a thorough understanding of you and your needs.

   It is also important to know what you don't know. Even with all the learning in the world, even with the help of the best financial advisor, it is impossible to understand everything. Investing is not a perfect science. There are no correct answers to be found even after years of research. In fact, we would argue it is more of an art, with a number of scientific tools to help you make better judgments. Only through realizing what you don't know—about a company you are investing in, about the direction of interest rates, or about the overall economy—can you make sound investment decisions.

4. *Diversification.* We have all heard from a very early age, "Don't put all your eggs in one basket." Throughout this book you will hear it again and again. (In fact, Chapter 7 is dedicated to the topic.) Technology and growth stocks may be hot one year, perhaps the next year energy and commodities or fixed income, but no one can (or should even try to) pick the hot assets each and every week, month, or year. Diversify your investments over several categories that are best suited to your objectives. Over the long term, a well-diversified portfolio will always outperform a group of investments concentrated in one area, country, sector, or asset class.

5. *Risk.* While a huge amount of time is spent talking about return, few investors talk about risk, and even fewer properly factor risk into their investment decisions. Funds advertise their long-term returns and often have a graph showing how much money you would have if only you had invested $10,000 in the fund five years earlier. Every year there are countless write-ups of the top-returning stocks, bonds, and commodities. Yet from all that information, the one assumption you can make is that none of those funds, stocks, or bonds will be the top-returning ones in the following year. Check it yourself. No fund, stock, or commodity has been a top performer two years in a row.

What all those lists and charts lack is a measurement of risk. As we like to say, "Return is only half the equation." No decision, whether it be about finance, family, or any other activity, can be made without considering both the reward and the risk of the possible outcomes. While we are inundated with amazing detail about the returns of various investments (e.g., "this fund is up 38.23 percent in the past 52 weeks"), the best we can get on risk is "aggressive" or "balanced" or "three stars." It is crucial for any successful investment decision that the risk be fully understood.

These five principles in 1990 guided Sir Dennis Weatherstone, now the retired chairman of J.P. Morgan, to organize a team of traders, managers, and Ph.D.s to develop a system that would enable him to better understand the risk of his firm. Four years later, in answer to Weatherstone's request, J.P. Morgan launched RiskMetrics and made the substantive research and analysis freely available to all market participants. J.P. Morgan did so to promote greater transparency of market risks, to establish a benchmark for market risk measurement, and to aid clients in understanding and evaluating advice on managing their market exposures.

RiskMetrics educated a global marketplace and gave institutions around the world the tools to make better, more informed investment decisions. RiskMetrics quickly became the standard approach for professionals to manage and measure their financial investments.

For four years I managed the RiskMetrics group at J.P. Morgan and was responsible for working with J.P. Morgan clients to improve their risk understanding and investment process. We worked with banks, regulators, multinational corporations, and money managers. We also invested significant resources in researching and developing new techniques for ever evolving financial markets. Given the tremendous demand for our services, in 1998 we decided to spin off the group from J.P. Morgan and set up RiskMetrics as a separate company, devoted solely to helping institutions around the world make better investment decisions. J.P. Morgan and Reuters, the world's largest financial information providers, funded the venture and remain today our largest shareholders.

One of our first clients was Long-Term Capital Management, a hedge fund that hired us shortly after its well-documented problems in the fall of 1998. Since that time we have added hundreds of new clients, including most of the so-called bulge bracket Wall Street firms, many of the Fortune 500, and over half of the world's central banks. We have published countless papers on financial assets, taught thousands of professionals about portfolio management, and developed new techniques for various markets, including credit and 401(k) plans. Today we distribute valuable information and analytics on over 150,000 different financial instruments every day. And we have added American Express, Deutsche Bank, Intel, Procter & Gamble, and Sony as strategic shareholders to expand our reach to a broader audience of market participants.

However, the reason for this book is not to discuss the history or growth of RiskMetrics. That is all background to the real story here. The real story is *you*, the newly empowered individual investor. Over the past decade there has been a dramatic change in the world of personal finance. Individuals like you and me all around the world have become more responsible for our own investment decisions. Gone are the days when governments or employers micromanaged our long-term finances and pensions. Because we all are living longer, our current and future financial investments will have a significant impact on our increasingly longer retirement lives. The success of these investments will eventually determine the standard of living we will have in the future. The good news is that technology offers all of us far greater access to information and understanding than ever before. As our financial decisions are becoming more important, technology is giving us more tools to act smarter.

It is precisely these three trends that led us at RiskMetrics to develop RiskGrades. RiskGrades are based on the same research we provide for the most sophisticated money managers and financial institutions, but are designed for use by individual investors or financial planners. Like the launch of RiskMetrics in 1994, RiskGrades aim to promote greater transparency of investment risks, to establish a standard for investment risk measurement, and to provide individuals with the tools and the discipline to become successful investors.

CNBC talks of "democratizing the markets," as individuals are given access to the same tools and information that the professionals use. The Securities and Exchange Commission (SEC) is requiring companies to disclose all pertinent data to all market participants simultaneously, no longer allowing Wall Street analysts first call on inside information. And freely available websites provide real-time data and news on investment opportunities around the world. Although we at RiskMetrics are proud of our tools and our data and work hard to keep them as the industry standard, we don't believe that the tools themselves are what make RiskGrades so valuable. Technology changes, graphs become more colorful, data is delivered even faster. But the basic tenets of successful investing remain the same. When you visit the RiskGrades website, www.riskgrades.com or use the RiskGrades functionality through your financial advisor or broker, you are accessing countless years of research and development by many of the smartest thinkers on Wall Street. But don't ooh and aah over the tools and charts—study the principles. Learn the thinking behind the data. Take the online course. And, of course, read this book. No one ever said investing was easy. If it were, there wouldn't be as much opportunity for those individual investors committed to doing it the right way—with an eye on *both* risk and return.

RiskMetrics and I are committed to teaching every investor out there what we have learned (and continue to learn) in our many years as professional investors. RiskGrades is not a tool but a service. A service to support each of you as you have chosen (or have been forced) to be more responsible for your own investment decisions.

I hope that this book begins to answer the question that marked the beginning of my career on Wall Street. I hope that our website and the financial advisors who use our tools provide you with more answers. These are not easy questions for anyone, even the professionals. There is no formula or magic bullet to tell you or anyone else what you should do. However, it is often said on Wall Street that markets are driven by fear and greed. The past few years, more than any in recent history, show that to be true. If you can learn to replace these two emotions with the five principles of Sir Dennis Weatherstone, and now RiskGrades, you will be well on your way to becoming a successful investor.

CHAPTER 1

Answer One Question

Here's one of the most important personal finance questions you'll ever be asked: How risky is your investment portfolio?

Quick. What's your answer? Very risky? Sort of risky? Not very risky?

No matter what kind of investor you are, it's likely you won't be able to answer this absolutely critical question with any degree of accuracy. Were you one of the lucky ones who avoided the implosion of the technology sector? Or does your portfolio contain a few technology stocks that are down 50 percent from their highs, or worse? What is the likelihood they will recover? What is the likelihood they will plummet even further?

Or maybe you're a conservative investor who, with the assistance of a financial advisor, has developed a set of financial goals and carefully allocated assets to stocks, bonds, and money markets. How much is your portfolio expected to drop in the next big market shock? How diversified is it really? And what is the probability that you'll actually reach those carefully conceived investment goals? It doesn't matter whether we're conservative investors, wild speculators, or something in between. When it comes to analyzing risk, most of us need to admit to ourselves that we don't know the answers.

Conversely, when it comes to the subject of returns, it seems we're all experts. The Internet has blessed us with enormous new resources that allow us to investigate returns at a level of granularity previously available to only the most sophisticated Wall Street institutional investor. Times have changed. Investors now have access to a myriad of research and investment sites from around the world. With the help of powerful search engines, we can study comprehensive sets of information effortlessly by asset class, geographic region, sector, rating, issuer, issue, and more.

This sort of access to information has done a great deal to level the playing field for individual investors. But even if we can compare returns down to the decimal point, many of us lack a basic understanding of how to compare the risk of one asset against another. We intuitively know that Cisco Systems is riskier than a U.S. Treasury bond, but by how much? Ten times? A hundred times? We may buy one mutual fund over another based on its return, but we don't stop and consider the additional risk the fund manager took to get those higher returns. Truth is, most of us are just as much in the dark about risk and diversifying our portfolios today as we were 10 years ago. We may add a new stock or a mutual fund to our portfolio in the hope of reducing our risk, but we don't really know how much diversification we've actually achieved.

What's an investor to do? The answer is, keep reading. Whether you manage your own investments or collaborate with an investment advisor, this book will help you meet your long-term financial objectives by providing you with resources to understand and manage the risks along the way. We'll help you become a competent investor by teaching you how to employ the basic principles of investing to overcome the market risks that stand between you and a financially secure future. We start by explaining the fundamentals of risk and introducing you to a new series of smart tools necessary to manage your investment portfolio, including the mechanics of portfolio risk, diversification, and returns. After reading this book, you will be able to understand the relationship between risk and opportunity, identify and measure your portfolio's exposure to risk, create an investment portfolio that matches your tolerance for risk, and manage your portfolio's risk on an ongoing basis.

And that's just the beginning. It needs to be. Because to really acquire a mastery of managing risk and creating wealth, it's not sufficient to simply read a book, this one included. No matter how good it is, the transfer of knowledge will not be complete. Learning is an ongoing process. To be truly effective, learning must occur progressively and provide trial-and-error experiences, offer multiple presentations of similar content, and feature creative techniques to reinforce learning over time. To acquire the investment skills we write about in *RiskGrade Your Investments,* you will need to take control of the concepts and practice. Learning to apply these skills also requires frequent interaction. Throughout the book we reinforce the material we present with pertinent examples and references to RiskGrades, a methodology developed by the RiskMetrics Group for measuring risk. RiskGrades is the featured component, or chassis, in the company's retail risk management platform, also aptly named RiskGrades.

A RiskGrade is an accurate and timely measure used by investors to evaluate the risk of individual securities and their portfolios on a daily basis. RiskGrades is the language for understanding volatility across all asset classes, regions, and currencies. It is founded on the very same principles as value-at-risk (VaR), the accepted risk measurement standard among Wall Street institutions. In fact, the RiskMetrics Group, while still at J.P. Morgan, introduced the idea of VaR in 1994. RiskGrades is simply a VaR calculation with a user-friendly face on it. What separates RiskGrades from VaR and other available measures is its ability to translate financial risk into a simple, easy-to-use format.

The RiskGrade measurement came into being as a result of our own preoccupation with measuring risk in the financial markets. In May 2000, RiskMetrics became the first Wall Street firm to launch a freely available, comprehensive, risk analysis website: RiskGrades (www.riskgrades.com). The impetus for RiskGrades was simple. We wanted to remind the world at large that all investments have some degree of risk associated with them. At the time, it was a lesson temporarily forgotten. The RiskGrades site was first and foremost a site designed to help investors and advisors understand the nature of risk and how to measure it. We reasoned that if we could help individuals and advisors to measure risk, then they could use the information to become smarter, more confident investors.

Unlike most financial websites being launched at the time, we refrained from adopting a fanciful website name (although www.silverback .com was briefly mentioned). We decided early on to make all of our content free, and we even declined a few solicitations to place advertisements on the site. With no marketing studies or business models to constrain us, a dozen or so RiskMetrics' employees dropped everything and committed all expendable energies to rigorously back-test our research, build the analytical tools, and create the website. Without any service remotely comparable to RiskGrades on the Web, we pondered the question, if we built it, would they come? After all, the idea to develop RiskGrades was conceived and green-lighted in the midst of the greatest bull market the world has ever seen. From August 1982 through March 2000, the S&P 500 Index returned an incredible 19.8 percent a year, according to Ibbotson Associates. With reference to the Rule of 72 (discussed in Chapter 8), this means that if your portfolio performed as well as the market, your money would double every three and a half years. With those types of returns available, calculating risk was not the foremost thought on peoples' minds.

Then, on April 4, 2001, a month and half prior to launch, both the Dow and the Nasdaq dropped roughly 500 points in intraday trading. Fortunately for investors, the market rebounded to finish the day with only modest losses. However, this date marked the beginning of the end for the bull market and set in motion an extremely volatile period in which Nasdaq would fall 23 percent by the time the RiskGrades website launched on May 23. The impact of tumbling markets on the demand for the site was felt immediately. Word-of-mouth referrals and positive reviews by the media fueled an even greater demand. The traffic on the site exceeded our most optimistic expectations.

In just two years, the RiskGrades website has been translated into seven languages and has registered more than 80,000 households from all 50 states and 168 countries around the world. More than 23 financial institutions, including J.P. Morgan, Merrill Lynch, American Express, Ameritrade, Bear Stearns, Deutsche Bank, Harrisdirect, and Intesa, are commercially distributing the service to their clients. In addition to financial firms, numerous financial portals provide RiskGrades data to their online audiences, including Reuters and Briefing.com. In the media, RiskGrades analysis has been featured by the *Wall Street Journal*, *New York Times*, *Business Week*, *Financial Times*, *Time* magazine, *Money* magazine, CNBC, and CNNfn. In June 2002, Forbes designated RiskGrades the "Best Asset Allocation site" on the Web. Needless to say, it's been a gratifying experience to see so many notable publications and journalists come to rely on RiskGrades to help readers make more informed investment decisions.

Buoyed by this success, our ceaseless fixation into the discipline of measuring risk and managing wealth led us to develop what we believe is a groundbreaking wealth management platform driven by what we call "the four pillars of personal finance"—multigoal planning, asset selection, managing risk and return, and developing efficient tax strategies. This soon-to-be-released platform, called WealthBench (the next-generation RiskGrades site), is designed to help investment advisors navigate their clients through the uncertainty of the financial markets with an integrated suite of sophisticated investment planning, portfolio construction, risk management, and portfolio monitoring tools. For more information on WealthBench, we invite advisors to visit www.wealthbench.com and register for a free trial offer.

For everyone else, if you haven't already registered for a free subscription to RiskGrades at www.riskgrades.com and entered your own personal portfolio, we invite you to do so now. Throughout the book, you will be learning more about portfolio construction, measuring and managing risk, and of course, RiskGrades. The model portfolios we present as examples are fine, but they will never replace the relevance of your own portfolio. Use this opportunity to humanize the science of wealth management by learning more about its methodology and values as they relate to your own personal portfolio.

This blended approach to learning is the key principle behind the RiskMetrics Group's own educational model and the reason you'll find this book so unique. At any point during your reading, you can practice your pre- and early wealth management skills in a structured online format, building on each new cognitive experience as it's presented in the book. *RiskGrade Your Investments* is one of the few personal finance books that includes this type of parallel online destination where readers can interact with advanced portfolio analytics, learn through discovery, and use their new skills in practical applications. We hope you take full advantage of it.

As for the book itself, *RiskGrade Your Investments* assumes a logical progression broken loosely into three parts. The first section introduces the notion of financial risk and highlights the growing implications of market risk in our everyday lives. We explore many topics that affect the face of investing, including the impact of new technology, the consequences of improved access to the markets, the rise of the 401(k) plan, and the ramifications of America's increasing life-expectancy rate. Contrary to popular opinion, we believe these advances have actually increased the likelihood that many investors will fall short of their retirement goals. We also examine investment behavior to understand the psychology behind investment decisions and identify a number of ill-advised habits that regularly afflict even the most experienced investor.

The second section of this book builds on what we learned in the first section and distills the basic tenets of modern portfolio theory into three chapters: asset allocation, diversification, and measuring risk. The chapters are intended to introduce readers to the fundamental building blocks of portfolio construction.

The second section begins with asset allocation. Because asset allocation is really risk allocation, our focus is on the relevancy of measuring risk in the asset selection process. We walk through the asset selection process and explain how the weighting you assign each asset class will be influenced by your long-term investment objectives and your tolerance for assuming risk. We explain the mechanics behind portfolio diversification, particularly how each element of a portfolio affects its overall risk. We demonstrate how correlation impacts portfolio risk and calculate the volatility of a portfolio using the RiskGrade measurement as well as other risk measures such as standard deviation and beta.

In the third and final section of the book we put all the concepts previously discussed into context. We do this by introducing readers to our own WealthBench software and demonstrating features that will help readers evaluate how risks are managed in their own portfolios. Our primary aim in these chapters is to encourage each reader to develop a thought process or framework that intertwines reason and risk; we want to encourage every individual to factor risk into broader-scale objectives. We demonstrate this thought process using real-life investment scenarios that will help you gain a better understanding of how a specific level of risk measurably translates into an expected level of return. Ultimately, seeing how fundamental risk management techniques can be applied in realistic investment scenarios will help you identify key risk-related issues to focus on in your own portfolios. These methods, combined with a healthy dose of discipline and reason, will help you make better investment decisions.

It's worth noting that the views expressed in this book are not solely those of the authors. Prior to writing this book we conducted a series of interviews and focus groups with selected advisors who are leaders, thinkers, and innovators in the investment advisory community. The viewpoints shared in the course of our discussions offer a variety of perspectives and insights into the world of wealth management. Not surprisingly, we found the depth, range, and background of each financial advisor unique. Some manage portfolios for and advise high-net-worth individuals, whereas others provide financial advice for those with average household incomes. Wealthier individuals naturally require a greater degree of watchful care, but the general approach to managing money—be it for a net worth of $100,000 or $50 million—ostensibly remains constant. Each client requires thoughtful investment analysis and advice tailored to his or her individual needs and goals. The advisors we spoke with help each client to carefully plan, frugally preserve, and appropriately harvest gains and losses in order to reach his or her long-term investment goals. With this in mind, we have included their viewpoints in the book to offer various perspectives on how your wealth can be managed with RiskGrades.

One final note: You will find that most of *RiskGrade Your Investments* focuses primarily on markets and trends in the United States, and the discussion dotes on equities and mutual funds. This is not due to any personal bias on our part, but a reflection of what we believe is most relevant for our readers. Still, the primary message, that risk management has to be an integral part of any investment strategy, transcends borders. Self-directed investing is charging full steam ahead in other parts of the world (even in areas where capital markets are not yet fully developed), from Europe to the Far East to Latin America. In fact, the stock market with the highest proportion of Internet trading is not, as you might think, in New York, but in Seoul. Accordingly, the principles of sound risk management are not only salient for U.S. investors; our central message is a global one.

CHAPTER 2

The Dilemma Facing Today's Investors

Before the days of computer networks, high-speed electronic transmissions, and the Internet, most investors monitored the performance of their portfolios quarterly as they received their brokerage statements in the mail. Back then, the closest an average investor could come to real-time pricing was to look up in the newspaper individual stock prices from the previous day's trading. Things have really changed. Today, optical networks deliver to the individual investor massive amounts of data at terabit speeds. It is no exaggeration that modern-day investors have virtually everything at their disposal and at their fingertips. Any piece of financial information, however profound or prosaic, can be found within minutes on any number of online links. From do-it-yourself trading tips to detailed research guides to general market commentaries, the electronic universe is filled with everything financial from A to Z. Other resources instrumental to making trading decisions, such as charting functionality and company-specific fundamentals, are also freely available on a host of financial Web page services.

High-speed transmission of data has become a primary driver in today's brave new world of personal finance. This free flow of information has replaced a guarded and opaque financial system that previously restricted widespread accessibility and kept the playing field imbalanced. Investment services now cater to every imaginable interest and all levels of net worth. The divide that has historically separated high- and low-end consumers has never been as narrow as it is currently. Retirement planning, tax planning, and money management are ubiquitous now. More important, these services are offered at a fraction of customary costs. Individual investors have more options and opportunities. If you can imagine it, it probably exists...or soon will. Digital finance has brought together a perfect blend of privilege and personalized attention to an audience with a wide range of interests.

Information Irony

The irony is that easy availability of vast amounts of information has seemingly created greater confusion, not greater clarity. Today's investors suffer more from a glut of information than a dearth of material facts and figures. Rather than making investment choices easier, the wealth of information has paradoxically led to making decisions more difficult for many. Data overload is a common condition among investors. Isn't technology supposed to simplify our lives? We are learning that even the wonders of technology, which can bring streams of the latest market information on command and execute trade orders at all hours of the day, cannot suspend the fundamental relationship between risk and return. Witness America's dalliance with day trading. A group of otherwise intelligent and prudent people succumbed to the temptation of shuffling their portfolio mixes with every rise and fall in market price. Their focus on very short term price swings worked well while the markets were going straight up, but proved to be an Achilles' heel when market conditions turned challenging. Some wrongly rationalize that because trading is now practically effortless (getting in is easy, so getting out should be easy, too), risk is somehow pardoned. Many confuse the ease of trading with serious investing.

Without a fundamental understanding of how enduring portfolios are built, managed, and sustained, extreme market conditions are much more difficult to negotiate. The same technology that has made wide-scale, self-directed investing permissible has also freely spread dangerous hazards, underscored by the greater fluidity in today's marketplace. The breadth of the Internet has created fresh concerns. Many investors in the digital age have been at one time or another duped by fallacious rumors, tricked by misleading advice, or misguided by self-proclaimed wonder strategies. Among the thousands of retire-rich schemes, how many actually hold any real secrets? Instead of leading us to serene waters, the global trend toward interconnectedness and the dramatic rise of Internet use has unknowingly steered many investors into stormy seas. Stock scams have penetrated much more quickly because of the extensive use of message boards and research postings. The widespread abuse of communication channels has led to hundreds of millions of dollars of losses and brought into question the extent of our First Amendment rights.

The *New York Times* magazine devoted the February 25, 2001, cover story to Jonathan Lebed, the teenage wonder trader who allegedly earned over $800,000 in six months after using several different Internet message boards to promote his stock picks to others.[1] Another case involved a bogus earnings report regarding Emulex Corporation, a technology company involved in manufacturing fiber-optic communications gear. A false statement released over the financial newswires on August 25, 2000, sent the company's stock into a free fall. The effect on the market was swift and dramatic. In 16 minutes, 2.3 million shares of Emulex traded, and the price plummeted almost $61, resulting in Emulex's losing $2.2 billion in market capitalization. At 10:29 A.M. EDT, Nasdaq halted trading after learning from Emulex that the release was false.[2] It was not until later that the press release was discovered to be a hoax. By day's end, the stock price was little changed on the day, but not before widespread losses occurred for both buyers and sellers. Moreover, of course, the dramatic collapse of Enron, WorldCom, and Global Crossings is cause for concern among vigilant investors looking to avoid companies whose highest levels of management may be playing a role in deceiving investors through improper financial reporting. Investors beware: Advances in technology come at a price; risk and reward now run much deeper and faster. In this vein, technology and the overabundance of data has been both a boon and a bust for investors.

The Market Matters More than Ever

For investors, the timing of this double-edged sword could not be worse. The difference between investing today and in years past is not necessarily the ease with which individuals can access information, build a portfolio, and invest. The primary difference is *why* we invest. Whether we recognize it or not, the markets matter because financial portfolios have replaced more traditional means of savings as the primary conduit to retirement. This is because the onus of retirement has shifted away from the public and private sectors and into our own hands. The early pioneers of the retail movement were inspired to seek change for the sake of progress. Now the result of their efforts, deregulation in the financial markets, is being assimilated by the mainstream as an indispensable component of how households plan for the future. Our blueprints for the futures will ultimately be shaped by a host of factors. Some will be personal (e.g., time to retirement and risk tolerance), and others will be beyond our control (e.g., the overall rate of return or the pace of inflation).

As new generations join the ranks of the investment community, the financial markets will have even further-reaching implications, not only on how we behave as consumers but also on how the overall economy performs. As the market itself grows in importance, individuals are increasingly coming to grips with the many subtleties of investing. They are awaking to the fact that without the financial markets, financial preparations for the future will fall short. Without another viable investment alternative capable of generating the future returns necessary to fund retirement, individuals will have no choice but to funnel their savings into the markets.

Will You Outlive Your Money?

Today's workers and retirees are living longer, healthier lives. When the Social Security program was created in 1935, a person was eligible to collect money at age 65—but life expectancy at the time was only 62. According to the IRS life expectancy table in Figure 2.1, today's retirees can expect a life span of 20 or more years past the traditional retirement age of 65.[3] For young adults just entering the workforce (born circa 1980), financial planners and insurance companies are projecting that you will spend fully one-third of your life in retirement. Thus it becomes critical that as an investor you do not underestimate your own life span in the investment planning process. Otherwise, in a perverse way, your real fear will not be dying early but outliving your money.

The Social Security Administration estimates that 76 million baby boomers will begin retiring in about 2010, and in about 30 years, there will be nearly twice as many older Americans as there are today. At the same time, the number of workers paying into Social Security per beneficiary will drop, creating further strain on our retirement system. As you can see in Figure 2.2, the percentage of population over age 65 was 8 percent in

Figure 2.1 IRS life expectancy table.

Age	Number of years the IRS expects you to live	Age	Number of years the IRS expects you to live	Age	Number of years the IRS expects you to live	Age	Number of years the IRS expects you to live
35	47.3	55	28.6	75	12.5	95	3.7
36	46.4	56	27.7	76	11.9	96	3.4
37	45.4	57	26.8	77	11.2	97	3.2
38	44.4	58	25.9	78	10.6	98	3.0
39	43.5	59	25.0	79	10.0	99	2.8
40	42.5	60	24.2	80	9.5	100	2.7
41	41.5	61	23.3	81	8.9	101	2.5
42	40.6	62	22.5	82	8.4	102	2.3
43	39.6	63	21.6	83	7.9	103	2.1
44	38.7	64	20.8	84	7.4	104	1.9
45	37.7	65	20.0	85	6.9	105	1.8
46	36.8	66	19.2	86	6.5	106	1.6
47	35.9	67	18.4	87	6.1	107	1.4
48	34.9	68	17.6	88	5.7	108	1.3
49	34.0	69	16.8	89	5.3	109	1.1
50	33.1	70	16.0	90	5.0	110	1.0
51	32.2	71	15.3	91	4.7		
52	31.3	72	14.6	92	4.4		
53	30.4	73	13.9	93	4.1		
54	29.5	74	13.2	94	3.9		

Source: Internal Revenue Service, 1999.

1946. Compare this with 13 percent in 1999 and an anticipated 20 percent in 2030. Looking at these numbers, it's extremely difficult to see how the United States will be able to provide its current level of Social Security benefits to its post-baby-boom generation. Thus far, policymakers have failed to appropriately plan for the shift in demographics.

What does this mean? Smaller Social Security benefits translate into one of two things: Either the individual alone must shoulder the burden of his or her retirement, or each person must find an alternative means of savings. Today, the Social Security Administration is taking in more in taxes than is currently being paid out in benefits; the excess funds are credited to Social Security's trust funds. There is now about $900 billion in the trust fund reserves; the reserves are projected to grow to more than $6 trillion in

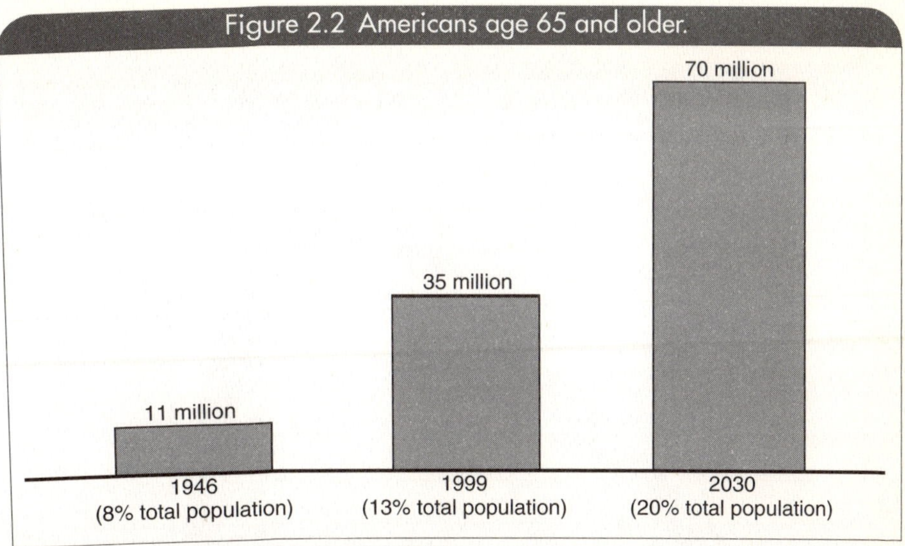

Source: Social Security Administration, 2000.

the next 25 years. However, benefit payments will begin to exceed taxes paid in 2015, and the trust funds will be exhausted by 2037. At that time, Social Security will be able to pay only about 73 percent of benefits owed—unless changes are made.[4] (See Figure 2.3.)

Birth of an Investor Nation

With the ability of the Social Security system to create supplemental income for Americans ages 65 and older in doubt, U.S. households have made investing in mutual funds, stocks, bonds, and bank deposits an integral part of their retirement plans. In the late 1950s, one out of every eight Americans owned stock. Today one out of two Americans are shareholders. How did the gap close so quickly? Ironically, it took a prolonged bear market in the early 1970s to dramatically alter the financial landscape for the average investor. After 1974, innovative investment vehicles began to emerge from Wall Street, from mutual fund selections (including low-cost index funds) to more advanced instruments such as futures and options. A series of deregulatory initiatives made lower commissions on brokerage accounts permissible, inviting a much wider audience of investors. The individual retirement account (IRA), a precursor to today's 401(k) plan, was also born at this time. For the first time, employees without formal

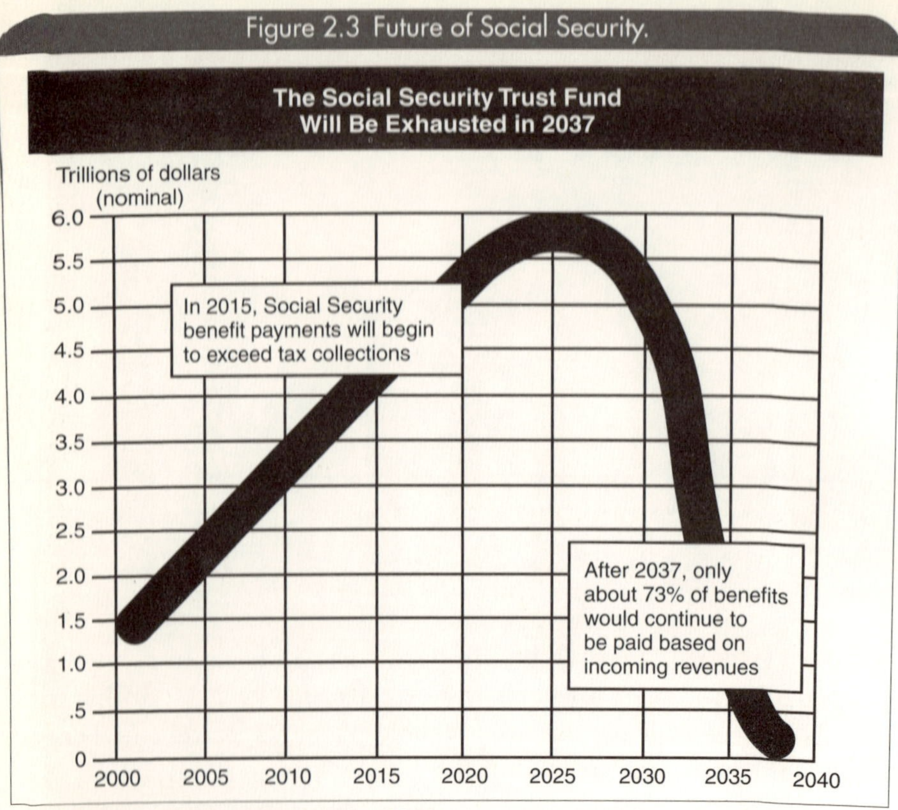

Source: Social Security Administration, 2000.

pensions finally found a reasonable way to fund retirement savings. Immediately, the average American started to become more proactive about investing.

As a result, the mutual fund industry experienced an explosion in growth. From 1980 to today, total net assets of mutual funds have grown over 5,000 percent. As money began to flood into the mutual fund industry, thousands of funds sprouted, and newly minted managers waited with open arms. The industry grew from 665 funds in 1981 to just over nearly 8,300 in 2001,[5] ostensibly driven by higher-than-average returns, professional management, and the ability to diversify. From the fund management perspective, a 2 percent load (or commission) was certainly an attractive proposition. Alas, a multi-trillion-dollar industry was born. (See Figure 2.4.)

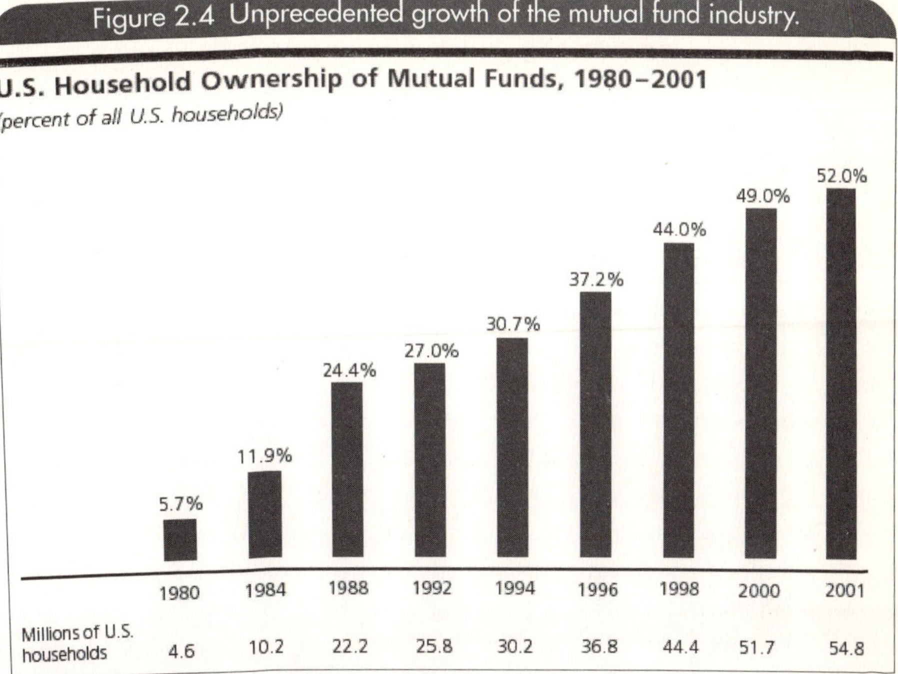

Source: Investment Company Institute, 2002.

According to the Investment Company Institute, in 2001, U.S households purchased $478 billion worth of financial assets, up from $312 billion in 2000. Of the total net purchases of financial assets by U.S. households, 58 percent, or $275 billion, was invested (including reinvested dividends) in mutual funds. The number of U.S. households owning mutual funds reached 54.8 million as of May 2001, up from 51.7 million in May 2000. As a result, more than half of the estimated 105.5 million households in the United States now own mutual funds, and an estimated 93.3 million individual shareholders in those households invest in funds. All totaled, U.S. households own $5.16 trillion in mutual fund assets.[6]

In line with this, investing is all but replacing our traditional means of savings, as evidenced by a negative personal savings rate in the United States. According to the Commerce Department, Americans are currently spending every penny (and then some) of their after-tax incomes. This is in stark contrast to 1982, when the U.S. personal savings rate stood at 9 percent. Today, personal savings has completely vanished. The message that we as individuals are ultimately responsible for our own financial welfare is being heard loud and clear. Offset the negative personal savings rate with the billions of dollars being invested in the financial markets each month and you can see how the direction of these markets will have an increasingly greater impact on our personal lives.

Do-It-Yourself Approach

In the face of such a complex and dynamic marketplace, many are opting to enter the investment game without the aid of an advisor. The *Wall Street Journal* has suggested in its online trading guide that the current generation of investors bears a Home Depot–like quality.[7] We are in effect a nation of do-it-yourselfers, reflecting a wide range of behavior from home gardening to wallpapering to stock trading. Many retail investors today can cite how fast a particular company is expected to grow, its trailing price-to-earnings ratio, or its latest gross margin. Terms like *slow and fast stochastics, downward channel,* and *a third leg in the advance* are not foreign to many individual investors.

The advantages of this type of do-it-yourself strategy are clear: Trading accounts at discount brokerages provide access to the markets at initially lower costs and greater convenience, along with research and an impressive array of financial tools. Accordingly, the response from investors around the globe has been profound. To gauge the impact we need only look at the facts: Stock market capitalization reached $35 trillion around the world in 2000, or 110 percent of global gross domestic product. The comparable figure just a decade ago was a mere 40 percent. There is no denying that the self-directed investment movement has penetrated investing to the core.

By all accounts, investing has come a long way in an abbreviated amount of time. Making these growth rates even more pronounced is the fact that these advances have been attained in the face of the most stressful financial events in the past half century—the Mexican peso devaluation in 1994, a widespread Asian currency crisis in 1997, the Russian default, the demise of Long-Term Capital Management in 1998, the tech wreck of 2000, and the September 11 terrorist attacks. In each case, individual investors demonstrated an uncanny resiliency in the face of some steep market corrections—each crisis was met with a steady stream of capital to bolster the markets. (See Figure 2.5.)

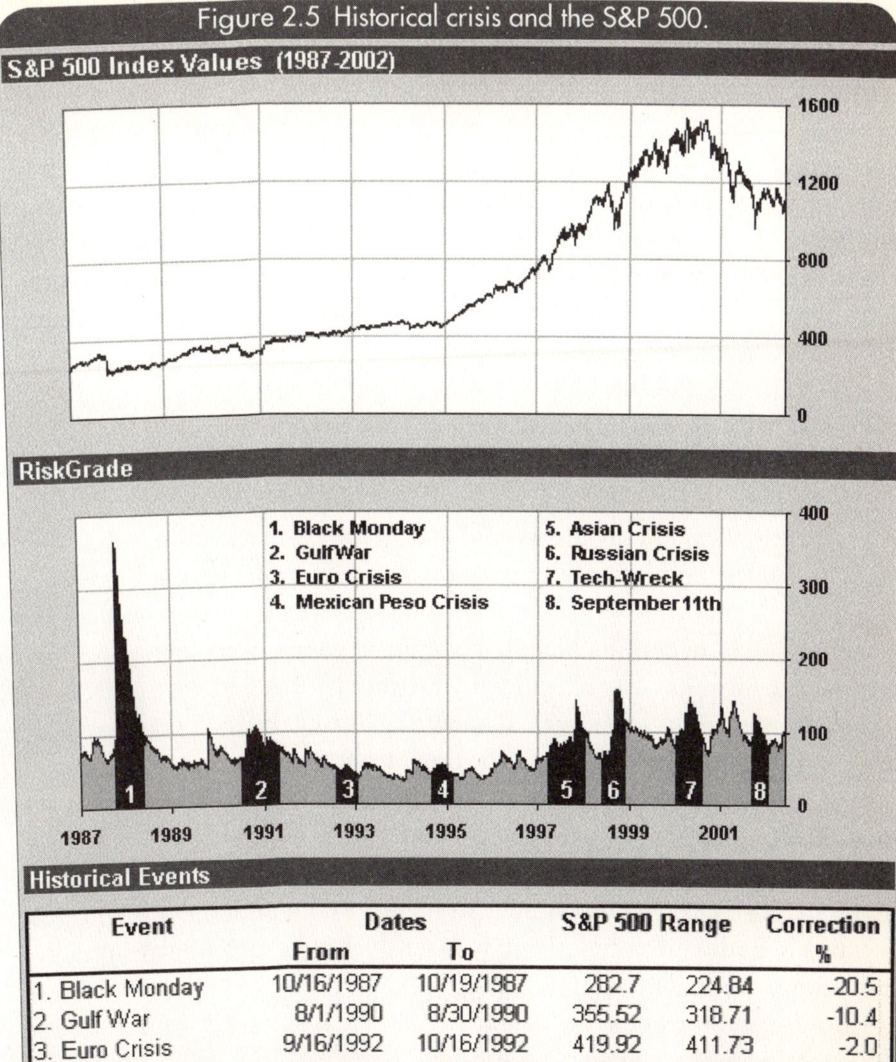

Historical Events

Event	Dates		S&P 500 Range		Correction %
	From	To			
1. Black Monday	10/16/1987	10/19/1987	282.7	224.84	-20.5
2. Gulf War	8/1/1990	8/30/1990	355.52	318.71	-10.4
3. Euro Crisis	9/16/1992	10/16/1992	419.92	411.73	-2.0
4. Mexican Peso Cris	12/20/1994	1/23/1995	457.1	465.82	1.9
5. Asian Crisis	10/24/1997	10/27/1997	941.64	876.99	-6.9
6. Russian Crisis	8/18/1998	10/8/1998	1101.2	959.44	-12.9
7. Tech Wreck	3/24/2000	4/14/2000	1527.46	1356.56	-11.2
8. September 11th	9/11/2001	9/20/2002	1092.54	983.79	-10.0

Source: WealthBench, RiskMetrics Group.

Prior to the bursting of the Internet bubble, investors who stood strong during the periods of uncertainty were rewarded almost immediately. During the five-year period from 1995 through 1999, the average annual return of the S&P 500 was 26.3 percent. As a result, investor enthusiasm spilled over into the growing number of online assets and fueled our fascination with the financial markets. This fascination was manifested in all areas of our social lives—at cocktail parties, little league baseball games, and church gatherings. The topic du jour in social circles is stock prices, direction of the market, and finding the next ten-bagger.[8] At the time, who could blame anyone for being so enthralled?

With the costs of building a portfolio significantly lower, coupled with a little bit of research and some timely moxie, investors proved they could produce superior market returns relative the market as a whole. Unfortunately to attain these results, investors cast a blind eye toward market risk. Nonetheless, they quickly discovered during the dramatic slide in 2000 and 2001 that investing successfully, particularly on one's own, is not as easy as it appears. A collection of technology stocks, as we all know now, does not constitute a conscientious plan. For the do-it-yourselfers, managing their own money without a well-guided investment plan led to excruciating losses. As many of us have learned, investing during difficult market conditions or in a declining market can be downright treacherous.

As investing shifts away from the hands of the professionals to the mousepads of the individuals, one concern is that individuals who manage their own retirement plans run the risk of being swept away by speculative urges and ill-conceived investment strategies. Without an investment process that includes discipline, do-it-yourself investors have shown a proclivity toward speculation, not long-term investing. Historian Edward Chancellor, author of *Devil Take the Hindmost,* has summed it up best: The difference between speculating and investing "is so thin that it has been said both that speculation is the name given to a failed investment and that investment is the name given to a successful speculation."[9] Given the availability of financial services today, we have to learn how to exploit the myriad choices and avoid being overwhelmed by them.

Looking back now, it's easy to observe the years of the Internet boom as a prime example of unstable speculation. Many of us were guilty of picking stocks without much regard for research, even placing buy orders absent any knowledge of what a company does. As investors, we need to rethink our overemphasis on returns. We should always be wary of market risks so that our speculative impulses never completely cloud our better judgments.

This can be very difficult when the scale of emotions run high and wide in the investment world, ranging from exhilaration to anxiety to disappointment to frustration. Although technology has been able to increase efficiency on many fronts, it has yet to find a solution for keeping raw human emotions from obfuscating our sensibilities when it comes to making sound investment decisions. Surf the endless stream of financial pages on the Web and you are likely to feel all of these emotions in the span of an hour. Regrettably, amid the sheer volume of market reports, the importance of maintaining a financial plan and adhering to its long-term objectives is being lost. A financial plan allows you to understand how each investment decision you make affects other areas of your finances, painting a broad picture of your current financial situation and where you would like to be in the future. It reflects your personal time horizon, financial situation, and feelings about risk. Only by viewing each investment decision as part of a whole can you consider its short- and long-term effects on achieving your goals.

Self-Directed or Full Service?

Investing, for the most part, involves a little bit of art, a little bit of science. Most of us believe that we can capably render the artistic aspect and sometimes even the scientific part. Unfortunately for us, this isn't a fair picture of reality. At the very least, the pros still have an abundance of full-time resources that can help uncover both unique opportunities and esoteric risks. Moreover, market information rewards the eyes and ears of those who are the first to listen. In this regard, even with the advantages of the Internet and other innovations, the playing field has yet to be completely leveled. Can we, as self-directed managers of our own financial welfare, dedicate the necessary amount of time and resources to successfully grow our money? Have we developed a proper skill set to succinctly synthesize and analyze the markets? The answers will undoubtedly be mixed.

In truth, most of us fall short of the business acumen and investment discipline of someone like Warren Buffett, John Neff, or Bill Miller. Nevertheless, that will not stop us from trying. Although blessed with a fair amount of general market knowledge, the average investor knows little about how to delicately balance immediate risks and intermediate returns.

However, without this essential skill, self-directed investing can be disastrous. Not surprisingly, in the wake of the frenzied dot-com era many are left feeling overwhelmed by the whole investment process. Consequently, many active trading accounts at discount brokerages became inactive accounts, as many do-it-yourself investors rightfully returned to the comforts of a full-service broker. Others emerged a little bruised, but more resolved than ever to rely on their own abilities to advance their investment scores through discipline, practice, and knowledge.

Going forward, the rocky road investors have endured since the market meltdown in 2000 will improve as the economic outlook improves, and a multitude of investment opportunities will follow, which will lead to competing advice on which path you should take. Self-directed or full service? There is no single correct answer to this question. Not all investors will or should follow the same path. Each person's investment approach should be based on his or her individual needs and goals. The right approach requires a financial plan with a systematic and rational strategy that can optimally balance risk and return. Finding a systematic approach that works for you is the first step in building a perfect portfolio.

Regardless of the path selected, one thing will be the same. Risk management tools and processes will grow in importance to individuals who will increasingly be encouraged to channel savings into the markets. As the pool expands, the presence of financial risk will carry increasing weight. This time around, we need to understand risk. Risk cannot be an afterthought. It must be a priority. And for good reason. The electronic investment environment will continue to make the markets easier to tap but trickier to crack. Without the foresight to manage the volatility this time around, risk will roam about even more rampantly. Making sense of the markets requires research and reflection and an ability to synthesize not only one aspect of investing, but also an entire picture of risk and return. Risk is not a new concept. Every investment guide, prospectus, or research report warns us about risk. However, in previous market cycles, many of us never read them or benefited from the tools available to analyze those risks properly. Now we can.

Will risk management have the ability to prevent future financial crises? No. It would be foolish to think that our investments could be completely insulated from the greater forces of the market. Whether we like it or not, periodic episodes of distress—manifested in the form of losses—are the price of doing business. Accepting this fact will not necessarily make the journey less stressful, but it will help you manage expectations and keep your sights on the end goal. Along the way, we should remind ourselves that sound judgment can help limit losses, which could be the difference between an early voluntary retirement and a late mandatory one. The key is in knowing your risks, taking control, and developing a financial plan where risk allocation and portfolio diversification work for you, not against you.

Our general thesis of investing, with one eye on risk and the other on return, is not a marked departure from other time-honored financial guides. Others have already listed the ingredients that are hallmarks of a successful investment program, which typically include a long-term time horizon, low transaction costs, and a risk profile that is well suited to meet individual tastes. The principal difference in our underlying approach is that we actually lend a hand to facilitate the process. It is easy to tell individuals to invest rationally. It is much more difficult to demonstrate what is required to do so, to provide hard information on the risks investors are taking, and to examine where those risks might lead them. Our outlook will give readers a better working framework for making future investment decisions.

CHAPTER 3

What Is Risk?

Risk is an elusive concept. Ask a roomful of people to define it, and more than a few unique responses are likely to be given. In the most general sense, risk is the uncertainty of the future value of financial assets. The greater the risk, the greater the potential range of one's future wealth, on both the upside and the downside, and therefore the greater the uncertainty about meeting one's financial goals. In the financial world, risk is often measured in terms of the volatility (or variability) in prices and returns.[1]

Whatever your definition, one thing is for sure: Most people view risk as a negative. Webster's dictionary defines risk as exposure to danger or hazard. That is only partially true, because it does not factor in the upside that comes with sometimes assuming a calculated risk. Perhaps the best description of risk comes from the Chinese characters denoting risk (see Figure 3.1).

The first character is the symbol for danger, and the second is the symbol for opportunity, making risk a mixture of danger and opportunity. This illustrates the trade-off that every investor has to make between the higher rewards that potentially come with the opportunity and the higher risk that has to be borne as a consequence of the danger.[2]

Although danger + opportunity = risk helps to capture the essence of risk, as a definition it is still too abstract to be practically applicable in the financial world. In order to show risk in a meaningful light, it needs to be

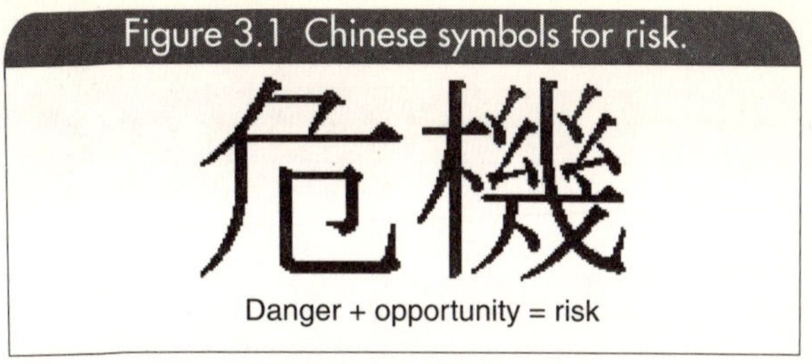

Figure 3.1 Chinese symbols for risk.

Danger + opportunity = risk

Source: Aswath Damodaran, *Applied Corporate Finance: A User's Manual,* John Wiley & Sons, New York, 1999, p. 35. Reprinted with permission.

translated from a descriptive concept into something more tangible. What is the extent of uncertainty? How difficult will it be to turn a profit? What are the chances of disappointment? In other words, financial risk needs to be put into a framework that can be measured on both a relative and an absolute scale. In this sense, risk is a numbers game.

In light of this, the market has gravitated toward a standard definition—*volatility.* Volatility (translated statistically as standard deviation) is defined as the degree an investment has historically fluctuated relative to its average (or expected) return. Volatility effectively quantifies the extent to which we are uncertain about the future value of our assets. Some investments fluctuate very little, whereas others experience wide swings in value. In general, the greater the variability or swing in an investment's value, the greater its overall risk.

Why RiskGrades?

Although the markets may *feel* more volatile now than at any time in recent memory, volatility in the equity market as a whole has failed to register significantly above longer-term trends as measured by the Chicago Board Options Exchange (CBOE) Volatility Index (see Figure 3.2), a broad measure of volatility in the U.S. equity market. In fact, even with the onslaught of the bear market in April 2000, the implied volatility reached only about 40 percent, far less than the spike to 152 percent on Black Monday, October 19, 1987.

Recent findings confirm that the broader markets have remained fairly stable with respect to longer-term averages, but individual stocks have been exhibiting greater instability as of late. The *Wall Street Journal* points to a study led by John Campbell and Burton Malkiel suggesting that the

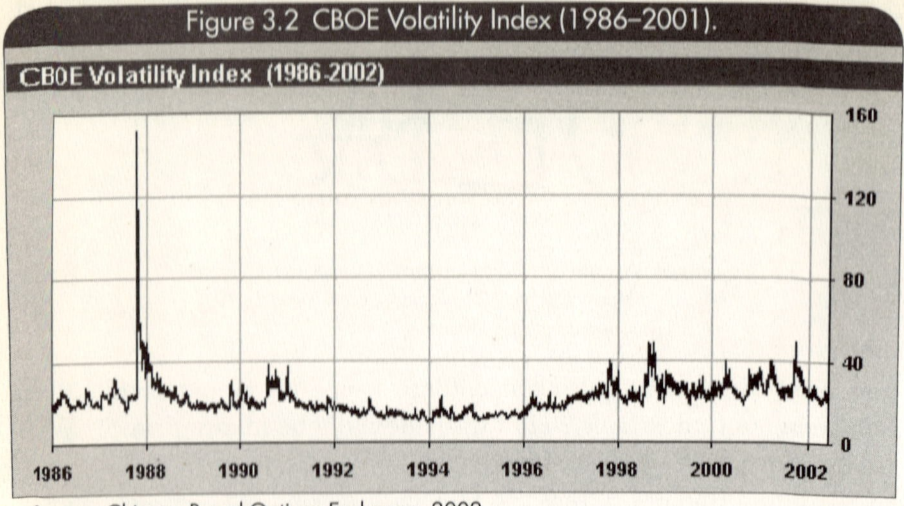

Figure 3.2 CBOE Volatility Index (1986–2001).

Source: Chicago Board Options Exchange, 2002.

real culprit for heightened volatility in many individual share prices is an increasing focus on specialization:

> **Once, an investor wanting to sock away a few big stocks could choose a conglomerate, whose exposure to disparate industries that ran on different cycles provided some protection. However, few such sprawling, diversified companies exist any more, as managements choose to concentrate on what the company does best. Individual stocks have become riskier bets with the decline in corporate diversification.[3]**

Whether this is the root cause of recent insecurity is debatable. What is clear is that with each spike in volatility has come increased talk of market risk. Financial commentators have tried to spin volatility in a practical if not dramatic light, citing such things as the enormity of the swings in the market. "Nasdaq tumbles 150 points," proclaim the newspaper headlines. While this may be good for news reports, the usefulness of such a statistic offers little to investors from a practical standpoint. An ill-advised interpretation of volatility can lead us down a misguided path. A volatile stock is not the same as a stock with a high degree of volatility. The regularity with which a stock moves up and down is quite different from the *extent* to which a stock swings in price. The subtle difference between volatility and variability of returns is important. A stock could be characterized by high volatility yet confined to a predictable range. In such cases, it is in fact appropriate to say that the stock is volatile, but not necessarily more risky. Understanding this point is critical in making sound decisions. Risk-averse investors would be wise to shy away from risky stocks, not necessarily volatile ones.

A classic case in point is Microsoft stock during the 1990s (Figure 3.3). The stock clearly had moments of downside risk, but overall rewarded those who remained faithful with once-in-a-lifetime returns. The stock ended on a high note at decade's close. What is striking is that the risk profile remained remarkably steady throughout the decade, with its RiskGrade level remaining largely between 150 and 200. Microsoft delivered astronomical returns with mostly predictable levels of risk. Investors should have found this stock respectable with regard to both risk and return.

In contrast, look at Kmart. Unlike Microsoft, returns for Kmart over the past decade were marked by instability (Figure 3.4). While Microsoft was enjoying higher highs and higher lows, Kmart actually delivered a

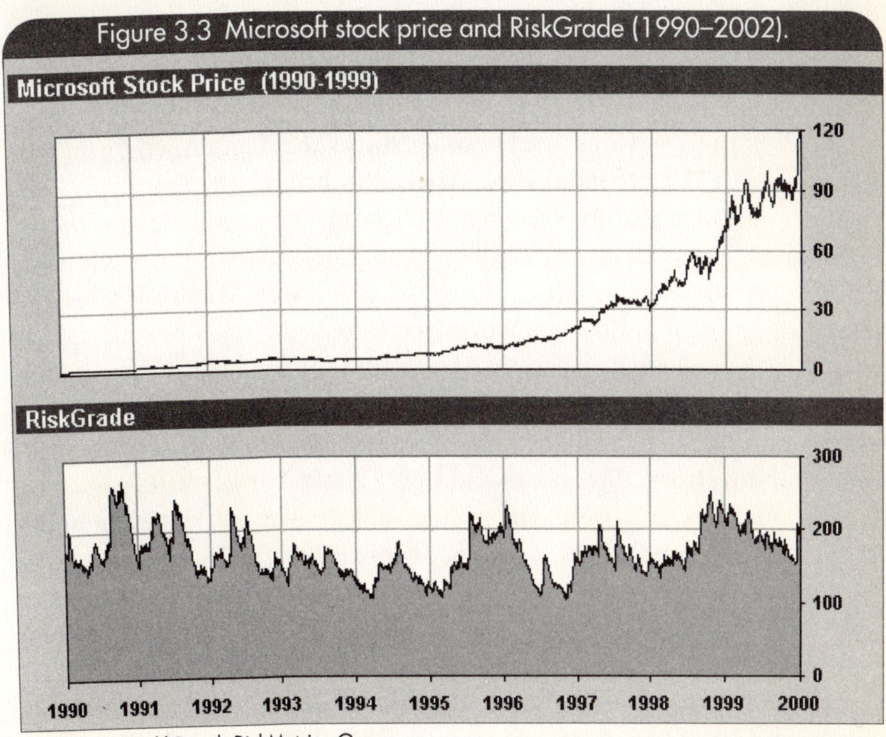

Source: WealthBench RiskMetrics Group.

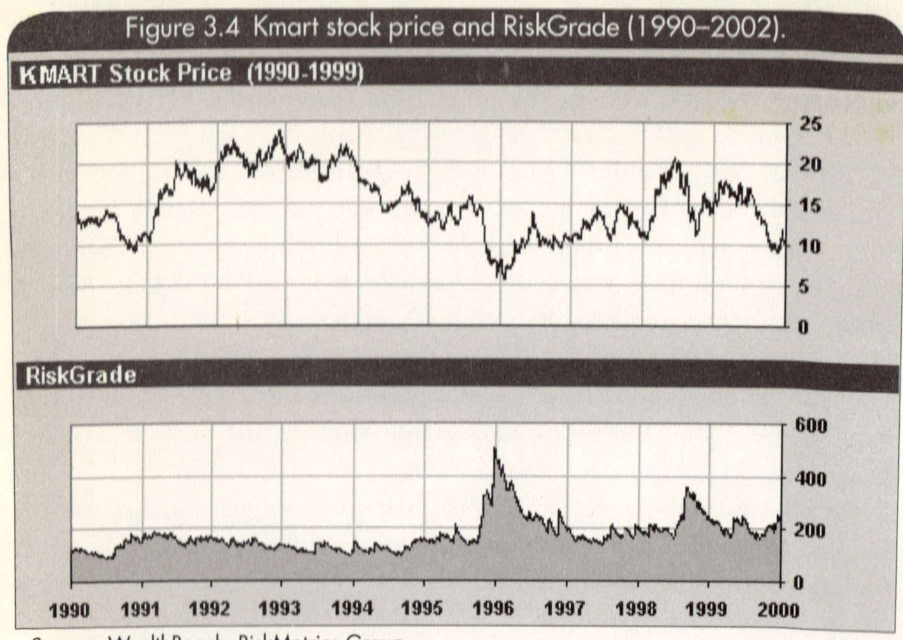

Source: WealthBench, RiskMetrics Group.

negative return for the period (excluding dividends). More important, risk was less predictable.

In all fairness to Kmart and to other stocks that languished during the 1990s, we should carry the story of Microsoft through the year 2002. Even the fairy-tale-like history of Microsoft could not overcome the thorny issues of high valuations, antitrust suits, and negative investor sentiment. Even before the U.S. Department of Justice declared Microsoft Corporation in violation of antitrust practices, its RiskGrade began to emit signs of trouble. After channeling between 100 and 250 for much of the decade, Microsoft's RiskGrade convincingly broke above the upper band, closing at 332 on April 3, 2000, its highest RiskGrade to date (Figure 3.5). Unfortunately for investors, this spike would be a harbinger of further risks up ahead. Although Microsoft's risk would subside over subsequent months, its RiskGrade leaped again in late September 2000. Those investors who grew uneasy with a heightened sense of risk earlier could have decided to scale back positions. The stock was still at a lofty $70 a share. Microsoft eventually crumbled to nearly $40 by year-end.

The frequency of larger price moves does not fully capture the magnitude of risk variation. In fact, we can be led astray just by following

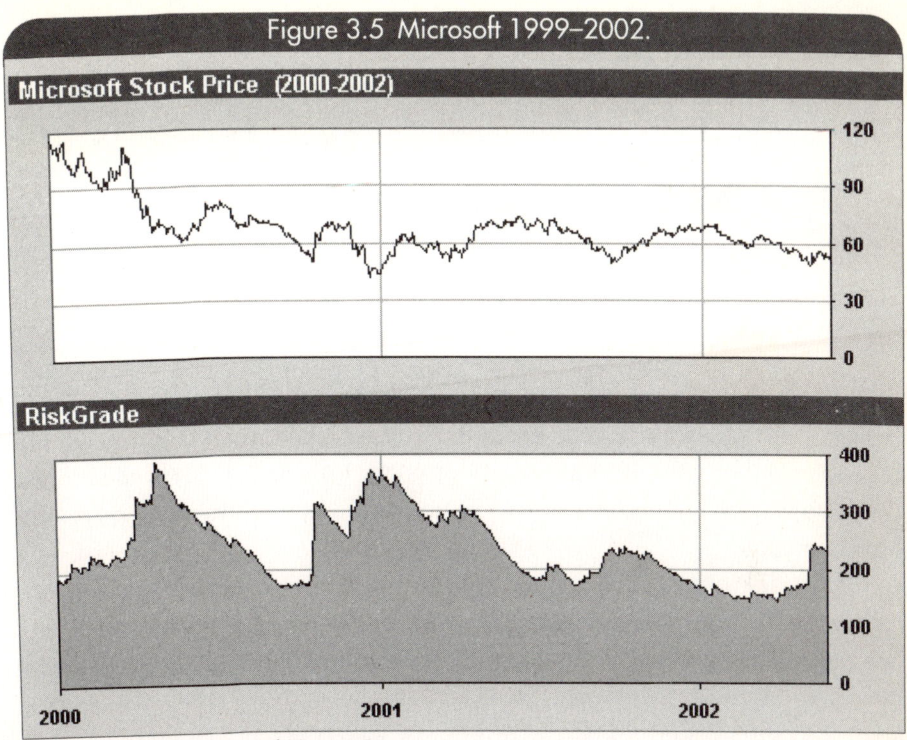

Source: WealthBench, RiskMetrics Group.

"frequency of moves" as a yardstick. In other words, using standard deviation alone as a test of risk can be somewhat misleading. Standard deviation is traditionally useful given a normal distribution or a stream of price points that revert to an average expected return (more on this later). However, as evidence shows, stock prices as a whole typically exhibit a positive bias over time. This implies that a stock can drift higher while regularly exceeding its daily standard deviation. Again, Microsoft is a prime example. Furthermore, standard deviation fails to adequately address the issue of relative risk. We may understand that a higher standard deviation implies greater risk, but how does our portfolio compare to the S&P 500? In other words, *"How much more risky is my portfolio?"* Risk needs a point of reference to offer greater insight.

RiskGrades were devised with these concerns in mind. A RiskGrade is first a measure of risk. RiskGrades measure the price volatility for individual securities and portfolios. By definition, a RiskGrade of 100 is equal to the long-term average volatility of global equity markets.[4] RiskGrades are

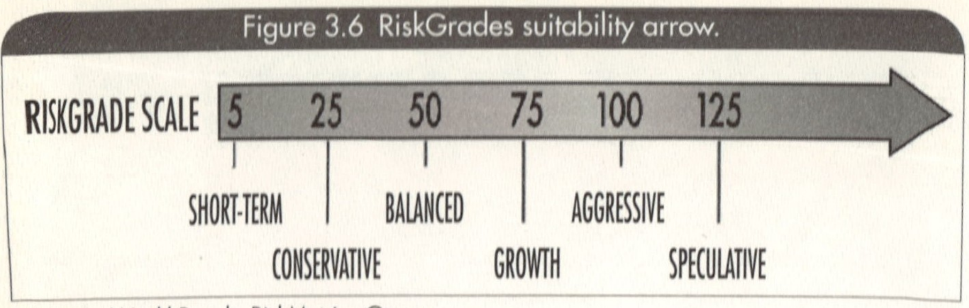

Source: WealthBench, RiskMetrics Group.

linearly scaled (Figure 3.6), meaning an asset with a higher RiskGrade is riskier than a lower one. For example, a RiskGrade of 300 is considered twice as risky or volatile as a security or portfolio with a RiskGrade of 150. A RiskGrade of 200 today versus 150 yesterday tells us that risk increased by 33 percent.

What distinguishes RiskGrades from other, more traditional barometers is RiskGrades ability to translate risk into a single, standardized number that can be compared on an equal basis across equities, mutual funds, bonds, and options. Moreover, RiskGrades factors in currency risk associated with purchasing foreign investments, which are not denominated in your portfolio's base currency. For example, advisors using RiskGrades can quickly counsel their American clients that purchasing shares of Daimler-Chrysler, denominated in euros on the Frankfurt exchange, with a RiskGrade of 160 is four times as risky as a Japanese bond fund denominated in yen with a RiskGrade measurement of 40. In addition, because each RiskGrade is computed on a daily basis, the value reflects the most current market conditions. Moreover, the answer to "How much more risky?" is provided as a point of reference, using a benchmark portfolio as a line in the sand of risk. In this way, a RiskGrade represents market risk more accurately than most measures.

Perhaps most important, RiskGrades can quantify a portfolio's diversification. With RiskGrades, investors will be able not only to identify the risk contribution of each asset to an overall portfolio, but also to manage it in such a way that portfolio risk can be optimized. At some point, we have all been reminded of the maxim not to put all our eggs into one basket. As we demonstrate in Chapter 7, diversification is the single most important component to effectively administering portfolio risk. Unfortunately even professional advisors make reference to diversification in an imprecise manner, encouraging general asset allocation strategies without any hard evidence that this is best for the investor. The appropriate asset allocation must be determined on an individual basis, dependent on each person's long-term financial goals. It's not until return is weighed against risk that you achieve an accurate and true assessment of how your investments are performing. By knowing how much risk stems from each position, investors will be able to actively manage risk right alongside return prospects. To our knowledge, no investment service other than RiskGrades has been able to identify the actual benefits of diversification in such a concrete way.

The Nasdaq Composite: A Case Study

There is no better way to demonstrate the applicability of RiskGrades than with a relevant case study. Let's take a closer look at an earlier snapshot of the Nasdaq Composite Index covering the period from 1998 to 2000. At the time, the Nasdaq in its ascent to an all-time high was the paragon of volatility. Look at the Nasdaq over this dizzying period, climbing from 1,500 to up over 2,500, then dramatically surging to 5,000, sliding to 3,000 shortly thereafter, briefly bouncing back, and ultimately experiencing a deep flush to 2,300—all in a 24-month span. The speed and magnitude of this market surge and correction were truly extraordinary.

All along the way, skeptics tried to warn of growing risks. However, reminders that previous run-ups ended badly did little to deter the herd of new investors. Standard risk measures failed to elucidate the growing perils in the market. It seemed investors cheerfully greeted every market dip as an opportunity to buy more. Moreover, for a long time the market appeared to compensate these aggressive investors handsomely. Even traditional valuation methods like the price-to-earnings ratio, a common ratio used by many professional and individual investors, were discarded by analysts, as they could not appropriately be applied to new-economy stocks that were annually growing revenues by more than 100 percent...but with no profits.

Unfortunately, investors would soon come to realize that it's almost never going to be "different this time around." As *The Economist* has described it in February 2000, "Another century, another technology, but the basic message remains the same: fundamental innovations rarely make shareholders rich in the long term."[5] In the aftermath of the technology bubble, many are left to ponder the lessons of history from a risk perspective. A large number of investors have finally realized that risk cuts both ways. The bravado that until recently was so pervasive among the current generation of investors has been replaced by a mind-set of hesitation, skepticism, and even fear. The markets, for most of the past decade, appeared to be a surefire ride to early retirement. The idea of monitoring risk was secondary as share prices soared. Investors fully realize now that it needs be a priority. Would it have ended differently if we had taken heed of risk along the way?

While it is arguable that the market was long overheating, the final surfeit of madness materialized in October 1999. At this time, the Nasdaq RiskGrade traversed in the mid-120s as the Composite edged toward the 3,000 level. By the first week of January 2000, with the Nasdaq up around the 4,000, the RiskGrade had leaped to more than 140. By early February, the RiskGrade inched up above 160, a third higher than just three months earlier. In mid-March, the Nasdaq RiskGrade rose to 170, then 180, and breached 200 by early April as the slide began. At its nadir, the Nasdaq RiskGrade reached 300, the damage reflected not only in a higher RiskGrade but, more important, in diminished portfolio values. (See Figure 3.7.)

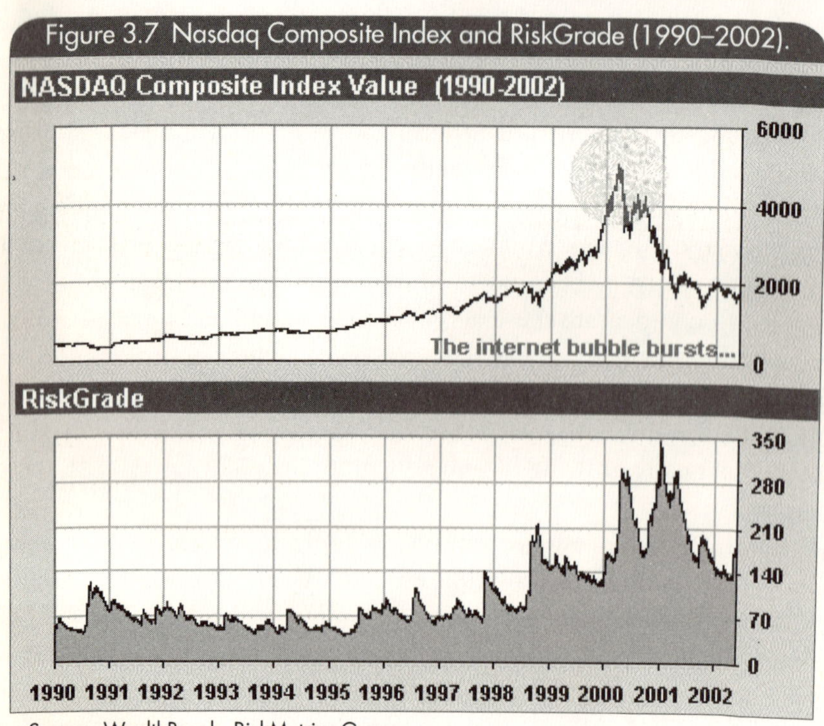

Source: WealthBench, RiskMetrics Group.

At the time, a RiskGrade of 300 was the highest ever recorded for the Nasdaq, a number representing a whopping three times more volatility than the average global basket of equities! (Almost a year later, as further steam was let out of the technology shares, the Nasdaq Composite Risk-Grade reached nearly 350 in January 2001.) By contrast, in early 2000, the S&P 500 edged up from the low 90s to a peak of 146, an increase of just about 60 percent. This was a clear indication of the broader base of assets in the S&P 500 compared to the concentration of high-flying technology stocks in the Nasdaq—exemplifying the benefits of diversification.

Astute investors will ask the obvious question: "Is RiskGrade a predictive tool?" The important thing to keep in mind is that RiskGrade was not developed to predict the direction of markets but rather to measure financial risk more precisely (see Table 3.1). A RiskGrade is only as good as its end user. For example, let's look at what RiskGrades would have revealed during the amazing tech run-up on the Nasdaq and its subsequent implosion. In 1995 the average RiskGrade for the Nasdaq Composite Index was 61. As the market rose to new heights day after day, so did its volatility. In 2000, the average RiskGrade ballooned to 218. Some investors may have been able to stomach investing in the Nasdaq with the risk in the 137 to mid-160s range (which represented about a 20 percent increase in the level of risk), or even a 180-level RiskGrade (which indicated a 33 percent

Table 3.1 Average Annual RiskGrades for Dow Jones Industrial, S&P Index, and Nasdaq Composite (1995–2002)

Year	DIJA RiskGrade	S&P 500 RiskGrade	Nasdaq RiskGrade
1995	45	40	61
1996	58	56	78
1997	86	83	84
1998	96	96	121
1999	83	93	140
2000	98	104	220
2001	103	107	221
2002 (through May 23)	99	101	156

Source: WealthBench, RiskMetrics Group.

jump); however, by April 10, 2000, the Nasdaq's RiskGrade was in excess of 225, representing an increase of more than 60 percent. At the very least, this enormous increase in risk should have signaled investors of the need to trim positions. At this point, the Nasdaq was still clinging to the 4,200 level, with about 17 months and 2,700 points separating it from its September 2001 lows.

Facing the first three-year stretch of falling prices since 1941, investors need to make use of concrete tools to measure financial risk instead of relying on vague observations of frequent market gyrations. RiskGrades, combined with an individual's own tolerance for risk, can significantly improve personal investment decisions. Needless to say, a strategy to exit whenever portfolio risk doubles would have far outperformed other financial plans that passively sit through market gyrations. For instance, when the Nasdaq breached the 225 RiskGrade level, perceptive investors could have concluded that the risks were simply too high. Those who decreased equity exposure at this time and stayed on the sidelines in safer assets saved not only valuable resources but also much heartache.

Other Measurements of Risk

We would be remiss if we did not fully explain some of the other popular measures of risk. RiskGrades, after all, is indebted to the overall progress that has been made in the area of risk measurement. Although there are a number of different ways to appraise financial volatility, we'll focus on the two most common references—standard deviation and beta—providing a brief synopsis of each. Let's first take a closer look at standard deviation.

Standard Deviation

Standard deviation as a statistical measure can be traced back to the 1700s, when the concept of normal distribution, or a bell curve, was first introduced. A normally shaped bell curve is intricately tied to a discovery known as *central limit theorem*, which posits that a greater pool of samplings will invariably lead to a centralized distribution curve, or a normal distribution. Early-eighteenth-century mathematicians—such as Jakob Bernoulli, Nikolaus Bernoulli, and Abraham de Moivre—were intrigued by the idea of producing accurate forecasts with an incomplete set of data. Standard deviation was the result of efforts to draw conclusions on mortality rates with just a small sampling of participants. *Standard deviation,* as it is applied to the financial markets today, can be defined as a statistical measure that captures the probable dispersion of returns from a mean. To help illustrate the concept of standard deviation, which can be difficult at times, please refer to the market primer in Box 3.1.

Box 3.1 Market Primer on Standard Deviation

Standard deviation is a general statistical measure of volatility. It measures historical variability of returns from their mean. A higher standard deviation implies more variable and uncertain returns. Standard deviation has been a classical portfolio risk measure since Nobel laureate Harry Markowitz used it in the 1950s to demonstrate risk reduction through diversification. Standard deviation is often used to define the normal distribution, which is the well-known bell-shaped distribution shown in Figure 3.8. The bell-shaped curve results from a statistical tendency for outcomes to cluster symmetrically around the mean (or average).

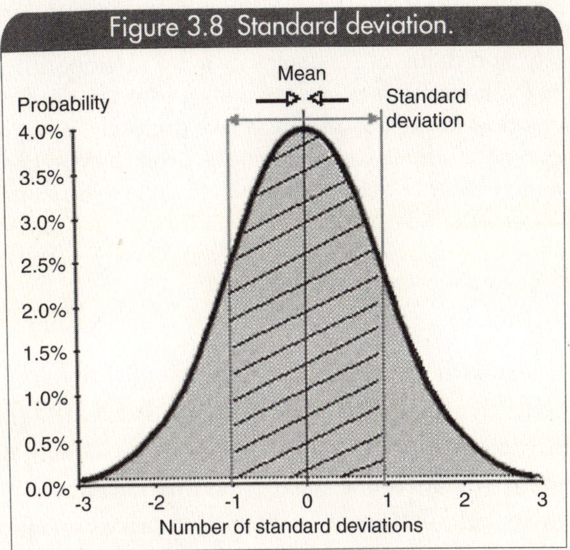

Source: RiskGrades, Understanding Risk online course.

Deviations from the mean are described in terms of standard deviations. In all normal distributions, 68 percent of outcomes will fall within 1 standard deviation to either side of the mean.

Let's illustrate the concept of mean and standard deviation with a simple

Continued

example. My New York subway commute every day is 30 minutes, on average, with a standard deviation of 5 minutes. Assuming a normal distribution for the time it takes me to get to work, this would imply the following:

- 68 percent of the time, I can expect my daily commute to be between 25 and 35 minutes (i.e., the mean of 30 minutes plus or minus 1 standard deviation, or 5 minutes).

- 16 percent of the time, my commute is less than 25 minutes (because the normal distribution is symmetrical around the mean, I expect this event to occur 16 percent of the time, or 100% – 68%/2).

- 16 percent of the time, my commute is greater than 35 minutes (again, because the normal distribution is symmetrical). In other words, my 84 percent confidence level for a worst-case commute is 35 minutes (only 16 percent of the time would I expect longer commute).

From this example, it makes sense that the more standard deviations we move away from the mean, the lower the probability of such an event occurring. For example, a delay of 10 minutes or more (2 standard deviations) has only a 2.5 percent chance of occurring compared to a 16 percent probability of a delay of 5 minutes or more (1 standard deviation).

Applied to the financial markets, we can use the standard deviation of returns to gauge how large market movements are likely to be, assuming that returns are normally distributed. For example, given 5.6 percent as the daily standard deviation for Yahoo! stock, we would expect its returns to fluctuate between +5.6 percent and –5.6 percent with 68 percent confidence.

Source: RiskGrades, Understanding Risk online course.

The use of standard deviation as a basis for measuring risk has proved to be quite an effective tool. The amount of risk is actually translated from the abstract into a working number. In short, risk is actually measured. However, standard deviation does have some weaknesses. For one, standard deviation bases its calculation on a stream of prices taken at face value. This means that every price point is treated equitably. A data point from a year ago is viewed as having the same effect as one from last week. While this does not necessarily pose a problem, investors should note that statistical studies have proved that forecasting accuracy can be greatly enhanced if more-recent events take precedence over long-standing incidents. RiskGrade addresses this concern by incorporating exponentially weighted data.[6]

Exponentially weighting data simply means that recent data points are weighted more heavily than older statistics. In other words, current market conditions and recent corporate changes are assumed to have much greater influence on a stock price than events of years past. The strength of exponential weighting can be likened to a Hall of Fame baseball player past his prime. While hitting like a perennial all-star early in his career, with batting averages close to .400, more recently this athlete has been relegated to platoon status because of a subpar batting average. In a big game, the manager must choose someone to pinch-hit. If the manager looked at this player's career batting average, it would be a no-brainer to send him in right away. With 5,000 career at-bats and a lifetime batting average of .333, this player has a 1 in 3 chance of getting a hit. However, if the manager employs exponential weighting, he will look more closely at the player's most recent at-bats to make his decision. Because the player's batting average is .200 in his last 500 at-bats, his likelihood of getting a hit drops to 1 in 5. Another weakness evident with the use of standard deviation stems from the fact that the final number is lacking a relative point of reference. In other words, the final analysis has no point of comparison—it tells us *how risky,* but not by *how much.*

Beta

In financial markets, beta is commonly used to measure how much an individual stock or portfolio is likely to move vis-à-vis a broader market barometer, typically the S&P 500 Index. (See the market primer in Box 3.2.)

The return of the overall market is defined by a beta of 1.0. A portfolio with a beta of 1.0 suggests perfect correlation with the broader market. A beta of 1.5 implies that a stock or portfolio will move in the same direction by an additional factor of 50 percent. Empirical studies conducted on U.S. stock market returns over almost three decades have attacked beta as an incomplete measure of risk, arguing that higher returns have not necessarily been accompanied by higher beta securities. A study by Eugene Fama of the University of Chicago, known for his contributions to research on market efficiency, and Kenneth French, finance professor at the Massachusetts Institute of Technology and an expert in the behavior of security prices, conclude that beta "is not a useful measure to capture the relationship between risk and return."[7] It's not unfair to say that a risk measure should

---

Box 3.2 Market Primer on Beta

In the financial markets, beta is commonly used to measure how much an individual stock or portfolio is likely to move vis-à-vis a broader market barometer, typically the S&P 500 Index. A stock with a beta of 1.0 suggests that the stock's price moves exactly in tandem with the overall market. If the market goes up 30 percent, the stock price goes up 30 percent. If the market falls 20 percent, then the stock falls 20 percent.

A stock with a beta greater than 1.0 is considered more volatile than the market. If a stock or fund has a beta of 1.5, then it tends to go up at a 50 percent greater magnitude. For example, if the market goes up 10 percent, the stock goes up 15 percent. The higher the beta, the more volatile the stock. A beta of less than 1.0 indicates that the stock's price is generally more stable than the market over a long period of time. Conservative investors whose primary goal is preservation of capital often gravitate toward low-beta stocks and stock funds.

For more information on beta, refer to the capital asset pricing model (CAPM) market primer in Box 3.3.

Source: RiskGrades, Understanding Risk online course.

---

link risk and returns together. However, it is far from clear that beta should be rendered meaningless on this basis alone. For example, beta can prove quite useful for any money manager or investor who uses a benchmark as a barometer of risk. The beta will always tell an investor how a particular investment is expected to perform relative to an index or another asset. Beta as a tool for measuring financial risk is good at indicating general risk, but limited in highlighting specific risk.

Because a beta is expressed in number format, it appears to be precise and robust. However, from a practical standpoint, beta has two principal limitations as an effective measure of risk. First, the concept of beta ignores company-specific risk, capturing only relative movements against the market. In this regard, beta can confuse investors into thinking that stocks sharing the same beta share the same risks—we'll see that this is far from the case. Another glaring weakness is that a stock's beta to the S&P 500, for example, may remain constant despite the fact that the market has grown significantly more risky. Compare the beta of Microsoft stock to the S&P 500 at year-end 1999 and 2000. Microsoft returned 68 percent in 1999 and a negative 63 percent in 2000 versus almost 20 percent for the S&P 500 in 1999 and negative 10 percent in 2000. Meanwhile, Microsoft's beta to the S&P 500 remained virtually the same. In other words, a beta is insensitive to recent market dynamics. "We must keep in mind that it is very difficult (indeed probably impossible) to measure beta with any degree of precision."[8] Because the recommended practice (according to CAPM) is to use a time series that dates back five years when available, the final number could prove to be somewhat stale. To put it differently, beta may not be sufficiently responsive to current trends—which may prove to be inconsequential in stable market conditions but is essential in a volatile environment. (See Box 3.3.)

Box 3.3 Market Primer on Capital Asset Pricing Model (CAPM)

The use of beta first burst onto the investment scene with the introduction of the capital asset pricing model, otherwise known as CAPM. Crystallized in the late 1960s, CAPM was the effort of three independent researchers—William Sharpe, John Lintner, and Jack Treynor—who drew on Markowitz's portfolio theory that explained why diversification reduced risk. The importance of CAPM to the field of finance did not go unnoticed. Sharpe won the Nobel Prize in 1990 for his contributions to the CAPM.

Although the CAPM takes into account many underlying assumptions about investor behavior, the logic behind CAPM can be reduced to a simple line of reasoning. Financial market returns consist of either a riskless or a risky component. A risk-free return can be realized exclusively through short-term Treasury bills. All other returns are effectively a combination of the risk-free rate and a market premium. This risk premium in turn is made up of two separate elements: market risk (systematic) and company-specific risk (unsystematic).

The pioneers of CAPM rigorously established that risk that can be diversified away, known as *unsystematic, idiosyncratic,* or *company-specific risk,* could *not* command a premium. This is because holding other, similar, stocks can offset risk related to a single company. For instance, consider the personal computer industry. Despite bright overall prospects, some companies will invariably provide less-than-enviable returns. What is good for Dell will not necessarily benefit Compaq and

Continued

Gateway. However, holding a handful of PC-related stocks will ensure a balance between admirable leaders and invariable letdowns.[9] To wit, the CAPM assumes that over time investors will not be rewarded for needlessly taking unsystematic risk. In contrast, "because systematic risk cannot be avoided, investors demand and, over the long run receive, compensation for bearing such risk in the form of an excess return."[10] This concept is represented in Figure 3.9 by the *security market line* and *beta*.

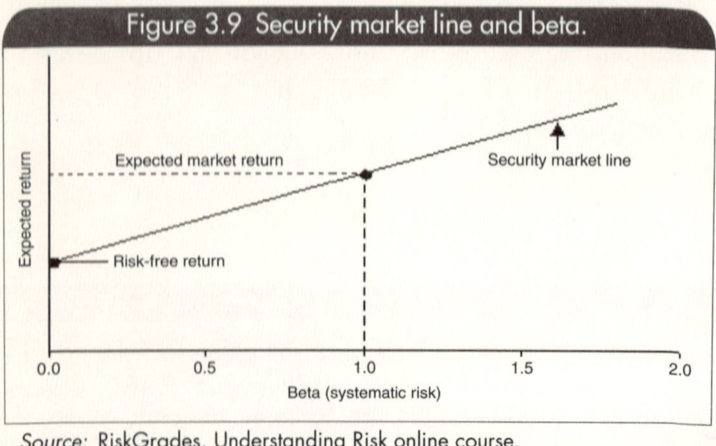

Source: RiskGrades, Understanding Risk online course.

RiskGrades versus Beta

For illustrative purposes, we compared the RiskGrades of the 29 widely held stocks with corresponding betas on the S&P 500 Index as a basis of comparison at the end of 2000. Tables 3.2 and 3.3 list stocks sorted by RiskGrades and by beta. A higher RiskGrade or beta suggests higher risk.

Expectedly, some stocks top both lists. It doesn't come as a big shock to see blue-chip names such as Exxon Mobil and Johnson & Johnson high on both lists. By any assessment, such names are viewed as "safer" bets. Moreover, technology names are considered predominantly more risky by both beta and RiskGrades. The findings, though, offer a few surprises. The RiskGrade of the S&P 500 is lower than the RiskGrade on any single stock. In contrast, measured by beta, seven stocks, including AT&T and Pfizer, appear to be less risky than the overall market, with a beta of less than 1.0. This is due in part to the fact that a RiskGrade on a basket of assets will factor in diversification benefits. A diverse portfolio (which is,

Table 3.2 RiskGrades versus Beta, Sorted by RiskGrade

Company	Symbol	RiskGrades	Beta versus S&P	Beta versus Nasdaq
Johnson & Johnson	JNJ	118	0.30	−0.02
Exxon Mobil Corp.	XOM	123	0.21	−0.03
Merck & Company, Inc.	MRK	154	0.43	−0.01
SBC Communications Inc.	SBC	172	0.63	0.08
General Electric Co.	GE	181	1.16	0.38
Pfizer Inc.	PFE	182	0.51	0.02
Wal-Mart Stores Inc.	WMT	238	0.98	0.16
Microsoft Corp.	MSFT	266	1.31	0.58
Walt Disney Co.	DIS	274	0.64	0.21
AT&T	T	287	0.91	0.31
Int'l Business Machines Corp.	IBM	287	1.14	0.45
America Online Inc.	AOL	303	1.59	0.66
EMC Corp.	EMC	330	2.17	1.02
Compaq Computer Corp.	CPQ	357	1.44	0.65
Cisco Systems Inc.	CSCO	363	2.15	1.04
Motorola Inc.	MOT	368	1.71	0.77
Sun Microsystems Inc.	SUNW	378	2.15	1.03
Home Depot Inc.	HD	389	1.21	0.27
Intel Corp.	INTC	389	1.77	0.81
Nokia Corp.	NOK	427	1.97	0.79
Qualcomm Inc.	QCOM	428	2.06	0.98
Oracle Corp.	ORCL	454	2.20	1.05
Dell Computer Corp.	DELL	461	1.64	0.78
WorldCom Inc.	WCOM	482	1.40	0.54
Lucent Technologies Inc.	LU	494	1.56	0.64
Yahoo! Inc.	YHOO	494	2.17	1.05
Nortel Networks Corp.	NT	515	1.85	0.87
JDS Uniphase Corp.	JDSU	543	2.85	1.49
CMGI Inc.	CMGI	627	3.05	1.51
S&P 500 Index		101		
Nasdaq Composite		239		

Source: WealthBench, RiskMetrics Group.

Company	Symbol	RiskGrades	Beta versus S&P	Beta versus Nasdaq
Exxon Mobil Corp.	XOM	123	0.21	−0.03
Johnson & Johnson	JNJ	118	0.30	−0.02
Merck & Company, Inc.	MRK	154	0.43	−0.01
Pfizer Inc.	PFE	182	0.51	0.02
SBC Communications Inc.	SBC	172	0.63	0.08
Walt Disney Co.	DIS	274	0.64	0.21
Wal-Mart Stores Inc.	WMT	238	0.98	0.16
AT&T	T	287	0.91	0.31
Int'l Business Machines Corp.	IBM	287	1.14	0.45
General Electric Co.	GE	181	1.16	0.38
Home Depot Inc.	HD	389	1.21	0.27
Microsoft Corp.	MSFT	266	1.31	0.58
WorldCom Inc.	WCOM	482	1.40	0.54
Compaq Computer Corp.	CPQ	357	1.44	0.65
Lucent Technologies Inc.	LU	494	1.56	0.64
America Online Inc.	AOL	303	1.59	0.66
Dell Computer Corp.	DELL	461	1.64	0.78
Motorola Inc.	MOT	368	1.71	0.77
Intel Corp.	INTC	389	1.77	0.81
Nortel Networks Corp.	NT	515	1.85	0.87
Nokia Corp.	NOK	427	1.97	0.79
Qualcomm Inc.	QCOM	428	2.06	0.98
Cisco Systems Inc.	CSCO	363	2.15	1.04
Sun Microsystems Inc.	SUNW	378	2.15	1.03
EMC Corp.	EMC	330	2.17	1.02
Yahoo! Inc.	YHOO	494	2.17	1.05
Oracle Corp.	ORCL	454	2.20	1.05
JDS Uniphase Corp.	JDSU	543	2.85	1.49
CMGI Inc.	CMGI	627	3.05	1.51
S&P 500 Index		101		
Nasdaq Composite		239		

Source: WealthBench, RiskMetrics Group.

in effect, the S&P 500) will exhibit less risk than any one name, which makes intuitive sense.

The concept of beta can mislead one into believing that a smaller number constitutes lower risk and a larger number higher risk. Take AT&T as an example (see Figure 3.10). At the time we ran our analysis, most would have perceived Ma Bell to be a fairly stable long-term investment. And a beta of 0.91 certainly provided support for that conclusion. In fact, as measured by beta, AT&T registered as one of the lower-risk stocks among the 29 selected. Measured by beta, the giant telecommunications provider appears to be about 10 percent less risky than the market, with a beta of 0.91.

In comparison, AT&T's RiskGrade measurement was 287. This elevated RiskGrade infers AT&T stock (at the time we ran our numbers) was almost three times as risky as the S&P 500, which had a RiskGrade of 101 (see Figure 3.11). Which measure is more accurate?

A closer examination of our example demonstrates that RiskGrades capture the essence of AT&T more accurately. AT&T traded up to $60 a share by late March 2000, close to its all-time high, only to lose steam as the summer months unfolded. The S&P began to slide from recent highs in early April 2000, rebounding during the months of June, July, and August. This divergence contributed to the lower beta, as the two moved essentially in incongruent directions. However, if we look at the performance of

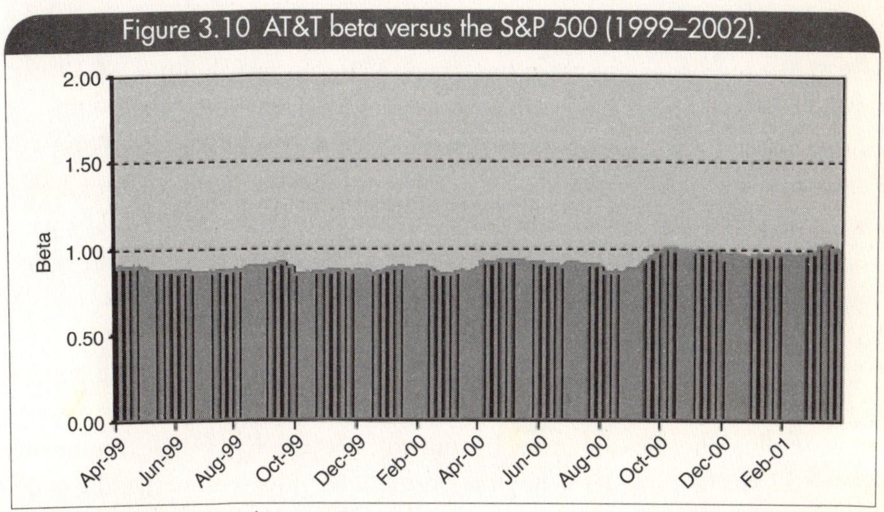

Source: WealthBench, RiskMetrics Group.

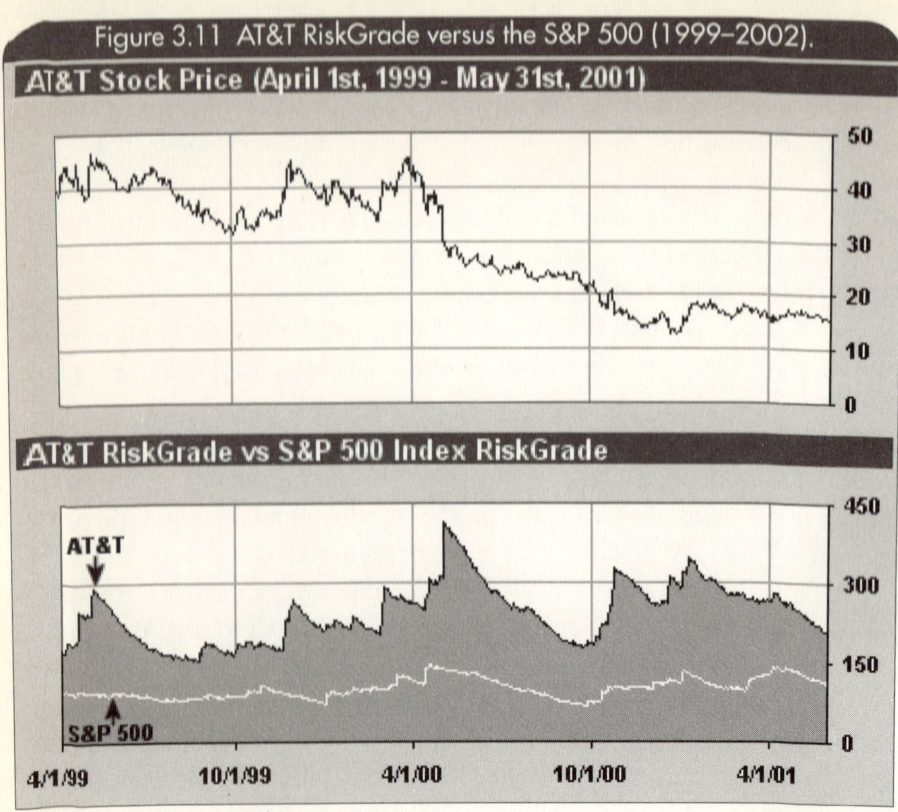

Source: WealthBench, RiskMetrics Group.

AT&T relative to the S&P 500 at that time, we see that the relationship of risk and return does not seem fully reasonable. In fact, holders of AT&T would likely argue that the stock posed more risk than the S&P 500 from both a short-term and long-term perspective. For instance, the five-year return ending in 2000 on AT&T was a whopping negative 60 percent; however, the S&P 500 in the same period delivered returns totaling 114 percent. For the year 2000, the S&P 500 fell by 10 percent; AT&T, on the other hand, was down 66 percent. It is tough to argue that AT&T is less volatile than the broader market by any standpoint.

Because beta treats time as static, recent market conditions are poorly reflected. Using beta as a yardstick to make near-term decisions can lead to some unpleasant consequences. In contrast, because RiskGrades exponentially weights historic data, the final output looks much more like the market today.[11] For all its limitations (unresponsive, inaccurate with respect to returns), beta is not entirely useless. Beta is fairly good at capturing the extent of long-term movements relative to the general market. This could prove useful in coming up with accurate long-term estimates and, when used in conjunction with a RiskGrade, in painting a more complete picture of risk for the investor.

An Empirical Observation: The Dow, the S&P, and the Nasdaq

In recent years, the Dow Jones Industrial Average and the S&P 500 Index have taken somewhat of a backseat to the Nasdaq Composite. A $10,000 investment in the Nasdaq at the outset of 1995 would have returned a profit of over $44,000, a whopping 400 percent gain by the end of 1999. By comparison, an equal investment in the S&P 500 Index would have profited by close to $22,000, or roughly half. Not bad, but bad enough to develop an inferiority complex next to the Nasdaq if your investment time horizon was five years. (See Table 3.4.)

The focus on the Nasdaq run-up during the late 1990s may have clouded our general perception of risk. Based on casual commentary and cursory observations, most investors sense the Nasdaq to be a far riskier venture than the Dow Jones Industrials or the S&P 500. In fact, such assessments are true based on most conventional measures of risk. Accordingly, financial advisors would probably suggest that the heavily tech-weighted

Table 3.4 How an Initial Investment of $10,000 Would Have Fared		
Year	**Dow Jones Ind End Value**	**S&P 500 Index End Value**	**Nasdaq Composite End Value**
1995	$13,345	$13,411	$13,992
1996	$16,816	$16,128	$17,170
1997	$20,624	$21,129	$20,885
1998	$23,944	$26,765	$29,162
1999	$29,982	$31,992	$54,121
2000	$28,132	$28,748	$32,857
2001	$26,135	$24,999	$25,941
2002 (as of August 23)	$23,022	$20,364	$18,091

Source: WealthBench, RiskMetrics Group.

index is not a place for widows and orphans. However, what if we compared the Nasdaq to the other indices from a risk-return perspective? Would we have a change of heart? More to the point, did the Nasdaq adequately compensate investors for additional risk?

Table 3.5 depicts the average annual return of the Dow, the S&P 500 Index, and the Nasdaq Composite for the period 1995 to 2002. The return numbers speak for themselves—the Nasdaq far outshone both the S&P and Dow price increases over the period from 1995 thru 1999. However, from the viewpoint of risk, the nominal level of risk on the Nasdaq was consistently higher as well, marked by a larger nominal RiskGrade every year. On a percentage basis, from 1995 through 2001, the Nasdaq Risk-Grade went from 62 to 220, a substantial 258 percent increase. During the same period, the Dow and S&P RiskGrades rose by 130 percent and 166 percent, respectively. Although far from conclusive, Nasdaq investors seemed to have been provided with excessive returns for the incremental risk taken, at least for the time period. Let's see by how much.

In Figure 3.12, the scattergrams plot the S&P, Dow, and Nasdaq by risk and return parameters for each of the eight periods shown in Table 3.5. The most coveted area is the upper left-hand corner, where risk runs low but returns are high. The dark line that cuts through the scattergrams corresponds to what we call the *threshold of indifference*, the minimum rate of

Table 3.5 Risk and Return Statistics for Major U.S. Stock Indices (1995–2002)

Year	Dow Jones Industrials		S&P 500 Index		Nasdaq Composite Index	
	Avg. RG	Return	Avg. RG	Return	Avg. RG	Return
1995	45	33.45%	40	34.11%	61	39.92%
1996	58	26.01%	56	20.26%	78	22.71%
1997	86	22.64%	83	31.01%	84	21.64%
1998	96	16.10%	96	26.67%	121	39.63%
1999	83	25.22%	93	19.53%	140	85.59%
2000	98	−6.17%	104	−10.14%	220	−39.29%
2001	103	−7.10%	107	−13.04%	220	−21.05%
2002 (as of August 23)	99	−11.91%	101	−18.54%	156	−30.26%

Source: WealthBench, RiskMetrics Group.

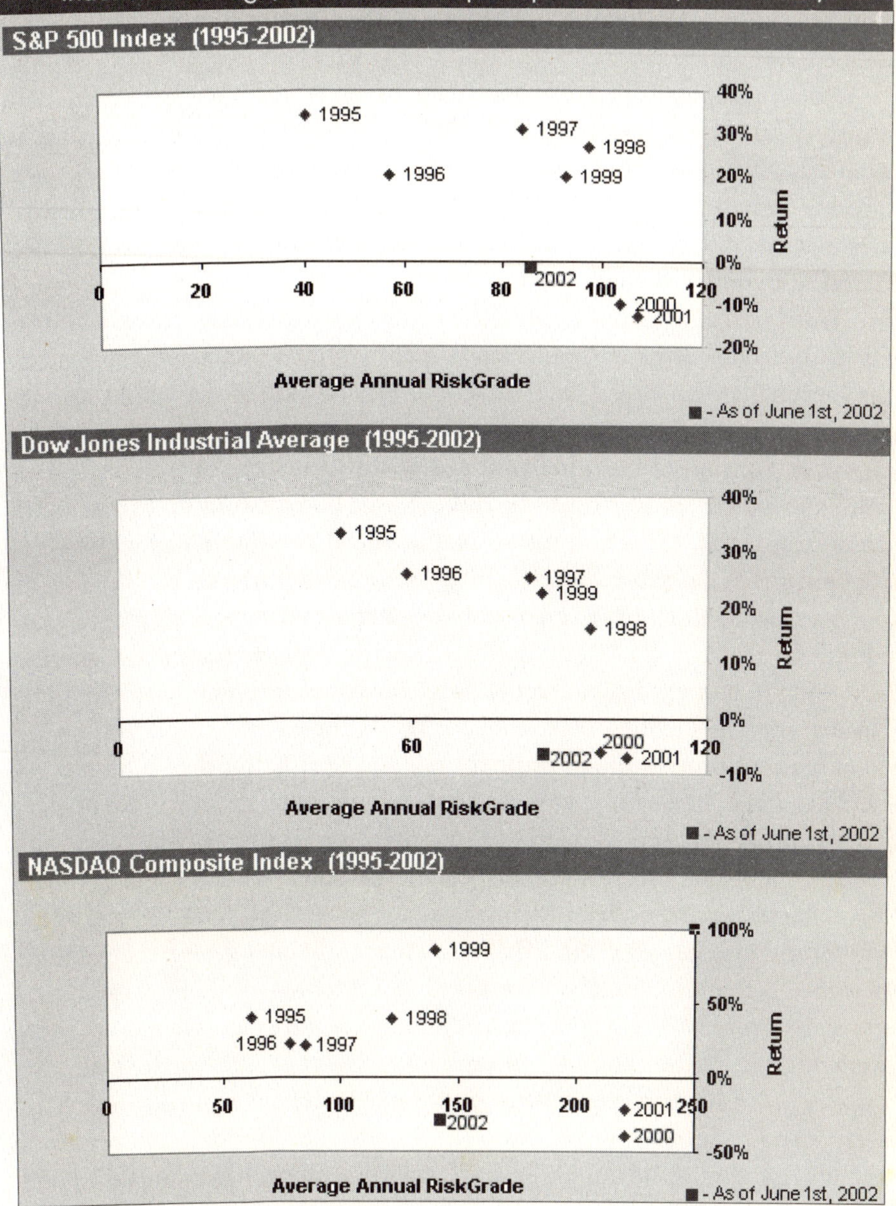

Source: WealthBench, RiskMetrics Group.

return an investor should expect given the risks. (As a point of reference, we are using a risk-free rate of 6 percent for our analysis. Naturally, a lower risk-free number will imply a flatter slope, or lower required return for each risk point.)

From a risk standpoint, the U.S. equity markets have generally paid investors for their investments in recent years. Isolating performance on an annual basis, we see that each index returned better than the minimum threshold every year until 2000. The Dow and S&P 500 rewarded investors most significantly in 1995, and 1999 was the best year for the Nasdaq when factoring in both risk and return.

As surprising as it may appear, the Nasdaq generally rewarded investors for taking additional risk in the second half of the 1990s (concurrent with the spectacular run-up). The Nasdaq Composite was, on the whole, a superior investment to the S&P 500 and Dow Jones even after factoring in risk. However, we should keep in mind that investments are not typically discrete one-year events. Witness how the Nasdaq went from first to worst in 2000, 2001, and 2002. The professional financial community may use one-year returns as a marker, but most of us value our returns on a rolling basis.

After we factor in the impact of the current bear market, we see how additional risk can knife into returns over the last three years. Carrying more risk in a declining market simply translated into deeper losses. The Nasdaq was the clear front-runner for the latter half of the 1990s, giving good reason for investors to smile for taking the risk, but then a nightmarish 2000 and 2001 decimated total returns. Consequently, the great disparity in returns between the three indices narrowed substantially.

In conclusion, investors should understand that an adequate amount of risk is necessary to position themselves for successful, long-term growth. We should also keep in mind that risk constantly changes. If the primary objective is to maintain a balanced profile, investors would be wise to target a risk level and rebalance accordingly. Investors can use market bellwethers such as the S&P 500 Index as a target risk guide. This naturally implies that market risk in our portfolios needs to be managed similarly to sectors and styles. If your portfolio RiskGrade exceeds your comfort level, overall risk should be scaled back. If risk dips below a certain threshold, risk should be increased. These thresholds must clearly be specified based on the appetite and tolerance for risk dictated by the individual circumstances of each investor.

CHAPTER 4

Return Is Only Half the Equation

As investors we face new risks every day. We consciously place our assets at risk in order to achieve an objective. This is the essence of investing and the reason that understanding risk and the practice of risk management is *the* central issue in investing today. We need to look no further than the horrific terrorist attacks on September 11, 2001, for evidence that difficult-to-measure, low-probability, yet extremely consequential events can and do happen. The tragic images and stories from that day, broadcast live on television, will be embedded in most people's minds forever.

For investors whose nerves were frayed even before the events of September 11, these are understandably emotional times. Since June 2000, investors have witnessed the collapse of Silicon Valley and dot-com valuations, September 11, recession, anthrax, the Enron scandal, the U.S. Department of Justice indictment of Arthur Andersen, 9 of the 18 largest U.S. corporate bankruptcies on record (including WorldCom), and Senate hearings investigating misleading advice by some of Wall Street's premier research analysts. To say the least, it has been an incredibly tumultuous period to be invested in the market.

In the wake of these events, one of the most important lessons an investor can learn is the significant role emotions play in all our investment decisions. More often than not, emotions are responsible for making us do things we later regret. In later chapters you will learn how to use Wealth-Bench's analytic models to simulate the potential impact that various disastrous financial events may have on your portfolio. Modeling these types of events before they happen will provide you with valuable insights into the composition of your portfolio. However, the burden will always be on you to assimilate, interpret, and act on the data. In times of crisis, emotions will affect your judgment. Trading decisions made in haste or born out of an emotive response to distress will inevitably be wrong. In order to make a sound investment decision we need the self-discipline to eliminate emotions from our decision-making process.

In this chapter we're going to explore the emotional side of investing otherwise known as *behavioral finance*. We examine the psychological characteristics that play a part in determining how we react to news, what we buy, when we sell, and even how well we manage our portfolios. After reading this chapter, you will better understand how behavioral tendencies influence your investment decision-making process.

Behavioral Finance

In early 2000, prior to the Nasdaq reaching its zenith, we presented a focus group of investors with two statements: (1) "In the real world, the road to finding financial security is laden with pitfalls, detours, and sharp turns." (2) "Technology stocks are valued too high." Not surprisingly, no one in the group dissented with either assessment. Interestingly, even after acknowledging both statements to be true, in a follow-up question we learned that more than half the group would continue to invest primarily in technology stocks. Why? To answer this, we're going to investigate the field of behavioral finance.

Behavioral finance is the study of how humans interpret and act on information to make investment decisions. Behavioral finance postulates that investors do not always behave in the rational, predictable, and unbiased manner suggested by quantitative models. In fact, we often see order where it does not exist and success amidst serendipity. These biases of judgment and decision making are sometimes referred to as *cognitive illusions*. Like visual illusions, the mistakes of intuitive reasoning are not easily eliminated. Consider the example shown in Figure 4.1. Although we can use a ruler to prove to ourselves that the two horizontal lines are of equal length, our eyes will continue to believe that the second line is longer than

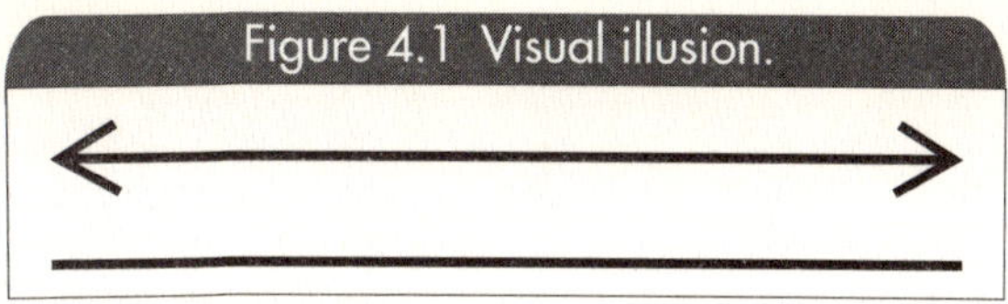

the first. Merely realizing the power of illusions does not take away from their ability to shape our minds.

Here's what David Kahneman, Eugene Higgins, and Mark Riepe have to say in the *Journal of Portfolio Management:*

> **The goal of learning about cognitive illusions and decision making is to develop the skill of recognizing situations in which a particular error is likely. In such situations, as in the case of [Figure 4.1], intuition cannot be trusted and it must be supplemented or replaced by more critical or analytical thinking—the equivalent of using a ruler to avoid a visual illusion.[1]**

Let's put our newly acquired conceptual skills to the test with another exercise. Out of 100 people gathered in a room, 90 are engineers and the remaining 10 are artists. Among the 100 is a man draped in black, wearing a beret, goatee, and dark sunglasses. Is he an engineer or an artist? Most observers, focusing on his attire, would guess the man is an artist. But a better guess would be an engineer, given that 9 of every 10 people in the room are engineers. The chance of being correct using this line of reasoning is 90 percent. However, most people tend to classify objects by *representativeness,* or immediate observable characteristics, instead of relying on more rational evidence. When applied to financial decisions, representativeness can severely hinder our investment performance. For example, if an investor regards a stock as good, he or she is likely to classify it as good well past the point where it becomes a bad stock. In this case, an investor who is susceptible to representativeness is likely to overreact to positive news and underreact to negative news, potentially missing a window of opportunity to profitably sell the stock.

In recent years, behavioral finance has reached mainstream status. Recent studies by Professors Terrence Odean and Brad Barber of the University of California at Davis, bolstered by other recognized experts in the field such as Daniel Kahneman (Princeton), Meir Statman (Santa Clara), Richard Thaler (University of Chicago), Robert J. Shiller (Yale), and the founding father, the late Amos Tversky, have brought behavioral finance to the forefront of issues affecting investor performance. Behavioral finance has helped to shed new light on inefficiencies in the financial markets and to explain the causes of stock market anomalies such as bubbles and crashes. The theories of behavioral finance are in direct conflict with financial economics, which is based on the assumption that investors make decisions based on rational expectations. Behavioral finance challenges this notion by proposing that people are, more often than not, less than rational. Leveraging the group's collective research, we highlight typical human behavioral tendencies and their implications for "rational" investment decisions.

The 10 principles of behavioral finance may be summarized as follows:

1. *Investors avoid selling stocks that have gone down in order to avoid the pain and regret of having made a bad investment.* As a result, investors are more likely to sell winners and hold losers.

2. *Investors are much more distressed by prospective losses than they are happy with equivalent gains.* Investors typically consider the loss of $1 dollar twice as painful as the pleasure received from a $1 gain.

3. *Investors follow the crowd and conventional wisdom to avoid the possibility of feeling regret in the event that their decisions prove to be incorrect—a tendency that lies at the root of many bubbles and crashes.*

4. *Investors tend to become too optimistic when the market goes up and too pessimistic when the market goes down.* Many believe that when high percentages of investors become overly optimistic or pessimistic about the future, it is a signal that the opposite scenario will occur.

5. *People often see order where it does not exist and interpret accidental success as the result of skill.* Most money managers, advisors, and investors are overconfident in their own abilities; however, high levels of confidence frequently show no correlation to greater success. For instance, overconfident investors tend to trade too much and underperform the market.

6. *People often see other people's decisions as the result of disposition, but they see their own choices as rational. Investors trade on information they believe to be superior.* For instance, there are two sides to a trade, a buyer and a seller; each believes his or her decision is superior, yet they can't both be right.

7. *The penchant to gamble and assume unnecessary risks is a basic human trait.* Entertainment and ego appear to be some of the motivations

for people's tendency to speculate. People also tend to remember successes more than failures, thereby unjustifiably increasing their confidence.

8. *In some cases, investors (individuals and institutional) hire full-service brokers and advisors for no other reason than to have someone else to take the blame.* Hiring an advisor or money manager diffuses an individual's responsibility and deflects blame if an investment strategy fails. If the strategy is successful, the individual can share in the credit.

9. *An individual's traits play a significant role in determining investment decisions.* The Bailard, Biehl & Kaiser Five-Way Model divides investors into five categories: *Adventurers* are risk takers and are particularly difficult to advise. *Celebrities* like to be where the action is and make easy prey for persuasive brokers. *Individualists* tend to avoid extreme risk, do their own research, and act rationally. *Guardians* are typically older, more careful, and more risk averse. *Straight arrows* fall in between the other four personalities and are typically very balanced.

10. *Many investors believe that they can consistently time the financial markets when there exists an overwhelming amount of evidence to the contrary.* The same can be true in attempting to select the hottest mutual fund or investment managers. By focusing only on recent investment performance, investors set themselves up for disappointment.

Recognize any of these characteristics? Many of these traits are human qualities that are not easily turned off. In fact, we are all guilty in some ways. When it comes to money, we all have the tendency to behave irrationally at times. As the 1990s came to a close, the endless wonders of the new economy convinced even the most rational of us to suspend reason, at least for a few years. A prolonged bull market made us overconfident in our abilities to predict the markets. Cognitive dissonance restrained us from acting properly, and when the question did arise about the soundness of valuations and the strength of the new economy, many of us just rationalized it away. Investors around the world tripped over themselves bidding up technology stocks and chasing initial public offerings (IPOs). A Bernstein Research paper summed it best: "The exceptional returns of Internet stocks can be seen as the equivalent of the lottery jackpot.... The jackpot has been huge and well publicized.... The number of people who play the lottery now represents half the adult population."[2] And although a large number of investors hit the equivalent of the jackpot in the stock market, very few held onto it in the ensuing market plunge. When the party ended, sobriety quickly replaced irrational exuberance. And just like partygoers who had too much of a good thing the night before, we're now left rubbing our heads, promising that next time our behavior will be different.

Overcoming Behavioral Finance in Your Investment Decisions

To be successful in the years ahead, it will be critical for investors to identify their own biases and find ways to minimize the negative effects. Just as it is important for investors to understand the concepts of diversification, asset allocation, and risk and return, it's important to know ourselves. In the words of Gavin Quill, Financial Research Corporation's director of research, "Good financial decisions require a combination of financial knowledge, self-knowledge, and the discipline to implement a plan dispassionately. Very few people can do all three well."[3]

The typical human urges and behavioral tendencies that impede investors can be controlled with discipline. We provide the following list of guidelines to help you avoid behavioral biases that impede sound financial decisions.

- Guard against overconfidence. All investors need a healthy dose of optimism to achieve their goals, but it must be tempered with reasonable expectations of their abilities.
- Because investors are more likely than not to remember past successes and forget failures, keep a list of trades or decisions that were not successful.
- For couples who share investment responsibilities, recognize your partner's strengths, but prevent only one opinion from overly influencing all investment decisions.
- Before making a trade, consider the possibility that the trade is a loser. What's the impact on the rest of your portfolio, both immediately and long term?
- Avoid using biased information and analysis; obtain an independent second opinion.
- Before buying a security, evaluate the time frame and conditions under which a sale is made.

- Know your tolerance for risk before assuming risk.
- If you're a long-term investor, don't react to short-term fluctuations.

Investors Behaving Badly

In an effort to explore investor behavior and its impact on long-term investment success, Phoenix Investment Partners, a leading U.S. investment management company, commissioned Financial Research Corporation (FRC) to perform a comprehensive analysis of investor behavior in the spring of 2000.[4] The full study, *Investors Behaving Badly—An Analysis of Investor Trading Patterns in Mutual Funds*, examines trading patterns in the mutual fund industry and the impact of behavioral finance on investors' returns during the 1990s. The results are eye-opening, if not frightening. The research concludes that investor behavior is often detrimental to the long-term success of our financial plans. The findings expose the negative influence of psychological, emotional, and behavioral drivers on trading activity in mutual funds. The study also finds that investors who use financial advisors tend to experience slightly better returns than those who do not rely on professional advice. Among its chief findings are the following.[5]

- Excessive portfolio turnover, combined with a propensity to buy relatively overvalued investments and ignore relatively undervalued ones, has caused the average mutual fund investor to underperform over the past decade.
- Investors' propensity for chasing returns is the major reason for underperformance. Buying high and selling low caused a shortfall of 20 percent to the average mutual fund investor over the past decade. Specifically, on a rolling return basis from January 1990 through March 2000, the average long-term mutual fund's mean three-year return was 10.92 percent, whereas the average invested dollar gained only 8.7 percent over the same period.
- On average, $91 billion of new cash flowed into funds after their best-performing quarters. But only $6.5 billion in new money flowed into the funds after their worst-performing quarters.
- Investors are trading funds at higher levels, which in most cases does not serve their long-term financial goals. The study found that investors think long term in theory, but act according to short-term influences.

- For the past several years, redemption rates have been on the rise.[6] In 1996, redemption rates were 17.4 percent, but by 2000, those rates rose to an incredible 32.1 percent.
- The implied holding period for long-term mutual funds in 1996 was 5.5 years. In 2000, it was only 2.9 years.
- Individual investors have consistently higher redemption rates and shorter implied holding periods than those investors who use a financial advisor. Advisor-assisted investors, the study found, also are more likely to stick to their declared intentions to invest for the long term.
- The study found that investors think long term in theory, but act according to short-term influences.

The *Investors Behaving Badly* study is neatly divided into two parts. The first part answers the question, do investors behave rationally? The second section provides answers to why investors actually do behave badly. Rather than recite the full details of the study, we'll look closely at a few key excerpts. We trust that these figures will be troubling to you. Accelerating redemption rates and falling holding periods are responsible for a 20 percent loss of returns to the average mutual fund investor. As incredible as this underperformance may seem, note that it came in the midst of an amazing bull run. We have every reason to believe that if investors repeat this behavior in sharply declining markets, the degree to which investors underperform will be dramatically worse. With so much at stake, we encourage everyone to visit the Phoenix Investment Partners' or FRC's website and read the study in its entirety.[7]

Redemption Rates and Holding Periods

During the magnificent bull market of late 1990s, investors wrung their hands with regret over one thing: not investing more capital sooner. The unfortunate consequence of this mind-set is an overconfidence on the part of investors that making money in the markets is an easy endeavor.

Prior to the recent burst of stock market activity (pre-1995), investors at least entertained the thought of managing volatility and the risk of a potential market decline. However, from the mid-1990s onward, a large segment of the investment community assumed a new perspective on risk. Fear of losing money was replaced with the fear of not making enough money. By the end of the decade, beating the S&P 500 by a few percentage points seemed to be an outdated objective. For many of us, as the 1990s came to a close, greed was the overriding factor in how we approached the investment game. Instead of being grateful about market returns in excess of 20 percent, we eyed the returns generated by red-hot technology sector as the true barometer of success.

The fallout from this newfound short-term mind-set was immediate:

- During the period from 1996 to 2000, long-term mutual fund redemption rates have been rising.
- During the 1996 to 1997 period, redemption rates averaged 18.6 percent. During the first quarter of 2000, redemption rates rose to an average of 32.1 percent.

Mutual Fund Redemption Rates: Nearly Doubled in Four Years

Every redemption rate can be translated into an implied holding period. (A mutual fund investor's *annual redemption rate* is defined as total dollars redeemed from a mutual fund in a given year as a percent of an investor's starting assets in that fund.) For example, as shown in Figure 4.2, if an investor consistently has 50 percent redemption rates, half of the assets are redeemed each year; over a two-year period, all the assets will be liquidated. This yields an implied holding period of two years. Table 4.1 illustrates how redemption rates translate into implied holding periods.

Long-term investing is generally considered to be a period of 10 years or more. According to Table 4.1, a mutual fund investor is considered a long-term investor if annual redemption rates are no greater than 10 percent.

An analysis was performed on aggregate fund industry data during the past four years for long-term funds, excluding data on short-term money market funds. By calculating monthly redemption rates (redemptions divided by starting fund assets) and then annualizing these figures, the Phoenix/FRC study found that average long-term mutual fund holding periods declined steadily from 1996 to 2000. The implied holding period for long-term mutual funds in 2000 was 2.9 years, compared to a 5.5-year holding period in 1996 (see Figure 4.3). As markets have gone up, holding periods have gone down.

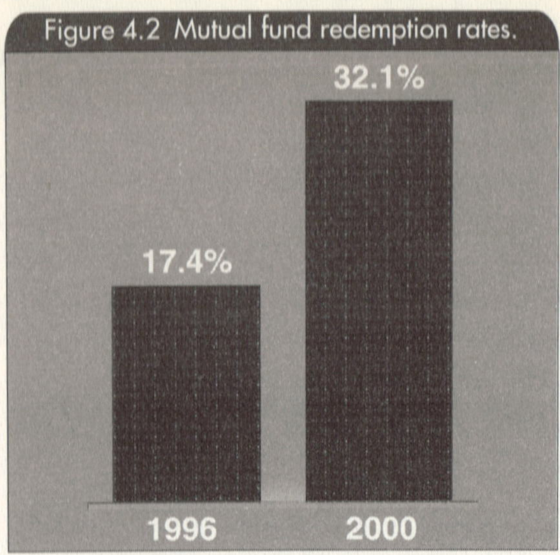

Source: Phoenix Investment Partners, research conducted by Financial Research Corporation (FRC). Reprinted with permission.

Short-term holding periods have a diminutive effect on returns; investors who continuously redeem one fund for another pay additional sales commissions, 12b-1 (marketing) fees, management fees, operating expenses, and taxes. These seemingly small incremental fees translate into significant differences over time. For example, if you invested $25,000 in a stock fund that provides a 12 percent annual return before expenses and had annual operating expenses of 2.5 percent, after 15 years you would have

Table 4.1 Translating Redemption Rates to Holding Periods	
Annual Redemption Rate	**Implied Holding Period**
5%	20 years
10%	10 years
20%	5 years
33%	3 years
50%	2 years
100%	1 year
200%	6 months

Source: Phoenix Investment Partners, research conducted by Financial Research Corporation (FRC). Reprinted with permission.

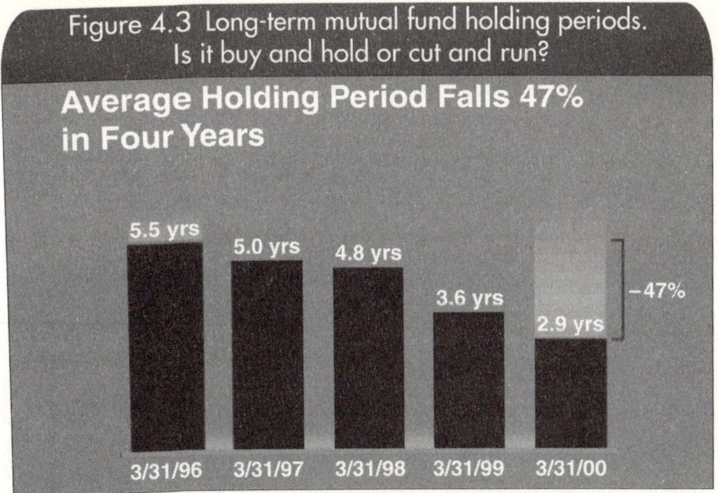

Source: Phoenix Investment Partners, research conducted by Financial Research Corporation (FRC). Reprinted with permission.

approximately $93,600. But if the fund had expenses of only 1 percent, you would end up with $109,082, which is an additional $15,482, or a 14 percent difference.

The Role of Financial Advisors and Professional Advice

In order to assess the impact of a financial advisor's advice on individual returns, this study also examined data for wholesale funds (those sold by an advisor) versus funds directly marketed to individual investors from 1996 to 2000. The categories—wholesale funds versus direct-marketed funds—were then used as proxies for funds that come with some degree of professional advice versus those that are bought by do-it-yourself individual investors.

The findings reveal a rather fickle individual investor who fails to stay the course without the assistance of a financial advisor. Individual investors redeemed their funds more often than investors with advisors in every month examined except one. These redemptions averaged 18 percent in 1996 and increased to 30.5 percent in 2000. During the same time span, the rates of redemption among investors with advisors increased from 13.8 percent to 25.4 percent, according to the data. The differential between redemption rates for individual investors versus investors with advisors marginally widened in 2000, to 5.1 percentage points. (Wholesale funds had redemption rates of 25.4 percent, versus 30.5 percent for individual investors.) While somewhat arguable, the numbers suggest that investors who have access to advisors are less likely to chase performance.

Fund Returns versus Investor Returns

Research on net cash flows in the mutual fund industry over the past 10 years shows that investors too frequently buy and sell at suboptimal times. Examining net inflows (new investor deposits minus investor redemptions) suggests that investors have a tendency to invest on a momentum basis: heavily purchasing funds in sectors that have had stellar recent performance and ignoring or selling funds in sectors that have recently underperformed. Not surprisingly, this type of behavior lends itself to consistent underperformance, a reflection of excessive turnover.

To create a proxy for average investor return during the 1990s, the study weighted the flows in and out of funds to determine actual investor average returns provided by long-term mutual funds in each Morningstar investment category (see Figure 4.4). Data for each month across the decade was gathered and subsequent returns for the following one-, two-, and three-year holding periods were calculated. All collective return figures were totaled and averaged to produce an average unweighted Morningstar category return for each of the three holding periods. These unweighted figures, which we call *fund returns*, serve as a proxy for returns that an investor who had used dollar cost averaging across the entire period might have achieved.

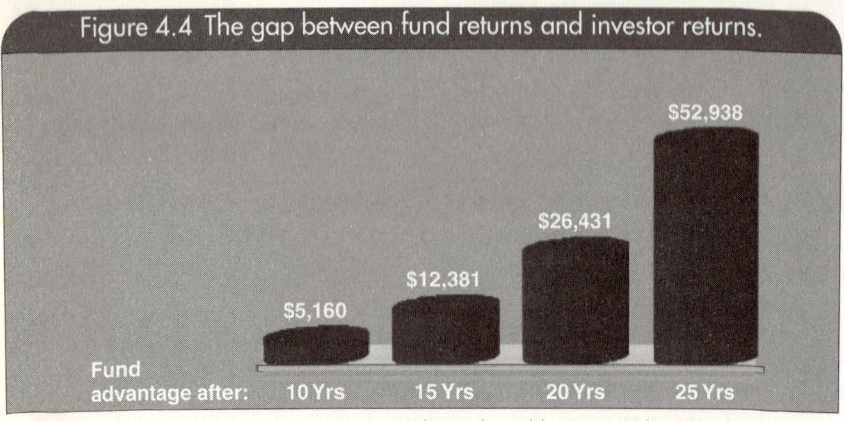

Source: Phoenix Investment Partners, research conducted by Financial Research Corporation (FRC). Reprinted with permission.

Figure 4.5 Fund returns versus investor returns.

Fund return versus investor returns

Annualized returns:	1 Year	2 Years	3 Years
Average fund	11.74	11.01	10.92
Average investor	6.68	7.13	8.7
Number of investment categories in which average fund returns surpassed average investor returns (out of 48)	37	42	37
Percent of investment categories in which average fund returns surpassed average investor returns (out of 48)	77%	88%	77%
Cumulative returns:	1 Year	2 Years	3 Years
Average fund	11.74	23.23	36.47
Average investor	6.68	14.71	28.44
Growth of $10,000 investment:	1 Year	2 Years	3 Years
Average fund Morningstar category return	$11,174	$12,323	$13,647
Average investor Morningstar category return	$10,668	$11,477	$12,844

Source: Phoenix Investment Partners, research conducted by Financial Research Corporation (FRC). Reprinted with permission.

Figures for the actual net flows into these funds (new investor deposits minus investor redemptions) throughout the period were weighted. When investors placed a bigger bet on a particular category or month, it was weighted more heavily. If flows were smaller, representing lack of investor interest or net redemptions, that month was weighted less heavily. These flow-weighted returns provide a general proxy for the returns that the average investor received.

What did we learn from this study? On the basis of the study, average returns achieved by long-term mutual funds exceed the returns realized by the average investor in the vast majority of cases. The differential between average returns and the actual return received by the investor is usually significant. The average return achieved by investors for the one-year period after the investment is made is more than five percentage points less than straightforward dollar cost averaging. Investor results underperformed average results of long-term mutual funds in roughly 80 percent of the Morningstar categories across all three time periods (see Figure 4.5).

Fund Flows versus Fund Returns

In an effort to assess whether investors are following the maxim of buying low and selling high, FRC examined mutual fund investments, or flows, to determine where investor money is going. In theory, an investor buying low would purchase a fund cheaply, *before* meteoric rise begins in value, rather than after the fact, when a fund's upward momentum may have peaked but its price remains high. However in reality, the research suggests that investors are largely acting contrary to this winning technique, placing more money into funds near their peak rather than selecting these funds when valuations are low—a clear mark of performance chasing.

Performance chasers (otherwise known as the *fund du jour crowd* or *Morningstar gazers*) are investors who pursue the headline-grabbing mutual fund winners of the moment. A prime example of this activity is illustrated in Figure 4.6. When technology funds were hot or considered winners, these funds witnessed a massive net inflow of cash. However, when the same funds started to slip, redemption rates increased. In light of this, chasing performance can be considered tantamount to buying high and selling low. As hard evidence indicates, today's hot funds are rarely tomorrow's winners. FRC found that, on average, funds that recorded a top 10 performance in one year reverted to the mean in the following year.

Investors would be wise to keep this study in mind. Across all Morningstar categories, the average quarterly return in best-performing

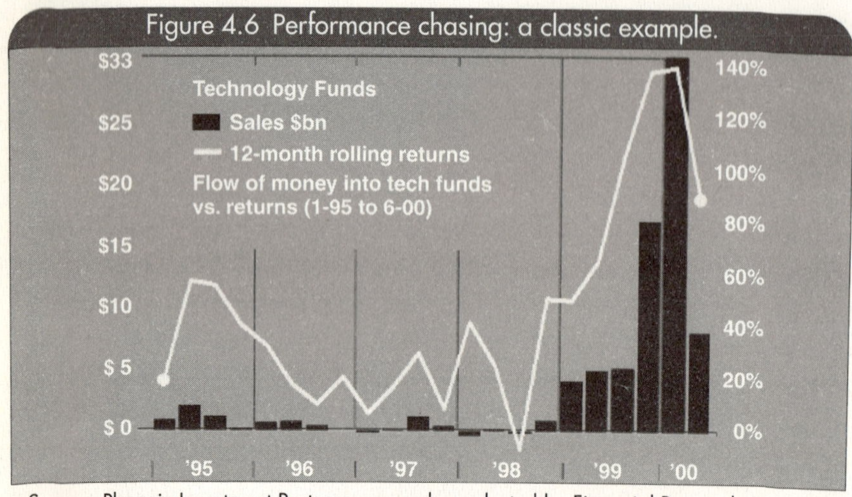

Source: Phoenix Investment Partners, research conducted by Financial Research Corporation (FRC). Reprinted with permission.

quarters was 14 percent, as opposed to 9 percent in worst-performing quarters. Following best quarters, net sales averaged $91 billion per quarter, compared with just $6.5 billion after worst quarters. Of the 48 Morningstar categories examined, trailing net sales in 42 cases were higher in the best versus worst case. Of the six exceptions, four were international/global categories and two were domestic sector categories. The pattern of flows following returns held true for all mainstream domestic equity objectives. Among core domestic equity categories, the differentials between best and worst quarterly sales rates were greatest for large-cap growth ($15.5 billion) and mid-cap growth ($8.1 billion).

All Eyes on Return

Where does this leave us? Although reason would suggest a cautious stance, we are lured by the seductiveness of high returns. That's normal for most all of us. The data of the Phoenix/FRC study bears this out. Returns are first and foremost self-serving. Money managers are still paid on total assets under their management.[8] Higher inflows naturally imply greater management fees, which in turn means a healthy living, with or without quality returns. And the best prescriptive that the fund industry has found to sustain this virtuous cycle is to promote returns, however accurate or misleading those return numbers may be. A typical marketing strategy of the fund industry is to wow potential investors with a circular showing some enviable returns. This is an expected tactic, as evidence shows that investors tend to migrate to funds with strong historic returns.

"In effect, the fund industry takes advantage of our psychological inclination to chase after history, which is in line with Tversky's argument that the recent past, while far from offering a comprehensive and reasonable picture, can incommensurately impact our behavior. A fund's performance is viewed as overly representative of a fund manager's skill and thus of the fund's future prospects. The abundance of mutual fund rankings and salient stories about successful fund managers reinforce the representativeness heuristic."[9] This line of logic has led to many unhappy returns, as high-flying performances by mutual fund managers are generally never repeated the following year.

Figure 4.7 shows a conventional representation of a major mutual fund during the 1990s. It underscores quite an impressive performance in U.S. equities during the final decade of the previous century. More specifically,

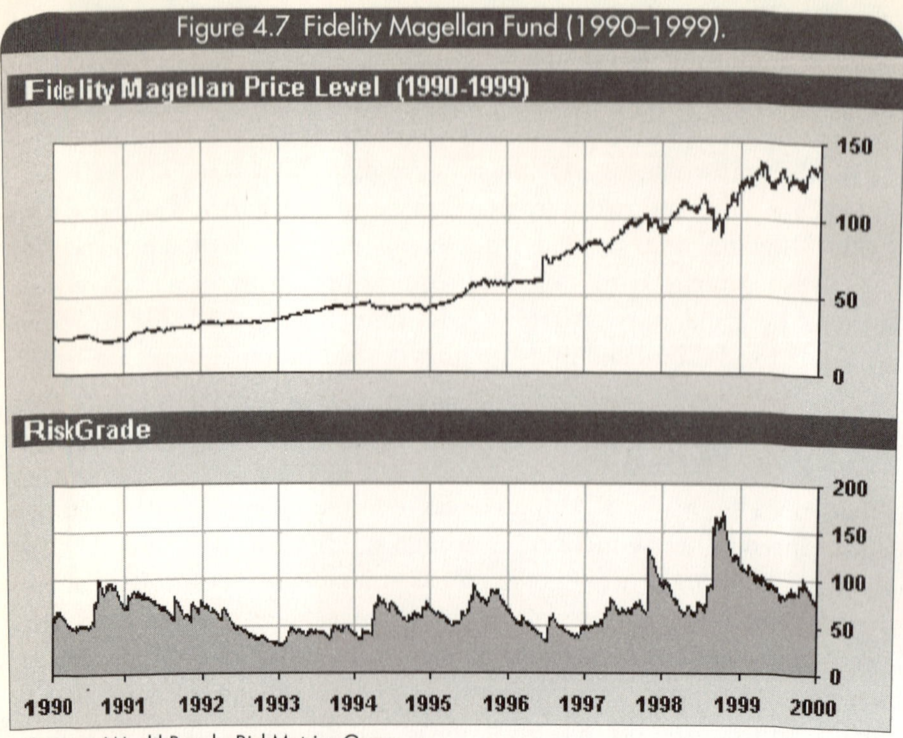

Source: WealthBench, RiskMetrics Group.

investors were handsomely rewarded by Fidelity's Magellan Fund, with an initial investment of $10,000 growing to over $54,000 by year-end 1999.

While it's easy to jump on Fidelity's bandwagon with the advantages of hindsight, particularly given the fruits of Magellan's labor in the final years of the past decade, it is much more difficult to stay the course when we are actually faced with a severe market downturn. In other words, gazing into the eyes of historic returns is far different from staring down the barrel of risk today. The final numbers are less meaningful if not put in the context of the time, effort, and energy spent along the way. What we don't see from this static viewpoint is our potential for downside volatility. How would we feel if we had chased after Magellan's returns at the end of 1999? Had we focused only on Magellan's generous 24 percent return in 1999 and ignored the fact that risk and return are like a DNA strand, interlocked and interdependent, we may have chased it at the outset of 2000 irrespective of our tolerance for assuming risk (see Figure 4.8).

As proof that past returns are no guarantee of future returns, investors who put $10,000 into Magellan at the start of 2000 found their initial

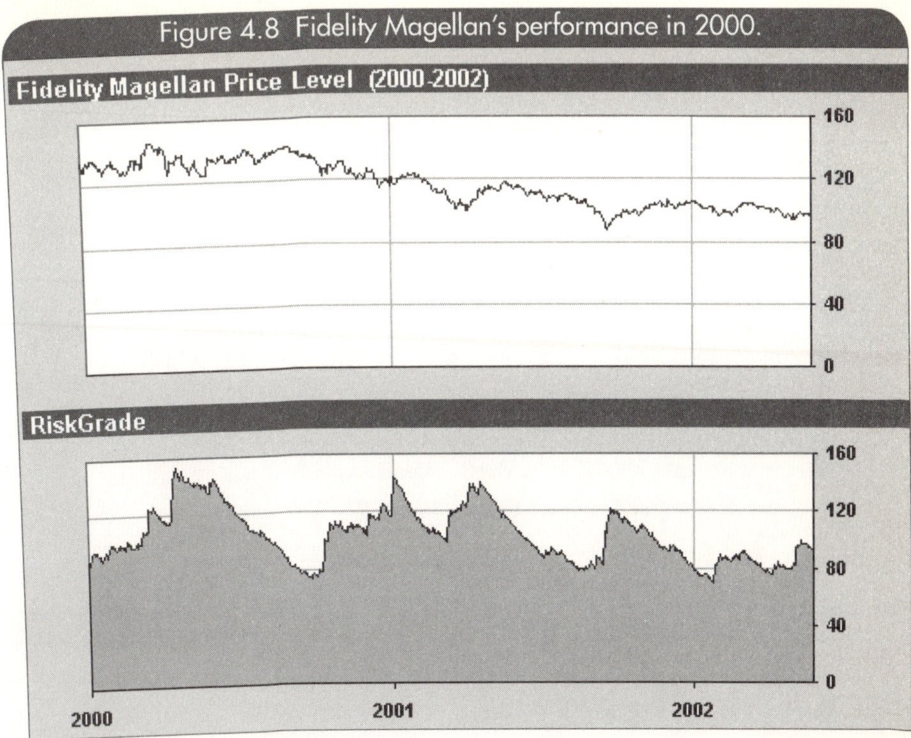

Source: WealthBench, RiskMetrics Group.

investment dwindling to a disappointing $9,159 by year's end. Although Magellan's 2000 performance was admirable given the prevailing conditions in the equity market,[10] it was also hardly what investors could have hoped for at the outset of the year.

In all fairness, the year 2000 represented one of the most difficult investment climates for market participants in over a decade. Confronted with a demanding environment, investors would have been better served with an accompanying picture of risk and not simply a marker of past returns. In other words, before plowing into Magellan or any other fund based on dated performance numbers, prudent investors should have previewed the apparent risks involved. Having done so, those put off by the risk profile may have sought haven in safer assets (see Figure 4.9).

As evident from a RiskGrades perspective, Magellan started to display a more unstable character beginning in late 1997. During this time, the fund's RiskGrade broke out of a stable range, climbing as high as 170 in October 1998. To Magellan's credit, higher returns accompanied the

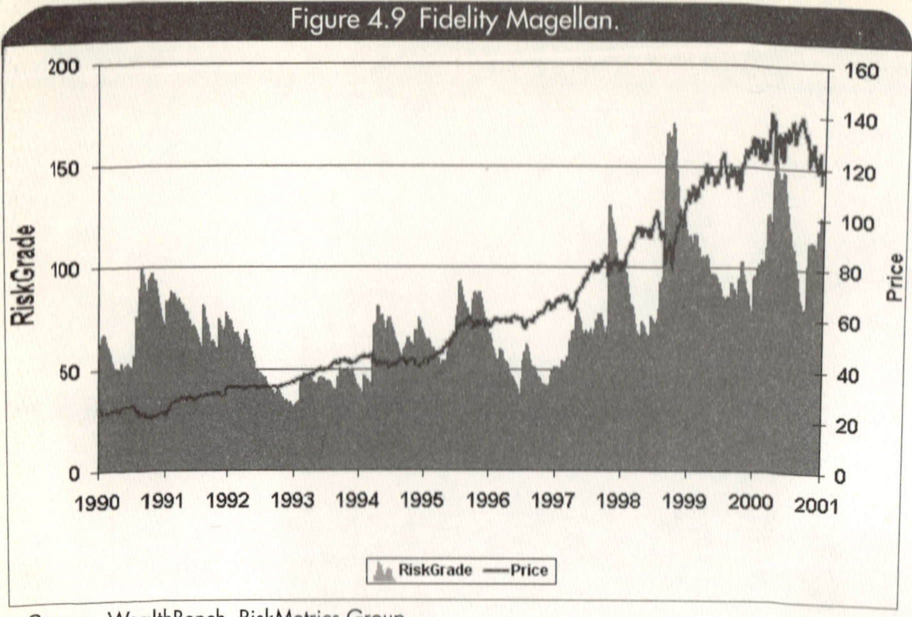

Source: WealthBench, RiskMetrics Group.

growing levels of risk. In late October 1997, the initial investment reached almost $33,000. By the close of the decade, the investment exceeded $54,000. In a little more than two years (late 1997 to 1999), Magellan almost matched the total dollar return achieved during the previous eight years (1990 to late 1997). Yet this great two-year run to close out the decade provided few signs of the tough months up ahead. In fact, by the end of the first quarter 2001, our initial $10,000 investment in 2000 had dwindled to $8,023, a fall of almost 20 percent in 15 months. In the face of this, can we stomach more downside volatility? Past returns are small comfort in the face of increased risk today.

Caveat Emptor: Let the Buyer Beware

Flip through the pages of your favorite business publication and you're bound to encounter mutual fund advertisements, lots of them. Strikingly, however, the layout, the images, and language used to describe each fund are all similar. Take a look. The name of each fund is displayed in large, bold fonts; the people featured in the ad all wear smiles; prominently displayed somewhere on the page is a series of star ratings from Morn-ingstar,[11] and the fine print is always located at the bottom of the page. Col-lectively, the print ads appear to have been generically created from a cookie cutter. Right?

Wrong. At first glance, you might think that, but we can assure you that's not the case. What many mutual funds lack in creative design they make up for in creative writing, especially when it comes to depicting the fund's performance. This is done in an attempt to prolong the inflow of cash by attracting new investors. In our review of fund marketing mate-rial—including fund websites, prospectuses, and advertisements—we found several overly aggressive practices used to delude investors.

As a case in point, we found that many mutual funds significantly mis-represent their fund performances by excluding recent negative perfor-mance information. The best example this type of fraud was reported in detail by Mercer Bullard in a series of specials to TheStreet.com.[12]

For example, in 2000, Jacob Internet Fund's 79.1 percent decline was one of the worst one-year performances in mutual fund history. But investors reading the fund's prospectus in January 2001 would never know it because this information was omitted. Ryan Jacob, the fund's manager, used legal chi-canery to its fullest extent to evade SEC reporting requirements and exclude his fund's dismal performance from its prospectus and marketing brochure— two important sources of information for prospective investors. As Bullard points out, the fact that Jacob can avoid mentioning that his portfolio lost nearly four-fifths of its value in one year shows how toothless SEC require-ments can be. Under current disclosure rules, the Jacob Internet Fund would not have to include its full year 2000 performance of −79.1 percent until Jan-uary 1, 2002—a full 25 months after the fact.[13]

Questionable disclosure practices are not isolated to Jacob Internet Fund; they're standard in the industry. A sampling of the online prospec-tuses for 14 other Internet funds established in 1999 and remaining in busi-ness throughout 2000 shows a pattern of hiding the facts. Three weeks into 2001, not one the mutual funds' prospectuses included their horrific per-formance results in 2000.

SEC rules require funds to prominently display their performance for that year in a bar chart near the front of the prospectus. In a footnote under the bar chart they're required to provide the fund's performance during the most recent quarter prior to the fund filing its prospectus. However, these funds were more interested in promulgating fiction than in disclosing

Figure 4.10 Disclosure Derby. Internet funds formed before 1999 trumpet their '99 performance and downplay 2000 results in their current prospectuses.

Fund	1999 Return in Bar Chart	Partial 2000 Return in Footnote	Actual 2000 Return
Monument Digital Technology	272%	−10%*	−57%
Amerindo Technology	251	−1**	−65
Kinetics Internet	217	−28***	−52
Munder NetNet	176	−15****	−54
WWW Internet	167	−19****	−57

Source: TheStreet.com, created by Mercer Bullard using data from SEC filings and Morningstar. Reprinted with permission. *July 1 through Sept. 30. **January 1 through March 31. ***January 1 through June 30. ****January 1 through September 30.

material facts to prospective investors. Either way, as you'll see in Figure 4.10, the results were perverse.

The Monument Digital Technology prospectus boasts a 272 percent return in 1999 in its bar chart, under which a footnote discloses the fund's negative 10 percent return from July 1 through September 30, 2000. The footnote skips over the fund's 0 percent and negative 22 percent returns in the first and second quarters of 2000. Nor is there any mention of the fund's 57 percent decline for the previous year.

And just as troubling to investors as funds that omit all pertinent performance information are funds that provide inaccurate performance numbers altogether. In Figure 4.11 shows a list of funds that misrepresented their actual returns for 2000.

Bait and Switch

The second example of deceptive advertising is the proclivity of the largest mutual funds to advertise their closed funds and deposit the money when it mistakenly arrives from new investors. A closed fund is essentially a mutual fund that has suspended sale of shares to new customers. Rather than making this fact readily apparent in the ad near the name of the fund or beside its prominently displayed return numbers, the funds bury this extremely pertinent fact in small print at the bottom of the ad.

Bait advertising as defined by the Federal Trade Commission is an alluring but insincere offer to sell a product or service that the advertiser in truth does not intend to sell. Its purpose is to lure consumers with the advertised merchandise and then sell them something else instead, usually at a higher price or on a basis more advantageous to the advertiser. The primary aim of bait and switch is to obtain leads to potential customers interested in buying the type of merchandise advertised.

So who advertises closed funds? According to an article published by the *Mutual Fund Market News,* a Thompson Financial Company publication, Janus Capital Management, American Century Investments, Strong Funds, and Van Kampen Funds have all advertised closed funds.

Upon receiving money from investors who are not eligible to invest in the advertised funds, Janus Capital Management deposits the money into a money market account. Other companies, including American Century Investments and Strong Funds, have service representatives contact investors who send in checks to inform them the fund they want to invest in is

Figure 4.11 Disclosure Derby II. For Internet funds launched in 1999, the return you see in the current prospectus isn't necessarily what you got in 2000.

Fund	Return Listed in Financial Highlights	Actual 2000 Return
Goldman Sachs Internet Tollkeeper	92%	–37%
Investec internet.com Index	82	–59
MetalMarkets.com Openfund	72	–42
ING Internet	41	–69
StockJungle.com Pure Play Internet	24	–67
RS Internet Age	22	–46
Firsthand E-Commerce	–2	–55
Enterprise Internet	–12	–51
Potomac Internet Plus	–15	–77

Source: TheStreet.com, created by Mercer Bullard using data from SEC filings and Morningstar. Reprinted with permission.

closed. They then try to sell a similar fund, but will return the investors' checks if they do not want to invest in those alternatives.

According to Janus, it deposits the money rather than returning it immediately to investors to save time. "We found that investors that send money to Janus want a Janus product." The company contacts investors by phone and mail and tries to sell a similar fund to those who have sent money for a closed fund.

Star Gazing

Another advertising ploy used by mutual funds to overcome recent negative returns is to ignore returns altogether. Instead of referencing a negative return, funds elect to publish only star ratings by Morningstar. Because Morningstar's ratings are based on performance compared with other funds for a period of three years, a fund can earn a five-star rating by virtue of *losing less money* than the others. According to a *Wall Street Journal* article, "Stars Don't Illuminate Performance Picture," one-third of U.S. stock funds with a five-star Morningstar rating had negative returns for the 12 months through February 2002.[14]

This trend toward providing stars and fund rankings rather than actual performance is in stark contrast to ads placed during the go-go years of the bull market. During that period, funds flaunted extraordinary returns in excess of 80, 90, and even 100 percent in their advertisements to draw investors into funds heavily concentrated in technology stocks. However since market's collapse in the spring of 2000, funds have had to find a new ruse to induce prospective investors.

Conclusion

For investors, the way to prevail over this objectionable behavior of mutual funds is straightforward. Before investing, we need to look at more than a fund's past performance. We need to explore beyond glitzy returns and star rankings. We might just discover many highly rated mutual funds are not what they appear. We need to know our own biases. Marketing departments are aware of our natural desire to pick winners and to time markets. Their advertising programs reflect this. We need the self-discipline to avoid the types of behavioral biases that impede us from making sound financial decisions.

The good news is that help is on the way. The Securities and Exchange Commission has not overlooked these deceptive advertising practices by mutual funds. In response, it has undertaken a series of initiatives to educate investors about the dangers of chasing fund performance and focusing on short-term returns of assets. In addition, on May 14, 2002, the SEC proposed rule amendments intended to encourage mutual fund advertisements to convey more-balanced information to prospective investors, particularly in regard to past performance. The proposed amendments are designed to raise standards for mutual fund performance advertising so that investors are informed, not misled.[15]

In June 2002, the RiskMetrics Group developed a method of evaluating mutual fund performance based on how funds compensate investors with additional return for bearing risk.

In RiskMetrics Group's evaluation metric, funds that provide excess return for the risk undertaken are identified as top performers, while funds with returns not commensurate with their risks are ranked poorly. The performance evaluations also take into account the degree to which the risks of a fund change over time, penalizing those with widely time-varying risk.

The "Best and Worst" fund evaluations are assigned within four style categories: conservative, balanced, growth, and aggressive. These categories are determined by the risk profiles of each fund. Only those funds with the statistically highest and lowest scores will be displayed. For an up-to-date list of the "Best and Worst" fund evaluations, see the RiskMetrics website.

CHAPTER 5

Buy, Hold, or Sell?

Throw a speculative investment idea on the table and the first thought that runs across many of our collective minds is the glimmer of quick profits. If you're in the market long enough, at some point you're bound to be swept off your feet by the allure of a "sure thing." Whether the sure thing pans out is never a certainty. For many of us, those sure things were tech stocks that quickly morphed into portfolio cellar dwellers after the tech boom went bust. A few of my sure things include optical network products companies Ciena and Network Appliances, network solutions providers Lucent and Nortel, and e-learning companies DigitalThink and Saba. Investors with similar collections of underperforming sure things, some off as much as 90 percent from their original purchase prices, inevitably all share the age-old problem of choosing a course of action now. Do I buy more, hold, or sell?

The way humans respond to crisis is shaped by recent memory. Cognitive psychologists believe it is not a particular event or environment that disturbs us, but our thought and beliefs about a situation that creates havoc in our lives. In an investing context, how we currently view the markets and react to prices is to a large degree defined by our perceptions of the current investment climate—just as the Crash of 1929 shaped how the public approached the stock market for many years thereafter. In hindsight, investors should have been piling into small-cap stocks as the market bottomed in 1932, but at that time the scar tissue was still healing. Fast-forward to today; in a sense, we have been conditioned in recent years to view the stock market as a sort of lottery. And who can blame us for having such a healthy dose of optimism after a decade that delivered average annualized returns of almost 17 percent on the S&P 500 Index? If not for a callous rout of the markets, U.S. equity investors may have been able to ignore market risk indefinitely.

By contrast, compare how we grapple with risk in other areas of our lives. We are not born risk takers per se. We have learned that life insurance pays, that fire alarms work, that safety belts can save lives. We take precautions because we understand that some risks are simply not worth taking. Although risk cannot be eliminated entirely, and certainly a healthy dose of risk is a necessary component in stimulating progress, taking risk for the sake of risk is dangerous.

Even though we are aware of all this, we still have a tendency to treat market risk differently. We speculate. We sacrifice our otherwise sound judgment in hopes of receiving a swift reward. Unfortunately, this type of behavior will ultimately catch up with us. Absent the rigors of a systematic approach, investing cannot be distinguished from speculation. If it is not obvious already, there is an important distinction between the two. Benjamin Graham summarized it this way. "Anyone who buys a so-called 'hot' common-stock issue is, or makes a purchase in any way similar thereto, is either speculating or gambling."[1]

The perils of speculating in the markets will always become most evident in a market downturn. For those who have only started their investment journeys, keep in mind that you have yet to live through years of protracted market weakness. As excruciating as the current bear market may seem, it pales in comparison to the years of aggravation endured by investors during the period of economic stagflation in the 1970s. The term *stagflation* was coined by economists to describe the previously unprecedented condition of simultaneous inflation and recession. It was the worst of both worlds: an economy that was contracting while prices continued to rise.

Although the term *bear markets* always seems to bring up the 1929 catastrophe or the 1987 crash, bear markets typically gnaw at us for years with slow and steady declines, knocking around our investment senses and draining every bit of enthusiasm. When the market turns bearish, risk is not simply an afterthought but instead a priority. Notes John Bogle, "Risk—

Figure 5.1 Where have all the good times gone?

Source: Copyright © The New York Collection 2001 Mick Stevens from cartoonbank.com. All rights reserved. Reprinted with permission.

however measured and however elusive a concept, except in retrospect—should be given the most careful consideration by the intelligent investor. Markets, no matter what you may have come to think, do not always rise."[2] In other words, risk management works best when used as part of our investment process, as a preventive measure. Adopting the principles of sound risk management after your portfolio takes a dive is too late. It's equivalent to shutting the barn doors after the last horse runs away. If *The New Yorker* is right (see Figure 5.1), we may already be yearning for the good times of the 1990s.

The Most Dangerous Words Ever Spoken

There's an old joke on Wall Street: What are the four most dangerous words in investing? The answer: "It's different this time." If anyone ever says to you, "It's different this time," don't walk away, run away.

Prior to the bursting of the Internet bubble, many wondered whether the markets today could experience a decline of the magnitude evidenced in 1929. From peak to bottom, the Crash of 1929 wiped out 89 percent of equity value over a three-year span. We heard so many pundits tell us that times change, and, for many different reasons, things would be different this time around. One reason was because the U.S. economy during the latter half of the 1990s performed like a Goldilocks fairy tale. It was blessed with just the right amount of monetary stimulus, a spurt in worker productivity, enormous strides in the field of technology, and an amenable global economy. Somehow the United States achieved a delicate balance between above-trend growth and full employment, all without inciting inflationary pressures. On the whole, economic conditions were not too cold, not too hot, but just right.

And for a while the markets responded gloriously. Between 1995 and 2000, the S&P and Nasdaq markets delivered an average return of 21.3 percent and 21.9 percent, respectively (Figure 5.2). Investors were delirious. Old rules (e.g., asset allocation, the importance of diversification, and investing according to your tolerance for risk) were discarded quicker than old bricks and mortar.

About this time, a new generation of market commentators digitally materialized and took over all forms of communication, including TV, radio, and online chat rooms. Armed with acerbic wit, they effortlessly dismissed all preexisting market theory as conventional. Only days into the

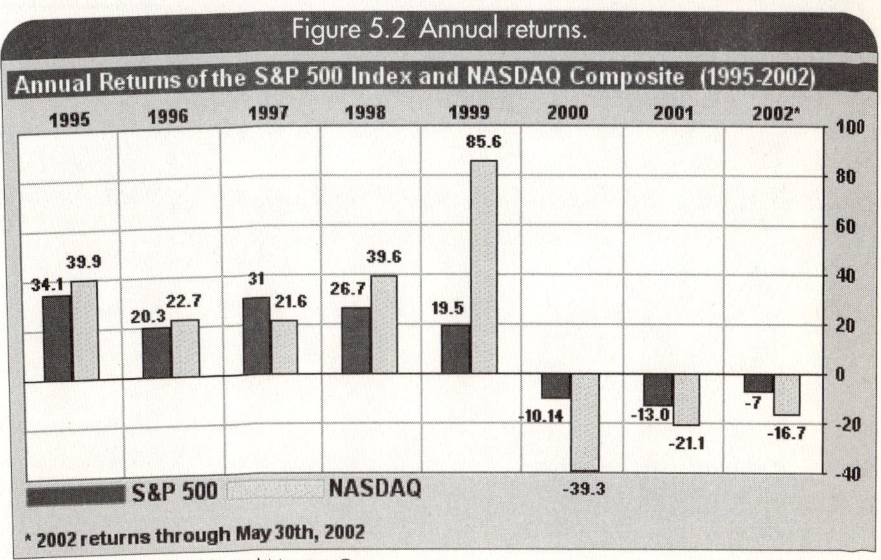

Source: WealthBench, RiskMetrics Group.

new millennium, we were being informed that the collective ideas and wisdom of such legendary investors as Charles H. Dow, Benjamin Graham, George Soros, Peter Lynch, Warren Buffett, John C. Bogle, and Sir John Templeton were relics from the past. The Dow Jones Industrial Average roared past 10,000 for the first time, two authors obtained their 15 minutes of fame arguing that the blue-chip index could just as easily smash 36,000.[3] All the while, the Nasdaq composite marched higher and higher as investors embraced shares of any company that promised to make technology smarter, faster or more accessible.

Then it happened: A combination of poor business planning, intense competition, and weak advertising pushed scores of dot-com companies off the precipice, wiping out hundreds of billions of dollars in market capitalization and sending share prices tumbling. The Nasdaq Composite, the technology bellwether, experienced a correction of 72 percent from top to bottom between March 2000 and September 2001—one of the swiftest and most damaging corrections in financial market history. (See Figure 5.3.) By comparison, the bear market that ravaged the Japanese Nikkei during the 1990s took over 11 years to fall by a similar magnitude. All told, at one

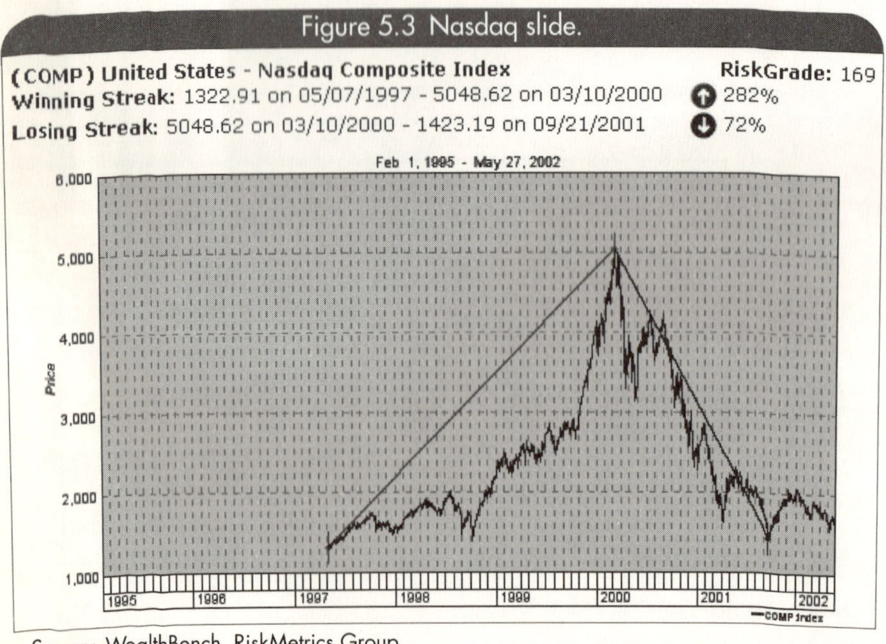

Figure 5.3 Nasdaq slide.

Source: WealthBench, RiskMetrics Group.

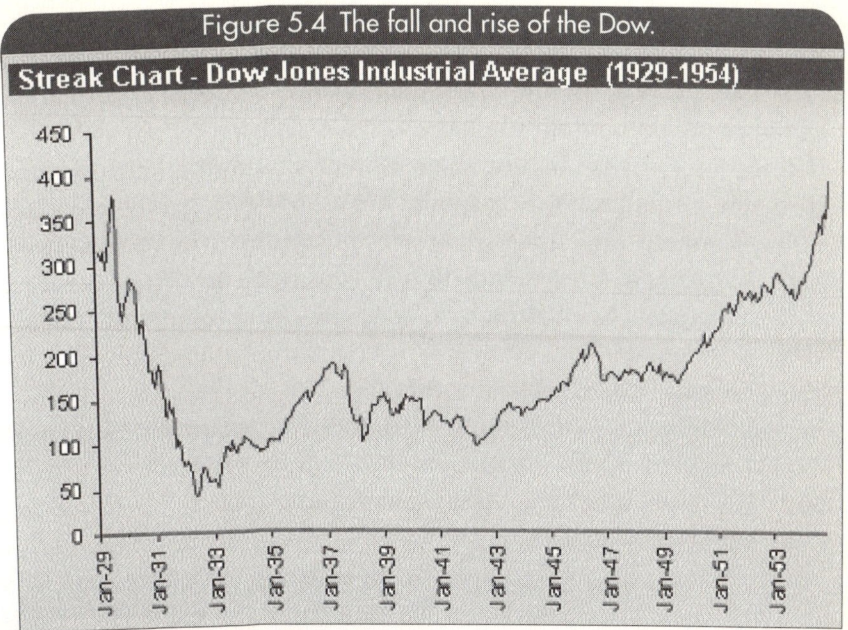

Figure 5.4 The fall and rise of the Dow.

Source: WealthBench, RiskMetrics Group.

point, over $4 trillion in wealth disappeared as a result of the slide in the U.S. equity market.

The dot-com industry imploded before our eyes—millions injured, one bull dead. Investors limped through Nasdaq's worst years ever in 2000 and 2001, as technology and telecommunications stocks were punished for having valuations that defied gravity amid a slowing economy. Broader stocks didn't fare much better, as the Standard & Poor's 500 Index put in its first down year since 1994, and the Dow Jones Industrial Average posted its first negative annual performance since 1990. It goes without saying, but we'll say it anyway: The investors who felt the most pain were the ones who disregarded the old rules—asset allocation, the importance of diversification, and investing according to your tolerance for risk.

Now let's compare the chart in Figure 5.3, depicting the slide of Nasdaq, with the one in Figure 5.4, showing the Crash of 1929. On a relative basis, only 17 percentage points separate the bottoms. Looking at Figure 5.4, a pessimist might well ponder the question, "What if investors' confidence in today's market continues to ebb, or corporate earnings fail to improve, or another Fortune 500 company like an Enron blows up? Who's to say we won't suffer the same prolonged losses today that the markets suffered in the Crash of 1929?" However, an *optimist* looking at the same chart might be struck by the tremendous upward pull—the fantastic rally from the lows notched in mid-1932—and wonder whether the market in 2003 and beyond will unfold similarly.

Indeed, the initial slide created an incredible window of opportunity, inspiring an eightfold increase from the lows set in 1932 to the highs set in 1954. The fortunate individuals who were not left destitute by the events of October 1929 were given a chance to take advantage of exceptionally discounted valuations. In the aftermath, adopting disciplined and consistent dollar cost averaging would ultimately have led to tremendous gains. Risk, as always, created numerous opportunities.

In reality, almost a generation separated the two peaks. The market sorely tested one of the primary tenets of a successful investment program: patience. For those who invested just prior to the Crash of 1929, it was a long haul back—almost 25 years to the day—to recoup the original principal amount. And this applied only to index-based investors (not widespread back then); individual shareholders fared much worse. Jeremy Siegel, author of *Stocks for the Long Run,* aptly summarized the severity of the collapse:

> The Dow utilities, once considered conservative by many investors, also fell 89 percent, while the Rail Average [the railroad sector that was a key component of the stock market in 1929] plummeted 93 percent! And the Dow consisted of the 'blue chip' stocks—the slaughter of the smaller stocks was even greater, as many fell 95 percent or became completely worthless.... No investor, institutional or individual, can tolerate that kind of trauma.[4]

The market showed no bias regarding style or sector (shades of 1929 clearly resurfaced in 2000). As the slide gained momentum, it was sell first, ask questions second. Under such distressed conditions, even the true believers had many reasons to lose faith along the way.

Playing the Hand We're Dealt

With so many conflicting reports and opinions over the immediate direction of the market and the timing of a rebound, we can't blame anyone for having more questions than answers. Here are the questions we're most frequently asked: What do I do now? How do I distinguish whether the market's worst is behind us or ahead of us? Is today's stock market over-priced, underpriced, or fairly priced? How can I better time my entry and exit points? The answers aren't easy. And because we're risk managers, the answers we provide generally do not thrill anyone. That's because each investor is unique. Without knowing each investor's distinctive goals, horizon, and tolerance for risk, we couldn't possibly offer a complete answer. A given investor may have short-term objectives that conflict with the blanket statement, "Invest for the long term." But that does not mean investors with a 1-, 5-, 10-, 20-year horizon cannot enjoy the fruits of the market.

The remainder of this chapter will address the question, "What do I do now?" However, since we don't know what you're holding in your hand, the information we present is going to steer you in three directions, to buy, to hold, or to sell. Hopefully, this data, when combined with your own sensibilities and understanding of your particular tolerance for risk, will enable you to build and maintain investments that deliver returns more closely aligned with your overall expectations.

Buy

Some perpetual bulls discount bear markets altogether. According to Peter Lynch, the famed fund manager who ran the Magellan Fund,

> The market itself is very volatile. In the 95 years so far, we've had 53 declines in the market of 10 percent or more.... That's once every two years. Of the 53, 15 of the 53 have been 25% or more. That's a bear market. So 15 in 95 years—about once every six years you're going to have a big decline. Now no one seems to know when they're gonna happen. At least if they know about 'em, they're not telling anybody about 'em. I don't remember anybody predicting the market right more than once, and they predict a lot. So they're gonna happen. If you're in the market, you have to know there's going to be declines.[5]

Those who favor the stock market over other alternatives suggest that focusing on the long term will mitigate any periodic episodes of distress. In fact, even major market corrections of over 40 percent seem minor when seen against the larger backdrop of a century's worth of higher prices. The broader U.S. equity market over any 30-year period has returned no less than an annualized rate of 3 percent.

Professor Jeremy Siegel of the Wharton School has contributed the most exhaustive empirical case for stocks in the long run.[6] His analysis, dating from 1997 back to 1802, demonstrates the steadiness of stock market returns despite what Siegel sees as three periods of fundamental change to the underlying U.S. economy over the course of almost two centuries. The first, from 1802 to 1870, was a period that witnessed the country shift away from its agrarian roots. The second period, from 1871 to 1925, was an era marked by incredible advances in manufacturing and production. The third period, from 1926 to 1997, saw the blossoming of the modern industrial age.

Contrary to what we would expect, real returns from the broader U.S. equity markets in all three periods remarkably gravitated toward 7 percent (see Table 5.1), this despite sweeping changes many times over in the larger economy. "The surprising constancy of the historical real return on equity cannot be denied. It may reflect economic forces far beyond our usual concepts of capital and investment," argues Siegel.[7] Most strikingly, $10 invested in stocks in 1802 was worth $5.59 million by 1997. Compare this to $8,000 for bonds in the same period. In light of this, there is little arguing that U.S. equities have proven to be solid long-term investments.

Not only have stocks proven to be good long-term bets, but longer holding periods have an efficacious effect on risk. Time has proven to be the best antiseptic to risk. Empirical studies, notably by Siegel, show that the volatility of expected returns declines with the advantage of time.

Table 5.1 U.S. Equity Returns

Historical Period	Years	Total Nominal Return	Inflation	Real Return
Agrarian age	1802–1870	7.1%	0.1%	7.0%
Manufacturing age	1871–1925	7.2%	0.6%	6.6%
Industrial age	1926–1997	10.6%	3.1%	7.2%
195 years of U.S. equity returns	1802–1997	8.4%	1.3%	7.0%

Source: *Stocks for the Long Run, Second Edition,* by Jeremy Siegel, copyright 1998 by McGraw-Hill Book Companies. Used with permission.

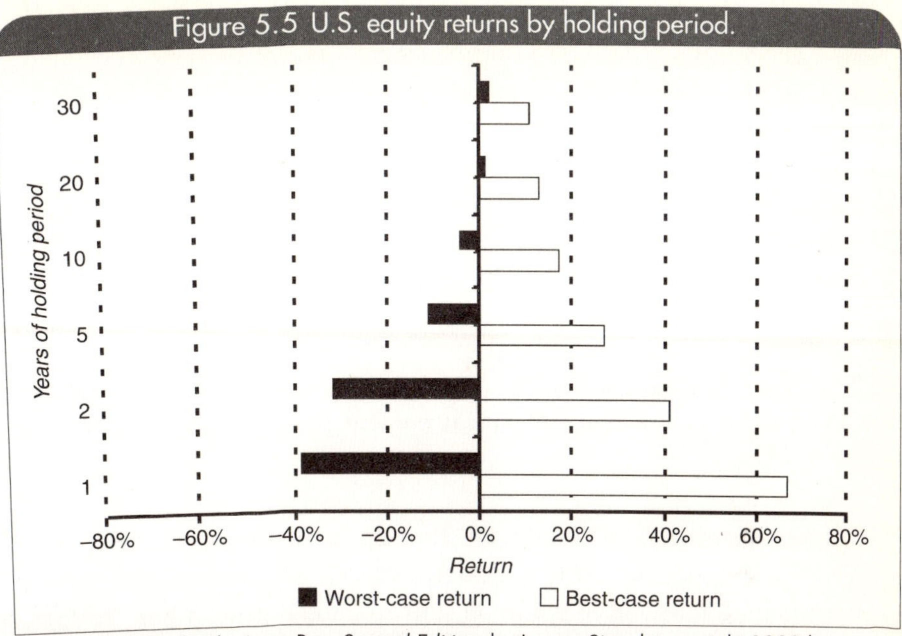

Figure 5.5 U.S. equity returns by holding period.

Source: *Stocks for the Long Run, Second Edition,* by Jeremy Siegel, copyright 1998 by McGraw-Hill Book Companies. Used with permission.

Again, using the period from 1802 to 1997 as the basis for our analysis, we see that the highest one-year real return on stocks was 66.6 percent (Figure 5.5). The largest one-year loss was 38.6 percent. In comparison, the largest compound annual return over 30 years was 10.6 percent; the smallest return in the same period was 2.6 percent.

Another way of illustrating these findings is to size up the difference between the best- and worst-case scenarios in each period. A one-year range can be restated as 105.2 percent versus 8 percent for a 30-year horizon. It is not unfair to conclude that the variability of returns narrows over time. In fact, that would be putting it mildly.

The numbers certainly give a ringing endorsement for stocks as superior long-term investments. Moving forward, there is little to dispute that U.S. equity markets will continue to offer sound investment returns for disciplined investors with long-term horizons.

Words of caution to long-term investors: Of equal importance, we must ensure that long-term investment advice is not blindly interpreted as a passive buy-and-hold strategy. Admittedly, this can prove exceptionally frustrating for investors who have espoused long-term strategies with the hope that everything would eventually be made right. But as evidence shows, whereas the broader equity markets have successfully delivered positive returns over many years, individual shares have been susceptible to complete failure. As such, a portfolio made up of a handful of individual equities can generate negligible or negative returns even after an extensive holding period. Failing to shave losers can be as disappointing as cutting winners too soon. We are reminded of the following exchange in Victor Niederhoffer's *The Education of a Speculator:*

> **"So how did it end?" I asked.**
> **"Well, let's just say I held on too long. I got reamed in the crash. But all my stock picks initially went up 50 percent. Now I'm a much smaller speculator."[8]**

An old business proverb suggests that no one ever got fired for taking profits. We are not advocating a hit-and-run strategy, but rather an investment guideline founded in common sense. You can grow a healthy forest without a single tree hitting the clouds, and so it is with even a long-term financial plan. Despite the emphasis on buying for the long run, the importance of realizing gains (whenever appropriate) should not be discounted. After all, the chance of building a buy-and-hold portfolio of several General Electric–like stocks is quite implausible.[9] In the real world, sometimes a prince who turns into a frog remains a frog. Value can change in an instant, without a lot of warning. Think about how many Enron, Tyco, Elan, and WorldCom investors would be happier today if they bolted after the first sign of accounting irregularities.

Words of caution to short-term investors: Can any of us afford to sit through a period of market malaise that mirrors the early 1970s? For some, even a handful of years will prove too costly. Even if we would like to heed the words of the wise, many of us simply cannot wait a decade or more for investments to pay off. To wit, those with a shorter-term outlook need to pay much more heed to risk, as greater fluctuations can wreak havoc on our senses and our net worth. To put it differently, a 5-year plan to retirement should look markedly different from a 10-year or a 30-year strategy. Although there is no single uniform recommendation, asset allocation will largely reflect our age, our investment goals, and our time to retirement. A near-term exit strategy should try to reduce the overall RiskGrade of the portfolio.

Hold

Perhaps no one champions the strengths of long-term value investing as fervently as Warren Buffett. Buffett's case for adopting a long-term horizon, echoed by other successful money managers, has been backed by an incredible performance over the past three and half decades. Under his command, Berkshire Hathaway has seen its per-share book value grow on average by more than 23 percent each year. Over this period, a single share of Berkshire stock has grown, incredibly, from $12 to $71,000 a share, an annualized growth rate of 27 percent. His legendary returns have given him the distinction of being labeled the "Oracle of Omaha." Buffett's success has been tied to a focused investing approach with the following characteristics:

- On average, select between 10 and 15 companies with solid histories and high probabilities of success.
- Hold onto these for a minimum of five years, if not longer.
- Ignore forecasts by the "experts."
- Disregard the day-to-day swings in market, which can be unsettling.

Despite the overwhelming mounds of evidence that urge us to adopt a long-term investment horizon and the true-to-life examples of Buffett, Lynch, and others, a common mistake repeated by even seasoned investors is to focus on short-term swings. We are creatures of believing what we see. As we learned in Chapter 2, the instantaneous dissemination of financial information cuts like a double-edged sword for modern-day investors. On the one hand, greater access to the markets has served as a great equalizer, making it possible for the masses to take control of personal financial decisions as never before. On the other hand, technology has fostered an environment of daily account voyeurs. Although this type of behavior was seen even during the Great Depression, today's technology has clearly brought it to a new level. The status of our online trading accounts is monitored more regularly than the balance in our checkbooks. The information age has allowed some of us to agonize over the status of our net worth minute by minute. The natural consequence of this compulsive behavior is a greater probability of reacting to short-term events. The more often we see change, the greater the likelihood that we will respond to it. Reacting to short-term moves in the market invites overtrading, which results in higher transaction costs that compromise returns.

Investors today are submersed in information. We are generally sur-rounded by information on all sides 365 days a year. Need proof? As you read this sentence you are likely within arm's reach of a radio, a television, a com-puter, a phone, or a handheld wireless device capable of delivering informa-tion. Such immediacy of information causes us to place greater faith in our ability to time the markets. And, over the long term, market timing is a losing proposition. The problem stems from our inability to consistently and cor-rectly interpret the massive amount of data available, much of it contradic-tory, and react fast enough to take advantage of opportunities and sidestep pitfalls. Although everything may turn out well, at least initially, over time decisions made in haste will lead to disaster. Some may argue that they can see events clearly as they unfold, but who can see beyond next week? Accord-ingly, we can buy and sell based on "correctly" anticipated market moves. Indeed, some investors will find a reasonable amount of trading success in condensed periods. But Benjamin Graham highlights a hollow logic in our ability to trust our judgment: "There is no basis either in logic or in experi-ence for assuming that any typical or average investor can anticipate market movements more successfully than the general public, of which he is himself a part."[10] By and large, adds Graham, "We are equally sure that if he places his emphasis on timing, in the sense of forecasting, he will end up as a spec-ulator and with a speculator's financial results."[11] Our pursuit of short-term profits will regrettably put us at risk of missing substantial upward gains. Conversely, notes Motley Fools David and Tom Gardner, "Fear sometimes causes people to lose sight of equity investing's superiority, always (it seems) at the wrong time…when the market has just hit bottom."[12] More often than not, our winners will invariably slip away too early, jeopardizing the prospects of capturing larger returns. Market timing, warns Bogle, is "a two-decision process that requires not only selling right, but knowing when the day comes to reverse engines and buying right. It is not easy."[13]

In recent memory, those who incrementally took profits as the market presumably reached "irrational" levels in the 1990s were worse off for it a few years later. Figures 5.6 and 5.7 chart the performance of Microsoft and Merck stock, respectively, in the second half of 1997. We focus on this period because of the negative confluence of events that was developing at this time and because of the spectacular run-up in share prices prior to this period.

As many will recall, the general global investment climate slowly began to deteriorate in the summer of 1997, after Thailand was forced to devalue its currency in early July. In the ensuing months, currency

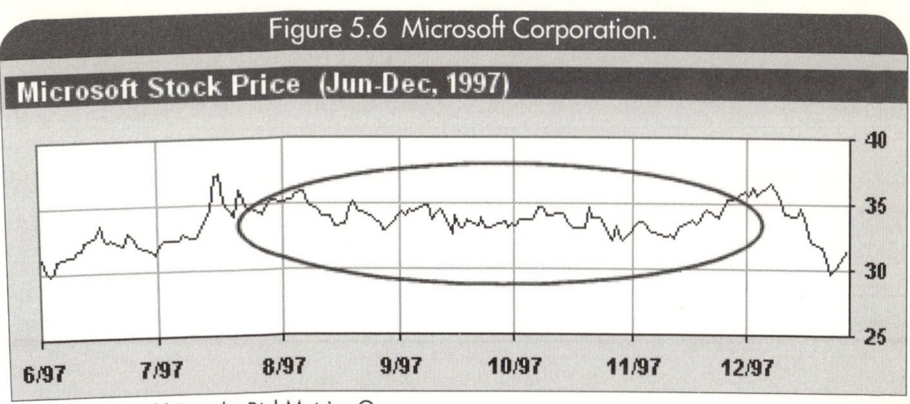

Figure 5.6 Microsoft Corporation.

Source: WealthBench, RiskMetrics Group.

devaluations spread like wildfire throughout Asia, jeopardizing regional stability. A year later, the Russian ruble became a victim. But the ruble devaluation, unlike its peers, was not simply provincial in nature. Instead, the Russian crisis plunged the global capital markets into deep panic, endangering the very foundation of the worldwide financial system. One of the most prominent hedge funds, Long-Term Capital Management led by famed ex–Salomon Brothers trader John Merriwether, fell victim to the financial shakeout. Ultimately, the New York Federal Reserve Bank, along with a consortium of 14 financial institutions, bailed out Long-Term Capital with a $3.6 billion equity investment. The consortium feared a rapid liquidation of Long-Term Capital's portfolio would upset the already jittery global bond market and thus devolve their own bond portfolios.

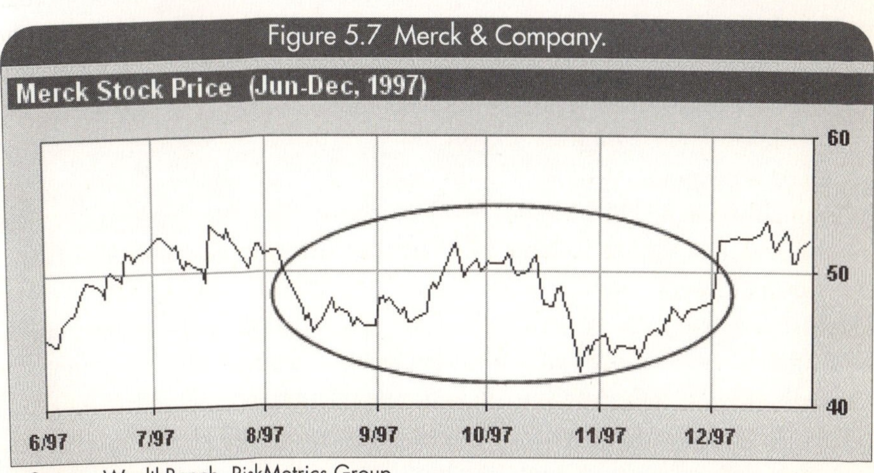

Figure 5.7 Merck & Company.

Source: WealthBench, RiskMetrics Group.

This was a perfect time to ignore one of the wise rules of Peter Lynch, that "[t]he key to making money in stocks is not to get scared out of them. . . . In dieting and in stocks, it is the gut and not the head that determines the results."[14] Even those strongly committed to the markets probably felt the urge to sell at least some shares between August and October, as many prices ground sideways or lower. After all, by July 1997, Microsoft and Merck had delivered very healthy gains of 2,485 percent and 385 percent, respectively, on a split-adjusted basis since 1990. At some point in time, we reminded ourselves, profits must be taken.

And for a short period, those who sold were right. But we know how the story ultimately played out for the remainder of the decade. As it turns out, the summer of 1997 was just another opportunity to buy the dip. U.S. equities subsequently climbed higher in the remainder of the decade despite deteriorating conditions in the Far East, South America, Eastern Europe, and a financial crisis of epic proportions. Microsoft ended the 1990s at an all-time high of almost $120 a share, up over 250 percent from year-end 1997. Merck closed up almost 50 percent from the summer doldrums of 1997. The unpredictable nature of the market stung those who tried to time it.

Naturally, the story of Microsoft, Merck, or any other stock doesn't remain frozen in time. Those who guessed right then may ultimately regret their decisions sometime down the road. Selling Microsoft in 1997 may have been a poor decision, but reducing exposure two years later appears to have been a brilliant move given the stock's slide in 2000. However, the story is far from finished. The performance bar is always being raised. If you made the right decision in 1997, to buy or hold 'em, did you also make the right decision in 2000 to fold 'em? Sellers in 2000 may one day have cause to regret their decision.

Sell

The second half of the 1990s was indeed generous to overall share prices. But not all stories ended the decade as happily as Microsoft and Merck. While the subsequent fall of dot-com mania failed to surprise anyone in hindsight, many mainstream stocks endured the pains of a bear market (lower highs and lower lows) even as the broader market rallied.

We have pointed to those who argue that a long-term, disciplined strategy is an important prerequisite in building a winning portfolio. We have also touched on evidence that shows the risk-reduction qualities that a longer-term perspective brings. But alongside this, we should add that risk should also be actively managed. As we see it, proper portfolio maintenance implies more than extending our investment horizons. What ultimately separates modern-day finance from mere gambling is our ability to actively fit the level of risk to our needs. A long stay at the blackjack table does not necessarily mean that losses will average out with gains over time. In fact, it's quite often the opposite: The longer you stay at the table, the more likely you are to lose. We will encounter instances when discomforting levels of risk should prompt us to act.

With this in mind, we regularly like to point to some key sobering events to maintain a sense of perspective. Although the overall U.S. equity market has proven to be a sound long-term investment, individual decisions often fail. Thus, making a generalization such as "Stocks have proven to go up in the long run and are therefore a sound investment" is, in our opinion, a misguided statement. Even one of the most ardent champions of long-term index investing, John Bogle, recognizes this fact. "No investor should forget, however, that odds should never be mistaken for certainties."[15] Too many professionals have referenced long-term horizons as a crutch. Indeed, the broader markets over time will drift higher, notes Niederhoffer, because "almost all price series move up with inflation"[16] and because of the power of compounding. But in an age when investors are as much exposed to individual stocks as to mutual funds, the message of risk control must be made transparent. California's power crisis in 2000 reinforces the notion that even utility stocks, once reserved for widows and orphans, are no longer sacred. The *Wall Street Journal* exposes the greater dangers in the marketplace this way:

> For those who invest by one traditional method—buying just a few well-chosen blue chips to hold for the long term—it has been a much bumpier ride. Big, industry-leading companies are being rocked by everything from deregulation to cutthroat competition to fast-changing technology that can shift an industry's balance overnight. The speed of change today is turning the concept of a few safe stocks, which you can just buy and sock away, into almost an investment relic.[17]

In other words, as long as companies are permitted to fail and the winds of business oscillate, no stock is completely immune from absolute disappointment.

In light of this, we need to accept that successful investing entails an ability to absorb losses. Unfortunately, just as we have traded away winners, we have been equally guilty of holding onto losers far too long. Even what appear to be rock-steady companies encounter difficulties as business prospects either decline or change. Notes Benjamin Graham, "The investor need not watch his companies' performance like a hawk; but he should give it a good, hard look from time to time." This is advice that should be well received.[18] Nothing is guaranteed, and every investment should be revalued at regular intervals, especially to see whether risk is dramatically changing. Xerox and Bethlehem Steel provide great examples of why we need to continually monitor and adjust the weights of even our core holdings.

For a time, Xerox was truly one of America's success stories. Founded in 1906, Xerox went on to wide acclaim with the success of the first electric copy machine, coined *Xerox* from the Greek words meaning "dry" and "writing." As recently as the late 1980s, Xerox was being heralded as an "American Samurai"[19] after successfully warding off an electronics assault by the Japanese. And Xerox shareholders benefited in the early 1990s, with shares experiencing over a tenfold increase between 1990 and an all-time high in 1999 (adjusted for splits). But times change. More recently, Xerox has been in deep financial trouble. At one time, its stock was off 93 percent from its high in May 1999 to its low in December 2000. Xerox is currently trading at 15. The market capitalization hovers around $6.5 billion, this for a company with global revenues of nearly $20 billion in 2000. While the story is far from over, certainly shareholders can't help but wonder whether they missed earlier sell signals. Should we have known better than to hold on for the long term?

If Xerox investors had properly taken into account risk readings, financial losses could have been limited. Xerox's RiskGrade measurement was generally range-bound for the better part of the 1990s (see Figure 5.8)— 100 on the low end, 200 on the upper end. Investors who were comfortable with risk appetites in this range should have become alarmed when Xerox's RiskGrade clearly breached 200 in early 1997. (As a reminder, a RiskGrade of 200 represents twice the variability of the broader market under normal trading conditions.) Xerox's RiskGrade soon subsided to more normal levels, and many investors may have reasonably discounted this spike as only momentary. Those investors who used the summer of 1997 as an excuse to sell the stock in the 40s were naturally disappointed when the stock climbed to the mid-60s two years later, a 50-plus percent return. However,

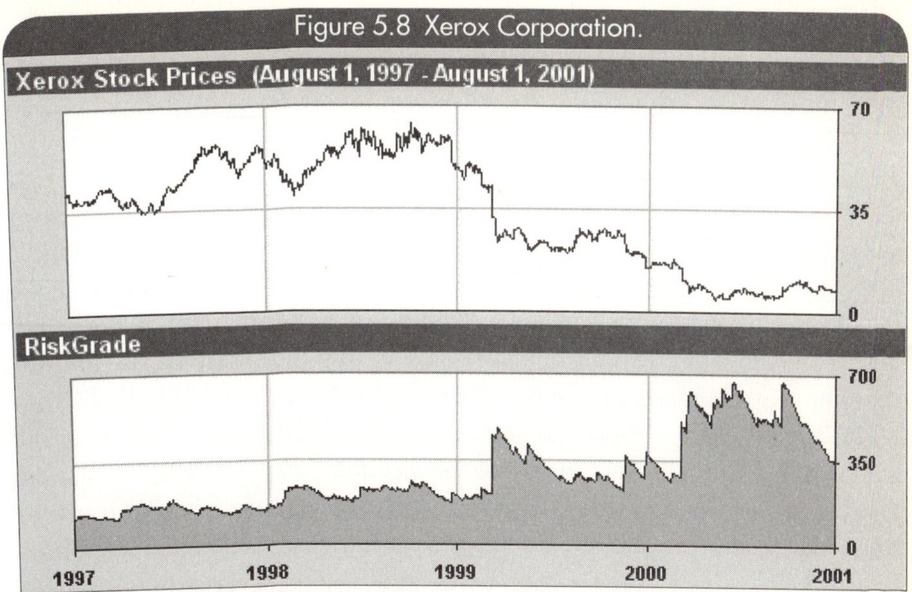

Source: WealthBench, RiskMetrics Group.

the situation at Xerox was clearly not right, and the RiskGrade captured the growing risks beginning in early 1999. Soon thereafter, the stock quickly plunged. Investors who had steeled themselves for the long haul had little comfort as the stock fell over 90 percent in about 18 months.

As we have seen, a radically changing business climate can push even the bluest of blue-chip companies out to pasture. Xerox is just one of countless thousands of companies that have disappointed long-term share-holders. The list seems endless. Woolworth's, a retailing giant for the better part of the past century, filed for bankruptcy some years ago. Rite Aid, once the largest drugstore chain in the United States, has teetered on the brink of Chapter 11 for some time as a result of accounting irregularities. Rite Aid is now trading at levels not seen since 1982. Although many of these companies will bounce back, others will not. When is a downdraft in shares merely an opportunity to purchase shares cheaply, and when is it a signal of the beginning of the end?

Needless to say, a large part of investment success relies on the ability to recognize shifting business trends. But more relevantly for average investors, success requires the ability to conform risk to meet personal standards. Benjamin Graham may have put it best in describing the vicissi-tudes of the marketplace when he stated:

There are two chief morals to this story. The first is that the stock market often goes far wrong, and sometimes an alert and courageous investor can take advantage of its patent errors. The other is that most businesses change in character and quality over the years, sometimes for the better, perhaps more often for the worse.[20]

The troubles at Xerox, Rite Aid, Woolworth, Texaco, Enron, WorldCom, and other companies should underscore the perils of a blind buy-and-hold long-term strategy. Individual companies carry risk that is ever changing. If the aforementioned stalwarts can crumble under the weight of corporate mismanagement or changing business cycles, other blue-chip names are susceptible as well. Many may disagree, citing such heavyweights as IBM or AT&T. Buffett has stressed that success rests on finding companies that will be dominant 10 to 20 years out. But the vast majority of public companies may be hard-pressed to survive the next 20 years. You often hear this phrase when discussing mutual funds: "Past success is no guarantee of future returns." The same is true for companies—the market reveres no one person or company. Who can be sure that the IBM of tomorrow will be the same dominant company that it is today? Certainly, Big Blue of the 1980s was no stranger to adversity. Ask the CEO of any Fortune 500 company today whether things have changed in the past 30 years...or even the past 10 years. It's difficult to forecast more than one year out with supreme confidence.

The experts may suggest holding on in the face of steep declines, and they may prove right more often than not, but be wary of accepting risk that is inconsistent with return objectives. Doing so will invariably throw us off course. Adhering to risk guidelines may mean that we sell too anxiously, forgoing upside possibilities, but it could also mean the difference between a 40 percent loss and a 90 percent walloping, which is especially important if our investment horizon or final objective does not have the advantage of time. Quite simply, many of us cannot wait for the next bullish cycle to begin. We need to be pragmatic. Heed the words of the mavens. Whether it's growth or value, try to focus on your long-term goals with regular appraisals of risk. Those who have more restricted horizons must understand that the undercurrents of higher risk can be allayed only with time. Taking unusual risks in an abbreviated period can certainly deliver exponential returns, but it can also nearly drain the tank with little time to refill it.

Investors should note that risk factors alone will not necessarily be able to predict performance. However, when analyzed in conjunction with other valuation measures, risk tolerance has proven to be a powerful indicator. "When a stock climbs without an increase in the attractiveness of the business fundamentals, don't be blinded by your good fortune. Your risk exposure is increasing with every upward trade."[21] Just as a good investor refrains from diverging completely from allocation targets, so, too, should risk be scrutinized. Let risk influence our decision. As they say on Wall Street, no one ever got fired for taking profits.

From a practical standpoint, disciplined investors should consider setting limits on risk, similar to stop-loss orders on stock prices. A simple way to do this is to reassess the composition of an entire portfolio or a particular stock when the overall RiskGrade breaches an acceptable level, either on the upside or downside. The decision to scale back or add to positions will naturally depend on elements in addition to risk alone. External market conditions and company-specific developments will ultimately enter into final decisions. However, a significant change in the underlying RiskGrade without any material improvements to accompany the shift could signal greater risks ahead.

Final Word on Timing the Market

We should make clear that we advocate taking a proactive stance against financial risk. This is quite different from a strategy predicated on market timing. That's not to say that timing can't help—it can. But timing the markets should not be confused with having good timing. "You are practicing another self-delusion if you buy a stock with the attitude that the performance of a newly purchased stock must please you quickly or shortly be sold," warn Metz and Stasen.[22] With the advantage of time, even poorly timed market decisions can ultimately provide solid returns insofar as the initial investment is sound. The same cannot be said for well-timed purchases in inferior companies. Metz and Stasen also wisely suggest that "buying right does little good if you are not prepared to hold on. Holding on will do you no good, it may even do great harm, if you did not buy right in the first place."[23] Because time is a critical element to performance, the interrelationship between time and risk cannot be overstated. When determining personally appropriate risk levels, investors must take into consideration not only absolute return objectives but also the consequence of risk on time. Investors who push investment horizons into the distant future can afford to exchange greater near-term flux for longer-term gains. In contrast, investors with more immediate needs for investment proceeds cannot run the risk of accepting wide swings, as near-term volatility could wipe out any chance of recouping losses. Remember, stocks in general exhibit a great deal of volatility in the short run.

Regrettably, many self-directed investors have misinterpreted this point, adopting a trading strategy that goes against the grain of time-tested investment logic. For example, recent data suggests that a typical investor now holds a stock fund for 2.9 years, on average, compared to over 12 years three decades ago. These short-term enthusiasts have wrongly concluded that the ease with which people can get in and out of the market today is tantamount to greater efficiency. This reflects hubris on their part. A short-term approach, by definition, implies that trading decisions must be more right than wrong. However, consider the following line of reasoning. Suppose that we subscribe to the efficient market theory, which holds that stock market patterns are not predictable. This would suggest that our short-term accuracy is no greater than 50 percent for any meaningful period. If our winners and losers cancel each other out, we are no further along than when we started. But factor in transaction costs and tax implications associated with short-term trades, and the final performance numbers will invariably be disappointing. An expense fee of 1 percent, while seemingly trite, will weigh more heavily on total returns with time. The difference between an expense ratio of 0.2 and 2.2 percent over a 10-year period on an initial investment of $10,000, with an annual rate of return of 9 percent, is $4,252, not an insignificant amount.

Some of our urgency can be blamed on our current environment, which holds immediate gratification in high esteem. However, the preponderance of data suggests that superior returns cannot be consistently achieved with frequent turnover of stock. The idea that entire portfolios can be removed when conditions deteriorate and restored when conditions improve is implausible. Other experts put it in more basic terms. "The factors that make an ideal investment are never all present at the same time. Even if such opportunity actually did exist, it would be almost impossible for anyone to recognize its existence."[24] One-hit sensations don't count. "It doesn't pay to be smart once; you've got to be right at probably 10 major market inflection points in an investment lifetime, and the odds against that are 1,024 to 1," argues the *Wall Street Journal*.[25] More to the point, the probability of outguessing the market on a consistent basis is a loser's game.

In light of all this, many have relied on the mutual fund industry as one solution. The idea of leaving some of the day-to-day decisions to the pros seems rather reasonable. But even the mutual fund industry has not been immune to poor judgment with respect to timing issues. Apart from some one-year wonders, the preponderance of mutual funds have consistently underperformed. In a five-year period ending in December 1999, only 16 percent of U.S. stock funds beat the S&P 500 Index.[26] An overwhelming number of managers consistently return less than the broader markets, mostly because of high turnover and disastrous timing decisions. It has been noted that fund managers now typically hold stocks in their portfolios for a little more than a year. In an era in which information flows freely, even our long-term performance is likely to suffer because many of us have failed to acquire a proper understanding of how risk plays with respect to both return prospects and return horizons. Although a bull market covered up many of our investment blemishes for much of the 1990s, the more volatile environment that we presently face will not be so forgiving.

CHAPTER 6

Asset Allocation

When embarking on our investment journeys, many of us mistakenly push off with an incomplete understanding of where we will come ashore. This is because we often set sail first and ask questions second. Rather than charting a course and a viable means to get there, we hope that some fortuitous current will take us where we want to go. Unbeknownst to us, the tides have a way of quietly steering us off course, deceiving our senses about where we are and what lies ahead. Christopher Columbus, for example, went to his deathbed convinced he had reached Chinese territory via a westward route. Had he not stumbled upon the fortunes of the New World, his legacy today might be relegated to a single footnote in an obscure history book.

Charting Our Course

Before jumping into an investment decision, we should remind ourselves of the misdirected Spanish expeditions to the Far East. As with Columbus, just starting off in a general direction does not guarantee that we will arrive at our desired destination. Even with a detailed map charting the vistas ahead, the travel itself is likely to be fraught with unexpected snares. After all, notes Alec Ellinger, "strategy in investment is very much the same as strategy in war; it is the formation of the broad general plan of campaign while the details lie in the province of tactics."[1] In this sense, proper planning is not an option, it's a requirement. The initial planning process may take a few hours, but it is in these moments of deliberation that the makings of a sound investment plan are born. For most of us, financial success will hinge on how we navigate the uncharted waters that lie ahead. Careful foresight can prepare us for some of the unseen travails that invariably come with the markets. Identifying an agreeable set of assets and applying a proper rank to each investment is imperative. Box 6.1 underscores the importance of formulating a suitable asset allocation plan.

Asset Allocation

In this chapter, we're going to explore asset allocation in more detail. Asset allocation refers to the process of allocating your assets among various asset classes such as equities, bonds, and money market funds. The primary goal of asset allocation is to constrain risk in our portfolios. Asset allocation is the cornerstone of modern portfolio theory and the single biggest determinant of our future investment performance. When done right, asset allocation provides us with an optimal mix of diversified assets that enhances the likelihood of us achieving our financial goals with the least amount of risk.

A study by Gary Brinson, Brian Singer, and Gil Beebower is often referenced as the final word regarding the impact of asset allocation on returns. This study reports that asset allocation accounts for over 90 percent of returns, whereas "relative skill in management of the asset allocation weights and in selecting specific securities" contributes less than 10 percent to final performance.[2] In other words, market timing and security selection is almost inconsequential to portfolio values. What is most paramount to the investor is owning the right category or class of securities rather than a particular security itself. By spreading assets among several different asset classes with different expected returns and RiskGrade levels, an investor is able to increase the likelihood that the components in each asset class will complement each other and improve the investor's overall risk-adjusted returns.

Box 6.1 Market Primer: When Do I Need the Money?

A good investment for an 18-year-old is probably not a good investment for an 81-year-old. If you're likely to need your money within five years, you should not allocate your entire wealth to stocks, which are highly volatile investments. On the other hand, if your investment horizon is long (20 to 30 years), you should be more willing to accept short-term fluctuations of the equity markets in exchange for long-term growth prospects. In addition to having more time to recoup losses, longer-term investors have the advantage of compounding returns over time. Small incremental returns can become significant over long horizons. Take the example shown in Figure 6.1. An investment in U.S. stocks outperformed government bonds by a mere 3.26 percent per annum from 1950 to 1999. That is, $1,000 invested in stocks in 1950 would have appreciated to $58,072 in 1999 (given an average annual return of 9.48 percent for the S&P 500), whereas the same investment in government bonds would have returned only $15,553 (given a 6.22 percent average annual return).

The chart shows the growth of $1,000 over time when invested in the S&P 500 versus U.S. 30-year bonds.

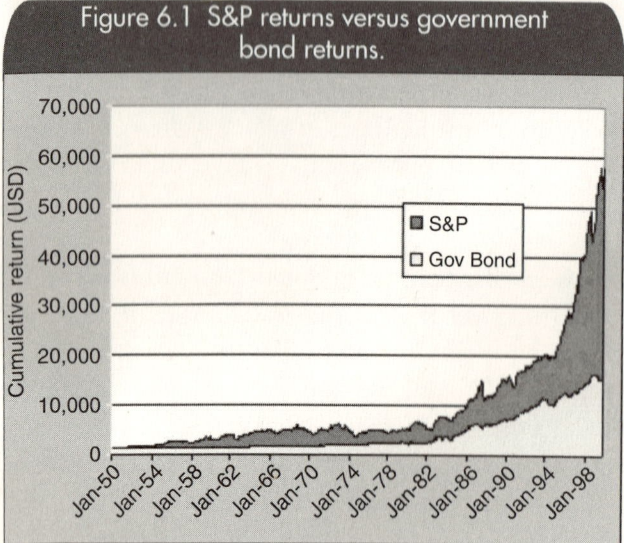

Source: RiskGrades, Understanding Risk online course.

Investment Profile

Like all processes, asset allocation can be broken down into steps. The first step is to determine an allocation plan that reflects personal dispositions and financial circumstances. First, a financial objective must be set. We must clearly establish the main purpose of our investment funds. While seemingly trivial, the significance of this decision cannot be overstated. As we have learned, our investment plans often fall short of objectives because we neglect to thoroughly factor in what we want and what we are willing to accept into our investment decisions. In other words, we fail to understand how much risk is necessary in order to meet our goals. Alec Ellinger points out that a common pitfall among investors is to express ambivalence, which leads to failed expectations: "It should be quite easy to form a clear opinion about the object of investment, *but one of the causes of failure for many investors is that they never make this simple decision but hover between investment for income and investment for appreciation without making a clean choice for one or the other*" (italics added).[3] An investor's objectives must be clear from the outset. After we concretely determine the main purpose of our investments, the second requisite is to identify a general allocation plan consistent with our ultimate objectives. This step addresses the pragmatic aspect of what should be held and how much should be allocated to each investment. The ultimate aim of any personal assessment is to determine a combination of assets that most accurately reflects an individual's time to retirement (or to a time when funds are required) and risk tolerance.

We start with a profile-building questionnaire. Investors will be able to find a standard customer profile questionnaire at most online brokerage or financial planning websites. The questionnaire is designed to help you better define your goals and determine your time frame and risk tolerance as they relate to the investments you select to help meet your investment goals. In turn, your responses to the questions help determine an appropriate asset allocation for you. In Figure 6.2, we've simplified our investment profile survey to include just a handful of questions that we feel are the most instrumental to the profile-building process. Are you the risky sort? Do you shy away from risk? Can you stomach volatility in excess of 10 percent…20 percent…50 percent? Do you grow squeamish at the earliest signs of a correction? Profile building is far from being an exact science, but it does provide a point of departure. The goal of long-term financial planning is to build an optimal portfolio that meets your personal expectations

---

Figure 6.2 WealthBench investment profile questionnaire (excerpt).

I. Stage in Life

Life stages are defined partly by our age and unique life experiences and partly by where we stand in relation to our retirement. As we move through various stages in life, our investment goals, needs, and concerns change. For example, strategies that suited you well as you accumulated assets in earlier years may not be effective when your focus shifts to providing for retirement income. Selecting the stage that best fits your current lifestyle will help us identify some general guidelines about how your portfolio should be allocated.

1. What is your current age?

   a. Under 30

   b. 30 to 45

   c. 46 to 58

   d. 59 to 64

   e. Over 65

2. Investment *time horizon* refers to the number of years you expect the portfolio to be invested before you must dip into principal. When do you anticipate the need for money from this portfolio?

   a. Less than 1 year (or already doing so)

   b. Between 1 and 5 years

   c. Between 5 and 10 years

   d. More than 10 years

3. Which of the following best describes your purpose for investing? Please select the most important one.

   a. I expect to use these funds for a large purchase or expenses within five years.

   b. I want to be certain that my capital is secure and that I have regular income now.

   c. I place dual emphasis on capital growth and income, with moderate fluctuation in year-to-year returns.

   d. I would like long-term growth and I am less concerned about income and return volatility at this time.

   e. I'm interested only in aggressive growth over the long run, and accept significant short-term fluctuations in returns.

4. Which of the following best describes your current stage in life?

   a. Single, with few financial burdens. I am eager to accumulate wealth for the future. However some funds must be kept available for enjoyment such as cars, travel, and entertainment.

   b. A couple without children. Life is grand. With dual incomes, my spouse and I are well off financially and preparing for the future by establishing a home, careers, and retirement accounts.

   c. Young family. This is the peak home-purchasing stage. I have a mortgage and maintain only small cash balances (bank savings, money markets, etc.) equal to 3 or 6 months of living expenses to cover emergencies. Saving for my children's education is top priority.

   d. Mature family. I am in the peak earning years and have the mortgage under control. My children are growing up and have either left home or require less supervision. I am starting to think about retirement, although it may be many years away.

Figure 6.2 (Continued)

I. Stage in Life

e. Preparing for retirement. I own my home and have few financial burdens. My primary concern is ensuring that I can afford a comfortable retirement. I am interested in pursuing other interests such as travel, recreation, and self-education.

f. Retired. No longer working, I rely on existing funds and income from investments to maintain my lifestyle. I am keen to enjoy life and maintain my health.

Step II. Investment Experience

As your personality characterizes who you are, your investment personality clarifies the investment strategy with which you'd be most comfortable with and what's appropriate to meet your goals. For this section, consider your trading history and select the answer that best describes you.

1. Which of the following statements best describes your current investment experience? (If you don't currently have any investments, choose the response that best describes how you think you would manage your investments.)

a. All of my investments to date have been in Treasury bills because I need the security of capital.

b. Most of my investments were made to generate income and preserve capital, but I now need some capital growth.

c. Most of my investments tend to be mutual funds or trusts, although they are generally not aggressive funds.

d. Most of my investments tend to be moderately aggressive. My objectives are long term; therefore I don't often make changes unless my reasons for investing have changed.

e. I tend to choose aggressive investments for long-term growth.

f. I currently do not have any investments; this is my initial attempt at long-term investment planning.

2. Over what period of time do you judge the performance of an investment?

a. Monthly

b. Quarterly

c. Annually

d. Between 2 and 5 years

3. Excluding short-term money market securities, how long do you typically hold a security?

a. Less than 3 months

b. 3 months to 1 year

c. Between 1 and 3 years

d. Between 3 and 5 years

e. More than 5 years

Step III. Tolerance for Risk

The final element in determining your investment strategy is your risk tolerance. Everyone has a different attitude toward risk. Some people can relax while their account balance goes up and down dramatically. Others get nervous if their account shows even the smallest drop in value.

Continued

Figure 6.2 (Continued)

Step III. Tolerance for Risk

These profiling questions are designed to assist you in determining your risk profile and the type of investor you can afford to be, based on your personal tolerance for risk and current lifestyle. In many instances, the profiles indicate that because of your financial situation, you can afford to take more risk than personal preferences alone would indicate. However, it is important to ensure that you are comfortable with the profile recommended for you.

As an investor, you need to be comfortable with the amount of risk you're taking and the potential consequences. If you stay up at night worrying about your investments, the returns you earn aren't worth the personal cost to your health. Keep in mind that your risk tolerance may change as you gain investing experience and confidence.

1. Which of the following statements best describes your investment philosophy?

   a. I am not comfortable taking risks with my capital, but I am prepared to do so with a small portion of my assets as I need some capital appreciation to offset inflation.

   b. I understand that the opportunity for greater returns comes with taking greater risks, but I am only prepared to do so with less than half of my assets.

   c. I understand that the opportunity for greater returns comes with taking greater risks, and I am prepared to do so with more than half of my assets.

   d. I have an aggressive investment approach and I am investing for the long-term. Therefore, I want to invest the majority or even all of my assets in the stock markets, as this is the best way to ensure higher returns over the long term.

2. If an investment offers the opportunity for higher long-term returns but also carries the chance of going down in the short term, how comfortable with it would you be?

   a. Very comfortable

   b. Not bothered

   c. Uncomfortable but prepared to try it

   d. Very uncomfortable with the prospect of any loss

3. How long would you be prepared to see your investment performing poorly before you cashed it in?

   a. Immediately sell if any loss in value

   b. Less than one year

   c. Between 1 and 3 years

   d. Between 3 and 5 years

   e. Between 5 and 10 years

   f. 10 years or more

4. On Black Monday, October 19, 1987, stocks declined more than 22 percent in a single day. If this happened again, how would you react?

   a. Sell all of my investments. Security of capital is critical to me and I do not intend to take risks.

   b. Sell some of my investments. It's time to cut my losses and transfer my funds into more secure investments.

Figure 6.2 *(Continued)*

Step III. Tolerance for Risk

c. Do nothing. This was a calculated risk and I will leave the investments in place, expecting performance to improve.

d. Buy more. I am a long-term investor and consider this sudden market correction as an opportunity to purchase additional shares at a lower cost basis.

5. The following chart shows the possible range of values for four different investments of $100,000 after one year. Which investment would you be most comfortable owning?

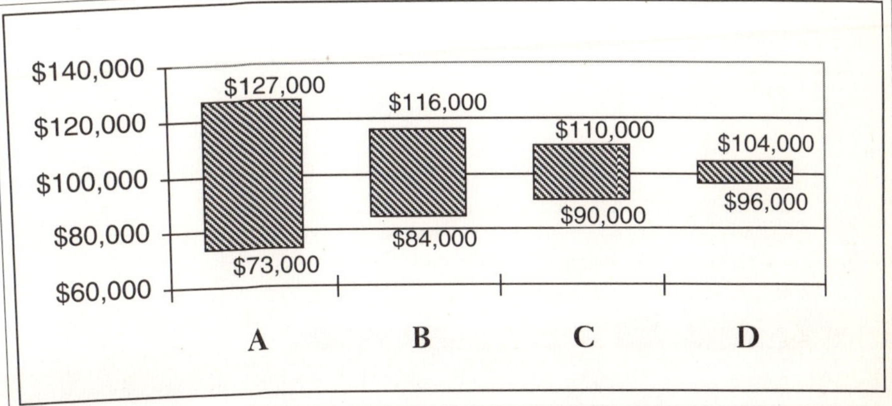

a. Investment A

b. Investment B

c. Investment C

d. Investment D

Source: WealthBench.com, RiskMetrics Group.

---

of risk and return. The following set of questions is designed to help us model an asset allocation mix that may be suitable to you. This asset mix is determined by several factors, including investment stage, portfolio size, time horizon, return objectives, and tolerance for risk.

To determine your personal investor profile, take a few minutes to answer the 12 questions in Figure 6.2. After completing the survey, refer to the scoring page in Figure 6.3.

After completing a questionnaire such as the one shown in Figure 6.2, the investor typically receives a scorecard that plots his or her investment profile, including a description of the profile and the general asset class mix that's representative of investors with a similar investment profile (see Figure 6.4). These types of profile questionnaires are popular because financial

Figure 6.3 Grading algorithm for profile questionnaire.

Investment Profile Scoring Sheet:

Check the answer you provided for each question. Award yourself the numerical value assigned to each answer. Add your scores up for each of the three sections to determine your cumulative score.

Part I. Stage in Life	a	b	c	d	e	f	g
Question 1	4	3	2	1	0	*	*
Question 2	0	1	3	5	*	*	*
Question 3	2	0	3	4	5	*	*
Question 4	7	5	4	3	2	0	*
Total Stage in Life Score	=						

Part II. Investment Experience	a	b	c	d	e	f	g
Question 1	0	2	3	5	7	2	*
Question 2	7	5	3	1	*	*	*
Question 3	7	5	3	2	1	*	*
Total Investment Experience Score	=						

Part III. Tolerance for Risk	a	b	c	d	e	f	g
Question 1	1	2	5	6	*	*	*
Question 2	7	4	2	0	*	*	*
Question 3	0	2	2	1	1	1	*
Question 4	0	2	4	7	*	*	*
Question 5	6	4	3	1	*	*	*
Your Tolerance for Risk Score	=						

Add all four parts together to determine your cumulative score:

Cumulative Score	=

If your cumulative score is:	Then your investment strategy is:
1 — 15	Short term
16 — 29	Conservative
30 — 39	Balanced
40 — 52	Growth
53 — 62	Aggressive
63 — 75	Speculative

Source: WealthBench.com, RiskMetrics Group.

advisors like to translate asset allocation into a language that is easily understood. The simplicity of pie charts makes the final analysis easy to digest, ostensibly casting an individual as a specific investment type and implicitly suggesting how much risk is appropriate. For example, an aggressive investor is very conscious of high returns, as the heavy posture in stocks indicates, whereas a short-term investor is concerned mainly with liquidity, represented by a significant amount apportioned to money markets.

The performance of the financial markets in 2000, 2001, and 2002 provides a prime illustration of the impact of asset allocation on returns. More than in previous years, asset allocation policy was instrumental to perfor-

Figure 6.4 What's your investor profile?

Investor Profiles

The following is a description of your investor profile that has the best fit for the answers you provided. WealthBench will apply this profile to build an investment portfolio that is suitable for you based on your investment horizon, retirement goals, and aversion to risk.

Investment Strategy	Description	Asset Allocation	
Short-Term Plan	Based upon your answers to the Investment Profile Questionnaire, you are considered a short-term investor. A short-term investor's primary financial goal is capital preservation. Typically, investors in this category require cash in a short period of time, and opt to invest in risk-free, highly liquid securities like US Treasuries.	RiskGrade Stocks Bonds Money Markets	5 0% 0% 100%
Conservative Plan	Based upon you answers to the Investment Profile Questionnaire, you are considered a conservative investor. Investors in this category typically seek to generate income from your investments while also decreasing the potential for loss of principal. Outpacing inflation is likely to be one of your primary concerns.	RiskGrade Stocks Bonds Money Markets	25 20% 70% 10%
Balanced Plan	Based upon your answers to the Investment Profile Questionnaire, you are considered a balanced investor. Typically balanced investors seek investments that generate income to help meet immediate or near-term financial needs.	RiskGrade Stocks Bonds Money Markets	50 60% 35% 5%
Growth Plan	Based upon your answers to the Investment Profile Questionnaire, you are considered a growth investor. Investors in this category typically seek to achieve long-term stable growth.	RiskGrade Stocks Bonds Money Markets	75 80% 20% 0%
Aggressive Plan	Based upon your answers to the Investment Profile Questionnaire, you are considered an aggressive investor. The typical objective of a growth-oriented investor is to accumulate above-average growth rather than obtain current income. In order to achieve this growth, an aggressive investor will accept the risk of price volatility.	RiskGrade Stocks Bonds Money Markets	100 100% 0% 0%
Speculative Plan	Based upon your answers to the Investment Profile Questionnaire, you are considered a speculative investor. Investors in this category seek to generate maximum growth over time. Speculative investors are willing to take on a substantial amount of risk in order to achieve above-average returns.	RiskGrade	125>

Source: WealthBench.com, RiskMetrics Group.

mance. Investors with a heavy concentration in either the technology sector or stocks endured significant pains since April 2000. By comparison, conservative portfolios that contain bonds with only a modicum of stocks suffered less from the costly whims of the market—this despite having general exposure to the stock market. On the whole, portfolios that were underweight in stocks fared much better than plans with large equity contributions. At the same time, a short-term investor with a prevalence for bonds considerably outpaced the market during this period. Investors with balance between stocks and bonds shielded their portfolios from erosion better than an aggressive investor focused on stocks alone.

Unfortunately for many investors, their due diligence into asset allocation stops here—looking at a series of pie charts. Pie charts are practical for their simplicity but lack the ability to convey a meaningful message. Though effective for initiating a discussion on expected return, the nicely divided pieces do not offer detailed descriptions of risk. It is next to impossible to distinguish the different nuances of every investment plan by just eyeing the various pie charts.

As a case in point, in less than a year Enron went from being one of the largest energy companies in the world to bankruptcy. The speed with which the company collapsed was unprecedented. In January 2001 a share of Enron stock was valued at $90; by year-end it was worth pennies. Shock waves from the collapse were felt immediately. Nowhere was the pain more acute than for the thousands of employees and retirees holding Enron stock in their 401(k) plans. The scandal effectively devoured the nest eggs of investors who had a concentration of Enron shares in their retirement plans. One of the many lessons learned from Enron is the importance of proper asset allocation, because investors don't always have time to react to risk in the markets. With Enron obfuscating its own financial condition, investors were denied the steady stream of quarterly loss reports that often portends failing companies. When accounting irregularities were finally disclosed, the shares went into a free fall. For individual shareholders, it was too late.

In response to the ensuing crisis in confidence regarding 401(k) plans, RiskMetrics' Alvin Lee and CEO Ethan Berman published a comprehensive guide for investors: *401(k) CheckUp: Best Practices in the Measurement and Disclosure of Risk in 401(k) Plans.*[4] The publication is an authoritative resource for investors anxious to learn how to quantify the level of risk and diversification in retirement portfolios as well as methods of reducing concentrations of risk. To help illustrate how understanding risk measures can lead to better investment decisions we're going to adapt an example from the document for our purposes.

Asset Allocation Should Be Risk Allocation

As discussed most individuals begin the investment process reading descriptions of investment strategies and/or answering questions about their own risk preferences. People are told that stocks are riskier than bonds, which are riskier than cash. They are asked questions like, "How much risk can you handle?" and "What would you do if your portfolio lost 25 percent of its value?" This leads individuals and their advisors to one of a number of defined investment strategies, often labeled as *short-term, conservative, balanced growth, aggressive,* or *speculative.*

Investors are then given some form of pie charts that link an asset allocation to an investment strategy or style. For example, an allocation of 95 percent equities and 5 percent cash maps to an "aggressive" strategy, or 60 percent equities and 40 percent bonds to "balanced." Based on these pie charts and their descriptors, investors select assets in their 401(k) plan.

However, there are at least two problems with this approach. First, two portfolios can have the same asset allocation but very different risk. In fact, some balanced funds could surprisingly carry more risk than aggressive ones. A conservative portfolio may see more variability in its returns than a balanced strategy. Thus, labels that demarcate the various investment styles (conservative, balanced, aggressive) can be rendered meaningless. Investors should prioritize the absolute level of risk above some generic investment label. Doing so will provide a better map of the financial landscape that lies ahead. Consider the two portfolios shown in Figure 6.5.

In this extreme example, even though both portfolios technically have an asset allocation of 80 percent equities and 20 percent fixed income, it is clear that portfolio 2 will have higher risk and less diversification than portfolio 1. Figure 6.6 provides a summary risk analysis of the two portfolios.

As shown, portfolio 1 has a RiskGrade level of 73, whereas portfolio 2 has a RiskGrade level of 219. Despite having the same asset allocation, portfolio 2 is approximately three times more risky. It should be noted that we could have created a portfolio of 80 percent large-cap equities and 20 percent in fixed income that would have *less* risk than a portfolio of 60 per-

Figure 6.5 Tale of two allocations.

Portfolio 1

Aggregate Tax-Deferred Assets

Stats

Market Value:	$100,000
RiskGrade:	73
Expected Return:	6.0%

Asset Allocation

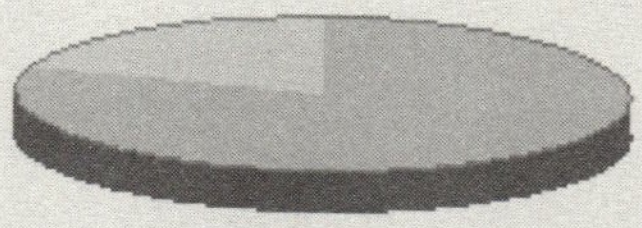

Asset Class	Taxable	Tax-Deferred	Non-Taxable
U.S. Large Cap Growth	-	80.00 %	-
U.S. Large Cap Value	-	-	-
U.S. Mid Cap	-	-	-
U.S. Small Cap	-	-	-
Intl. Equity	-	-	-
U.S. Bonds	-	20.00 %	-
U.S. Munis	-	-	-
Intl. Bonds	-	-	-
U.S. Cash	-	-	-

Portfolio 2

Aggregate Tax-Deferred Assets

Stats

Market Value:	$100,000
RiskGrade:	219
Expected Return:	6.0%

Asset Allocation

Asset Class	Taxable	Tax-Deferred	Non-Taxable
U.S. Large Cap Growth	-	80.00 %	-
U.S. Large Cap Value	-	-	-
U.S. Mid Cap	-	-	-
U.S. Small Cap	-	-	-
Intl. Equity	-	-	-
U.S. Bonds	-	20.00 %	-
U.S. Munis	-	-	-
Intl. Bonds	-	-	-
U.S. Cash	-	-	-

Source: WealthBench.com, RiskMetrics Group.

Figure 6.6 Portfolio overview and RiskGrade measurement.

Portfolio 1

Symbol	Risk Grade	Market Value
Vanguard S&P 500 Index Fund	94	$80,000
U.S. Large Cap Growth	**94**	**$80,000**
Vanguard Intermediate Treasury Fund	23	$20,000
U.S. Bonds	**23**	**$20,000**
Account	**73**	**$100,000**
Diversification Benefit	**7**	

Portfolio 2

Symbol	Risk Grade	Market Value
Cisco Systems	352	$40,000
Texas Instruments	240	$40,000
U.S. Large Cap Growth	**277**	**$80,000**
Vanguard Long-Term Corporate Fund	18	$20,000
U.S. Bonds	**18**	**$20,000**
Account	**219**	**$100,000**
Diversification Benefit	**21**	

Source: WealthBench.com, RiskMetrics Group.

cent large-cap equities and 40 percent fixed income, even though stocks are ostensibly riskier than bonds. Again, looking only at asset allocation to assess risk can be misleading.

Second, asset classes are volatile. Even when a portfolio holds investments that could reasonably be characterized by a common asset allocation strategy (e.g., each asset class represented by a broadly diversified fund), the risk may not be what you expect. By this we are referring to the fact that the volatility itself of financial assets fluctuates over time. For example, a low volatility level for an asset class indicates that daily fluctuations in price can be expected to lie within a relatively narrow range.[5] However, volatility may increase dramatically at times, indicating that the range of daily price fluctuations could widen greatly. Empirically, we have observed that the markets are quiet at times and very volatile at other times.

Using the asset allocation strategies and compositions shown in Figure 6.7, the RiskGrade of each strategy over time is shown in Figure 6.8. As shown, if you determined in 1996 that the right risk profile for you was a balanced asset allocation strategy, then you would have seen your risk profile increase by a factor of 4 over the next few years, even as you made no changes to your assets. As shown, the volatility of the markets increased dramatically over time. In fact, the risk of your portfolio three years later would be *more than double the most aggressive strategy you determined was too risky for you when you started the process.* A simple asset allocation fails to provide a good measure of risk.

Risk Allocation

Given the pitfalls of relying solely on asset allocation analysis to understand risk, we believe the solution lies in rethinking how an investor's risk

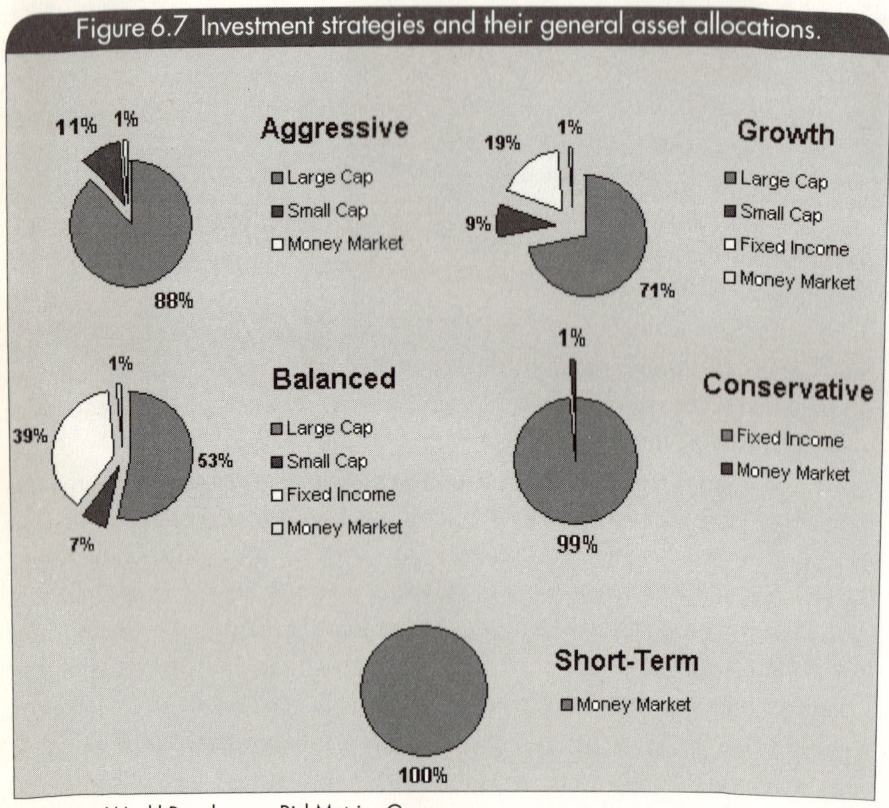

Source: WealthBench.com, RiskMetrics Group.

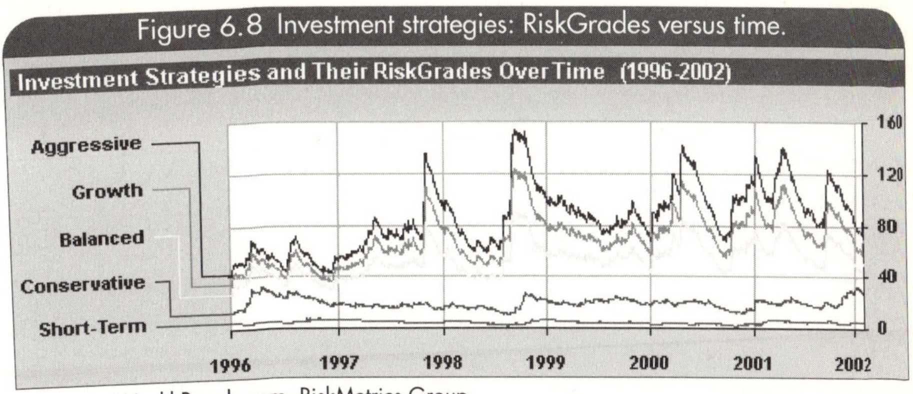

Source: WealthBench.com, RiskMetrics Group.

preferences should be translated into action. The conventional method of selecting a preset asset allocation strategy can be misleading and generally locks an investor into a portfolio whose risk can vary widely. It makes more intuitive sense to assign a specific, quantitative risk target that can directly reflect an investor's risk preferences and can be held constant over time. We refer to this process as *risk allocation*. Maintaining a constant risk allocation, though, requires shifting one's asset mix periodically as the risks of different asset classes fluctuate.

Individuals still need to specify their risk preferences, but those preferences should be defined by RiskGrades, diversification score, and the other measures in our framework—*not* by asset allocation. Investors do not care if they are invested in technology stocks or emerging-market equities as long as they are achieving the returns that they are expecting with an amount of risk that is comfortable. In Figure 6.9, we map investment strategy descriptions to a RiskGrade.

For each strategy, we select the target RiskGrade guided by the long-term average RiskGrade observed in accordance with the asset allocations shown in Figure 6.7. While adhering to one of these asset allocations may not be optimal at any given point in time, what we find valuable are the long-term average RiskGrades associated with each, since this yields a useful set of target ranges.

For example, an investor who is looking for stable returns with limited volatility might be characterized as having a balanced risk allocation and therefore seek to maintain a portfolio RiskGrade of about 50. That portfolio today might have a 50 percent equity weighting, though (as we saw in

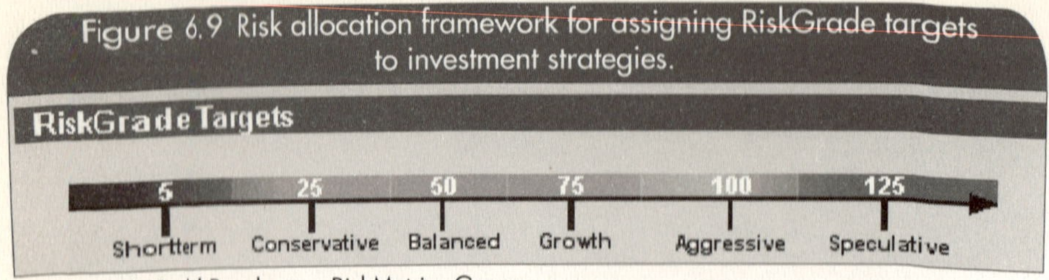

Figure 6.9 Risk allocation framework for assigning RiskGrade targets to investment strategies.

Source: WealthBench.com, RiskMetrics Group.

Figure 6.8) it might have had 80 percent equities in 1996 when the equity markets were less risky than today.

In addition, targets for other risk measures such as diversification score can help investors manage aspects of risk for their accounts other than just price volatility. Keeping an eye on volatility, diversification, and exposure to market shocks forms the basis of a multifaceted overall risk allocation strategy, which we discuss in more detail. The message here is that investors should be focusing on risk allocation, not asset allocation.

Monitoring and Rebalancing: A Habit Worth Learning

Identifying an appropriate risk allocation target in an investment plan is only a first step. As most investors intuitively know, the risk levels of financial assets constantly fluctuate. Thus, maintaining a specific risk allocation is an active process, not a passive one. In practice, this means setting a specific strategy for rebalancing one's portfolio to maintain the RiskGrade, diversification score, and other measures within target ranges. A rebalancing strategy may include the following:

- *Frequency.* The specification of how often the portfolio's risk measures will be monitored.

- *Threshold.* The level of deviation from the target that is tolerable.

A disciplined rebalancing strategy with clear guidelines regarding the frequency of monitoring an account and the degree to which deviations from target are tolerable helps set realistic parameters to manage rebalancing efforts and costs. Risk allocation targets are not single points, but rather ranges that guide the direction of one's investment process. When the risk of your account is outside the acceptable range, consider rebalancing the account holdings.

Current data suggests that the majority of plan participants do not have a rebalancing strategy. A Hewitt Associates survey found that only 30 percent of plan participants transferred balances in 2000, which suggests that many individuals are not aware of the importance of rebalancing. A lax approach to monitoring one's account, and failing to rebalance when appropriate, almost inevitably leads to deviation from one's risk allocation target.

To illustrate this point, consider a hypothetical employee of Cisco Systems in May 1997. As an employee who strongly believes in the company's prospects, he designates 40 percent of his 401(k) to Cisco Systems stock. As an investor who knows a little about the concepts of diversification, he puts 20 percent more in a pair of equity index funds, 39 percent in a fixed income fund and 1 percent in cash. (See Figure 6.10.)

On September 1, 1997, the RiskGrade of this account was 75, indicating a growth-oriented risk allocation based on the framework outlined previously. For simplicity's sake, we assume there are no additional contributions

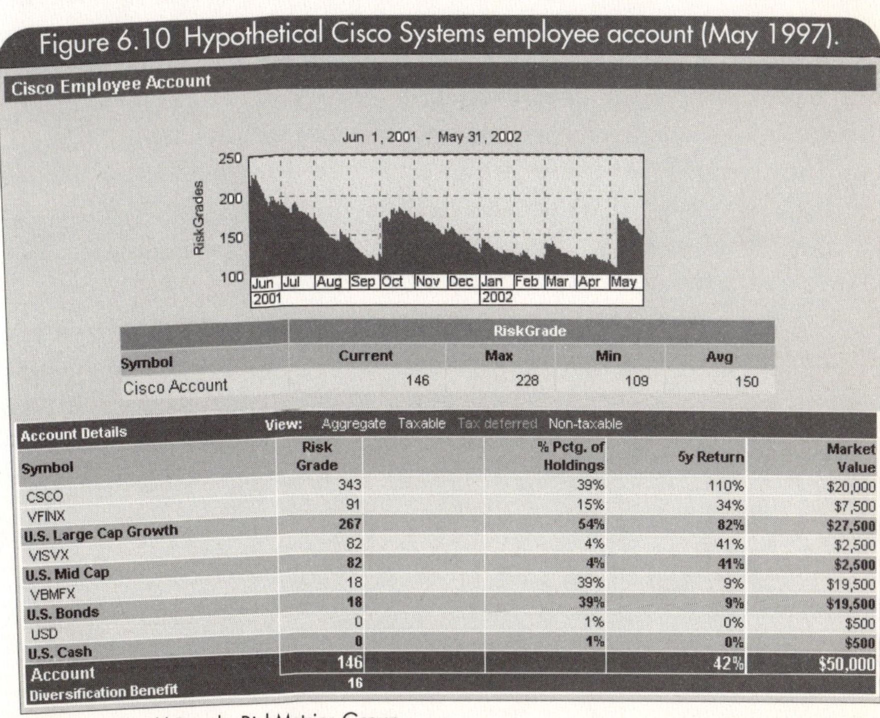

Figure 6.10 Hypothetical Cisco Systems employee account (May 1997).

Symbol	RiskGrade			
	Current	Max	Min	Avg
Cisco Account	146	228	109	150

View: Aggregate Taxable Tax deferred Non-taxable

Symbol	Risk Grade		% Pctg. of Holdings	5y Return	Market Value
CSCO	343		39%	110%	$20,000
VFINX	91		15%	34%	$7,500
U.S. Large Cap Growth	267		54%	82%	$27,500
VISVX	82		4%	41%	$2,500
U.S. Mid Cap	82		4%	41%	$2,500
VBMFX	18		39%	9%	$19,500
U.S. Bonds	18		39%	9%	$19,500
USD	0		1%	0%	$500
U.S. Cash	0		1%	0%	$500
Account	146			42%	$50,000
Diversification Benefit	16				

Source: WealthBench, RiskMetrics Group.

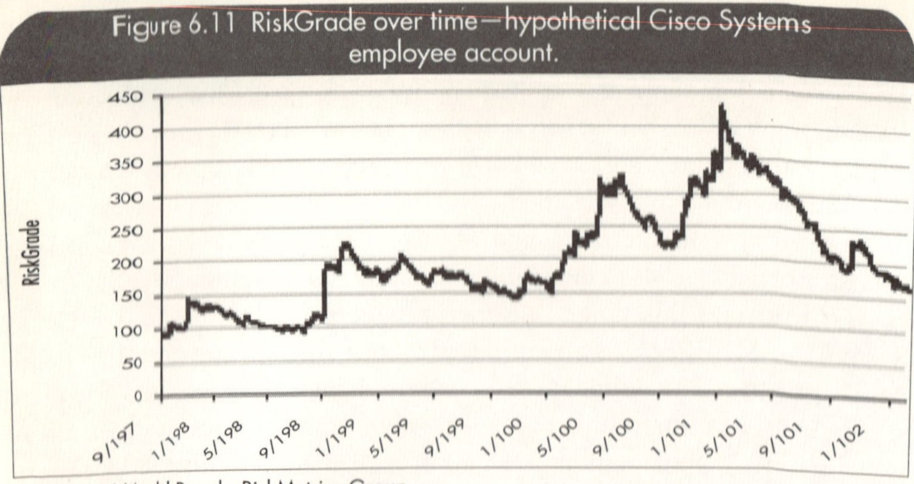

Source: WealthBench, RiskMetrics Group.

to or balance transfers in the account. The value of the account on February 1, 2002, was $81,443 with a RiskGrade of 173, indicating a speculative risk allocation. Thus, five years closer to the employee's retirement date, the account's RiskGrade had increased by more than 100 percent. As shown in Figure 6.11, the RiskGrade of the account varied widely during this time, with a peak of over 400 in early 2001 (or more than five times the risk of the portfolio when the employee did his original risk assessment). In addition, the diversification score of the account on February 1, 2002, was 14 percent, indicating that additional diversification could reduce the account's RiskGrade by 86 percent. (We discuss diversification score in more detail in the next chapter.)

Given the market movements over the past few years, it's absolutely crucial that all investors monitor their portfolios on a frequent enough basis to increase the chances that what they are trying to achieve will in fact be achieved.

Diversification

U nlike many of the physical ailments we regularly experience in our daily lives, a portfolio is much more difficult to diagnose and treat. The symptoms of a common cold, for example, are quite easy to recognize—runny nose, scratchy throat, fever. Over the years, we have learned how to treat the basics on our own—take two aspirin, drink plenty of water, rest, and if necessary consult the doctor. However, administering to the common ailments that afflict our portfolios remains for many a mystery. Often, we don't realize anything is wrong until trouble hits. Along the way, we misinterpret signals that should warn us against impending risks. Similar to diagnostic equipment at the doctor's office, the RiskGrades service helps investors identify the vitality of their own portfolios and provides a yardstick to measure any problem's severity. Our research focuses on finding effective and practical ways to prevent market risk from barring you from your long-term financial goals. In that sense, RiskGrades are good preventive care against more serious portfolio problems that may lie ahead.

With that said, subscribing to the RiskGrades or soon-to-be-released WealthBench service is not a shortcut to achieving your goals. The greatest software in the hands of the best investor will not stop the value of your portfolio from rising and falling with the whims of the market. RiskGrades have no predictive power regarding the markets. But that's the point: No one does. Smart investors don't try to forecast the future movements of the markets. Instead, they adhere to sound rules of portfolio management and diversify. Dispersing your money in a reasonable way over many investments will help you avoid excessive exposure to a single source of risk. If you're a mutual fund investor, this may mean investing in index funds that track the broader market or purchasing a bond fund to offset your equity growth funds. If you like to pick stocks, continue to purchase what you know, but avoid creating a portfolio that is affected by the same variables. For example, an employee of United Parcel Service (UPS) who owns a large number of company shares would be wise not to accumulate additional positions in other package shippers, airlines, or auto manufacturers because all are significantly affected by the price of oil and the direction of interest rates. Instead, it would be better to invest in companies of different sizes, both foreign and domestic, across different sectors, from basic materials to technology.

Because market cycles oscillate, a properly diversified portfolio allows investors to offset losses in one sector or investment type with gains in another. Though the impulsive side in us may argue, "Diversification never appears that smart, because investors always have at least some exposure to the market's most lackluster sectors," our sensible guts tell us, "Over the long haul, it is a much surer way to build wealth," as emphasized in Jonathan Clemens's article on market losses in the *Wall Street Journal*.[1] And that's the aim of diversification—capturing the market's overall returns while moderating volatility, thereby making it easier for investors to stay the course. Looking at the charts in Figures 7.1 and 7.2, the importance of diversification becomes remarkably apparent. Both illustrate just how dramatically market performance in the equity markets changes from year to year. Not only do different segments of the stock market behave differently, but leadership among these different segments changes drastically, too. For this reason, it's critical that investors maintain their long-term focus and refrain from reacting to short-term leadership changes in the market. Jack Sherry, president of the Phoenix Investment Partners' Private Client Group, strongly cautions investors against switching among the various equity styles in a vain attempt to time the shifts in leadership. This behavior has historically led to higher portfolio volatility and poor results. For evidence of this fact, refer to the

Figure 7.1 Diversification chart.

Diversification Is Key

Large-Cap Growth ■ Mid-Cap ■ Small-Cap
Large-Cap Value   International   S&P 500

BEST→WORST	'90	'91	'92	'93	'94	'95	'96	'97	'98	'99	'00
BEST	-0.3	46.1	18.4	32.6	7.8	38.4	23.1	35.2	38.7	33.2	8.25
	-3.1	41.5	16.3	18.9	2.7	37.5	23.0	33.4	28.6	27.3	7.01
	-8.1	41.2	13.8	18.1	1.3	37.2	21.6	30.5	20.0	21.3	-3.02
	-11.5	30.5	7.6	14.3	-1.8	34.5	19.0	29.0	15.0	21.0	-10.10
	-19.5	24.6	5.0	10.1	-2.0	28.4	16.5	22.4	10.1	18.2	-13.96
WORST	-23.5	12.1	-12.2	2.9	-2.1	11.2	6.1	1.8	-2.6	7.4	-22.42

Source: Phoenix Investment Partners, research conducted by Financial Research Corporation (FRC). Reprinted with permission.

Figure 7.2 Sector diversification.

Sector Diversification Is Also Key

BEST→WORST	'91	'92	'93	'94	'95	'96	'97	'98	'99	'00
BEST	Health Care	Finance	Tech	Tech	Health Care	Tech	Finance	Tech	Tech	Utilities
	Transport	Consumer Cyclicals	Capital Goods	Health Care	Finance	Finance	Health Care	Health Care	Basic Materials	Health Care
	Finance	Utilities	Transport	Consumer Staples	Capital Goods	Capital Goods	Consumer Cyclicals	Consumer Cyclicals	Consumer Cyclicals	Finance
	Consumer Staples	Basic Materials	Energy	Basic Materials	Transport	Energy	Utilities	Utilities	Capital Goods	Transport
	Consumer Cyclicals	Capital Goods	Utilities	Energy	Utilities	Consumer Staples	Consumer Staples	Consumer Staples	Energy	Energy
	Basic Materials	Transport	Consumer Cyclicals	Capital Goods	Tech	Health Care	Transport	Finance	Utilities	Consumer Staples
	Capital Goods	Consumer Staples	Basic Materials	Finance	Consumer Staples	Basic Materials	Tech	Capital Goods	Finance	Capital Goods
	Utilities	Tech	Finance	Utilities	Energy	Transport	Capital Goods	Energy	Transport	Basic Materials
	Tech	Energy	Consumer Staples	Consumer Cyclicals	Basic Materials	Consumer Cyclicals	Energy	Transport	Health Care	Consumer Cyclicals
WORST	Energy	Health Care	Health Care	Transport	Consumer Cyclicals	Utilities	Basic Materials	Basic Materials	Consumer Staples	Tech

Source: Phoenix Investment Partners, research conducted by Financial Research Corporation (FRC). Reprinted with permission.

best-to-worst performances turned in by the large-cap growth sector in 1999 and 2000 (Figures 7.1 and 7.2).

What Jelly Beans Can Tell Us

Another way of explaining the principles of diversification is to state that although a single investment may get it wrong, a group of investments is likely to get it right. In many instances, the masses have a way of arriving at the "right" conclusion. Diversification works similarly. A jarful of jelly beans may offer the clearest illustration of diversification at work. Consider the following experiment that we conducted with our RiskMetrics colleagues.

I brought a 64-ounce jarful of jellybeans into the office and asked everyone to guess the total number. Only my wife, who filled the jar, knew the actual answer. Predictably, to win the jar of jellybeans, some people (researchers) went to great lengths to try to determine the right answer—sizing up the mass of each jellybean, calculating the diameter and height of the jar, and coming up with an educated guess. Others simply gave off-the-cuff responses and went back to work, spending about the same amount of time to answer the question that I took to ask it. By the end of the day I received 44 guesses. Before submitting the final guess, I guaranteed my own victory. Without knowing the answer or counting the jellybeans, how did I win the contest?

The answer: I took the average of all 44 responses. Given that the likelihood of any one respondent being able to correctly guess the exact number of jelly beans was equivalent to relying on chance, I counted on a small percentage of respondents coming within a hair of the actual total and the majority of guesses being much higher or lower than the actual target number. Not surprisingly, the dispersion of responses was far and wide, and no single guess was correct. In the end, the average of all guesses was only four jellybeans away from the approximate number in the whole jar.

The real winner in this experiment was the law of large numbers.[2] It's clear that a larger group invariably produces a more accurate collective solution. There is something to be said for the will of the masses.

What does this have to do with diversification? Everything. Let's walk through it. Think of each individual guess as a single investment added to your new portfolio. In the end, your portfolio will contain 44 individual investments, or educated guesses. The contest is over; it's time to retire;

now let's see how you fared. Well…not one of those investments you made was a grand slam, which would be the equivalent of one of your guesses hitting the actual number of jelly beans in the jar. However, some were very close, a few did extremely well, and others fell far from the mark and were labeled losers. Does this mean your portfolio is a loser? No, not at all. Because the *average* of all those guesses (i.e., investment returns) is surprisingly accurate, it can be the equivalent of coming within inches of a grand slam. Keep this example in your mind just a little longer. What would happen if we increased the number of guesses, or stocks, from, say, 40 to 140? Averaging a greater number is likely to increase the precision even more.

In the real world, perhaps better than anyone, Warren Buffett has interpreted the message of diversification most effectively from a pragmatic standpoint. His investment style reflects the importance of diversification, yet Buffett is not one to simply diversify for diversity's sake. On the surface, his company, Berkshire Hathaway, is a conglomerate with operations in such unrelated industries as insurance, flight services, and furniture. However, Buffett has never been shy about building huge positions—in fact, buying out entire companies he truly believes in. In 2000, Buffett owned 32 separate companies, mostly in mundane lines of businesses including paint, roofing products, and rental furniture. Of the expected $1.9 billion in operating profits for Berkshire Hathaway in 2000, about 50 percent came from his insurance businesses alone. In terms of specific stocks, Berkshire Hathaway owns 9 percent of Gillette's float and 5 percent of Coca-Cola. Even with a concentrated approach, Buffett has been able to consistently post superior results. Berkshire Hathaway has been outpaced by the S&P 500 in only 4 out of the past 36 years, with average annual returns of 23.5 percent since 1965. In effect, his style has ideally spanned the divide between excessive diversification and too much concentration. In a nutshell, the secret to Buffett's initial success can be pinpointed to his knack for spotting good companies and sectors with proven business models and valuations that may not fully reflect a company's true worth and building a portfolio of such companies. Buffett's continued success lies in his ability to increase returns in the long term by minimizing risk across a variety of investments and reducing the negative effects of market volatility on his portfolio. To learn more about how to reduce volatility in your portfolio, read the brief market primer on diversification benefits in Box 7.1.

Box 7.1 Diversification Benefits

Diversification benefit is your risk reduction from having multiple invest-ments. The RiskGrade of any portfolio will always be less than the weighted average RiskGrade of its components because it's unlikely that all investments will go sour at the same time. The best way to diversify is to look for uncorrelated investments, because that minimizes the chance that their value would fall in tandem. As you've already learned, however, it's tough to find completely independent investments because of systemic risk. Nonetheless, you can eliminate unique risk by selecting multiple invest-ments with low correlations—for example, stocks from different industries or countries.

The graph shown in Figure 7.3 demonstrates the diversification benefit from investing in a portfolio consisting of Coke and GE (in equal weight-ing). You can see that the portfolio RiskGrade (bottom line) is consistently lower than either Coke or GE's individual RiskGrades.

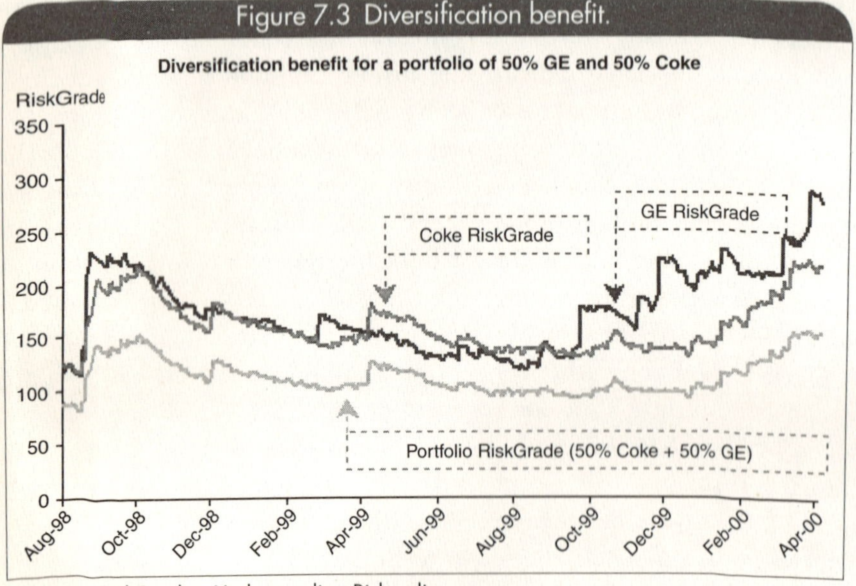

Figure 7.3 Diversification benefit.

Source: RiskGrades, Understanding Risk online course.

This example shows how you can easily reduce the risk of a single stock investment by over a third through selecting just one additional stock. You can continue to diversify your portfolio and eliminate unique (or firm-specific) risk until you have nothing but systemic market risk.

Source: RiskGrades, Understanding Risk online course.

Quality, Not Quantity

Now that you understand what diversification is and realize you can calculate its benefits using WealthBench, it's important to stress what diversification isn't. Diversification is not blindly filling up our portfolios with assets in an attempt to receive diversification's blessings. Unfortunately, just mixing up our investments without understanding how diversification bestows its benefits can be a recipe for disaster. A common misstep is to build and assess a portfolio rather than to assess first and build second. With such a haphazard approach, investors often run the risk of unwittingly increasing exposure to just a handful of names. Bigger is not always better, certainly if it's only size for the sake of size.

This can be an especially pronounced problem for mutual fund holders, given the opaque nature of funds' investment categories. Investors may think they are diversified because they have spread their investments across a handful of different mutual funds, but in truth they may be getting a duplicate set of stocks in every one of their funds. As it stands, an up-to-date list of holdings by each fund is often difficult to obtain and, moreover, not made available on a timely basis. Current industry standards require disclosure of information only on a semiannual basis. Thus, with funds, you never know where your eggs are being stored; consequently, pinpointing the source of risk is frustratingly difficult.

The following investment scenario is a tad immoderate but altogether helpful in depicting the challenge faced by mutual fund investors building a diversified 401(k) portfolio. Having just changed jobs, Sarah Jones elects to receive a lump-sum distribution from her previous employer's 401(k) provider and after a period of deliberation invests her $100,000 in three large, general stock funds from the same family of funds that administers her new company's 401(k) program. The family fund name, Vanguard, is widely recognizable and respected. Prior to making her selection, Sarah was advised by her uncle to choose index funds to help diversify her portfolio. Sarah researched the funds—Vanguard Total Stock Index (VTSMX), Vanguard Institutional Index (VINIX), and Vanguard 500 Index (VFINX)—and found that each performs extremely well. Two of the three have a four-star rating by Morningstar, and the other has a three-star rating. George Sauter, a director of the Vanguard Group who has managed portfolio investments since 1987, is in charge of the funds. Sarah, pursuing a growth strategy to fund her retirement (which is 30 years away), distributes her $100,000 equally and purchases the three funds. As an investor, what is Sarah Jones missing? (See Figure 7.4.)

Diversification, diversification, diversification. Except for the names, the three funds Sarah selected are essentially identical. Moreover, the extra fees and expenses Sarah will have to pay will diminish her future returns. Look at the mutual fund holdings report in Figure 7.5. The top holdings of all three funds are in the upper half of the figure, and the percentage of holding categories are at the bottom. Now look at the top 10 holdings for each fund. They are exactly the same. The same can be said for each fund's asset allocations. Even their sector weightings are nearly identical. Incredibly, adding up the percentages of top 10 holdings for all three funds, we find that 20.89, 25.66, and 24.69 percent of each fund is invested in the same 10 stocks. What does this mean to Sarah? That $71,240 of her total $100,000 investment is tied up in a small group of stocks. This certainly wasn't the diversification that Sarah originally sought. As you can see from Sarah's 401(k) portfolio in Figure 7.4, her diversification measurement, or benefit, is 0, or nonexistent. In light of her results, we expect that Sarah quickly sought the assistance of an advisor and asked, "*If diversification is so good for us, why is it so difficult to gauge?*"

From the eyes of a portfolio, most assets tend to shift in a conflicting manner in terms of direction and magnitude of move. A portfolio, under normal trading conditions, will see some assets increase in value and others

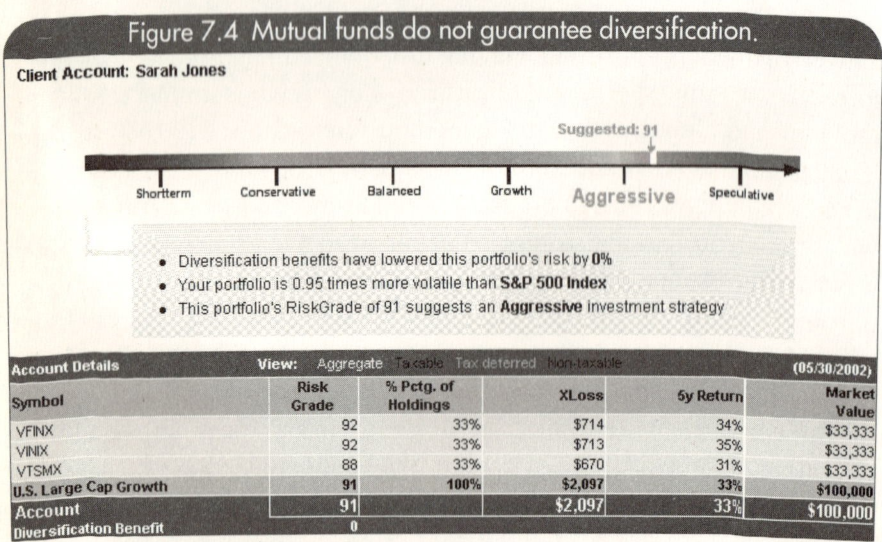

Account Details	View: Aggregate Taxable Tax deferred Non-taxable				(05/30/2002)
Symbol	Risk Grade	% Pctg. of Holdings	XLoss	5y Return	Market Value
VFINX	92	33%	$714	34%	$33,333
VINIX	92	33%	$713	35%	$33,333
VTSMX	88	33%	$670	31%	$33,333
U.S. Large Cap Growth	91	100%	$2,097	33%	$100,000
Account	91		$2,097	33%	$100,000
Diversification Benefit	0				

Source: WealthBench, RiskMetrics Group.

Figure 7.5 Mutual fund holdings report.

VFINX: TOP HOLDINGS — Vanguard 500 Index

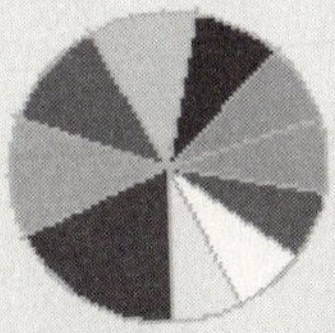

(02/28/2001)	Ticker	Name	Risk Grade	Percentage of Holdings
	GE	GENERAL ELECTRIC COMPANY (USA)	225	4.54 %
	MSFT	MICROSOFT CORP	264	3.07 %
	PFE	PFIZER INC	175	2.80 %
	XOM	EXXON MOBIL CORP	126	2.79 %
	WMT	WAL-MART STORES INC	187	2.20 %
	C	CITIGROUP, INC	219	2.05 %
	INTC	INTEL CORP	436	1.89 %
	MRK	MERCK & CO (USA)	155	1.82 %
	AIG	AMERICAN INTERNATIONAL GROUP I	151	1.78 %
	IBM	IBM CORP (USA)	248	1.75 %

VFINX: HOLDINGS CATEGORIES — Vanguard 500 Index

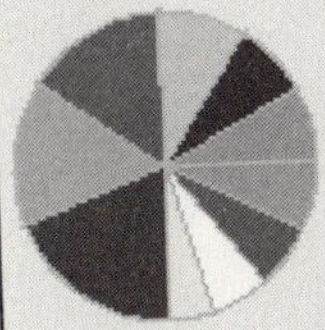

(02/28/2001)	Sector	Percentage in Sector
	Finance	16.87 %
	Electronic Technology	14.05 %
	Health Technology	13.38 %
	Producer Manufacturing	8.59 %
	Consumer Non-Durables	7.04 %
	Retail Trade	6.93 %
	Technology Services	6.48 %
	Energy Minerals	5.98 %
	Communications	5.28 %
	Consumer Services	4.49 %

Continued

Figure 7.5 (Continued)

VTSMX: **TOP HOLDINGS** **Vanguard Tot Stk Idx**

(02/28/2001)	Ticker	Name	RiskGrade	Percentage of Holdings
	GE	GENERAL ELECTRIC COMPANY (USA)	225	3.84 %
	MSFT	MICROSOFT CORP	264	2.59 %
	PFE	PFIZER INC.	175	2.37 %
	XOM	EXXON MOBIL CORP	126	2.36 %
	WMT	WAL-MART STORES	187	1.87 %
	C	CITIGROUP INC	219	1.73 %
	INTC	INTEL CORP	436	1.60 %
	MRK	MERCK & CO (USA)	155	1.54 %
	AIG	AMERICAN INTERNATIONAL GROUP I	151	1.51 %
	IBM	IBM CORP (USA)	248	1.48 %

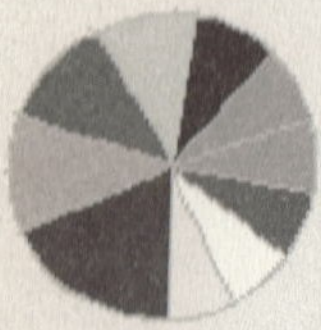

VTSMX: **HOLDINGS CATEGORIES** **Vanguard Tot Stk Idx**

(02/28/2001)	Sector	Percentage in Sector
	Finance	18.42 %
	Electronic Technology	13.80 %
	Health Technology	12.19 %
	Producer Manufacturing	7.05 %
	Consumer Non-Durables	6.67 %
	Retail Trade	6.62 %
	Technology Services	6.23 %
	Communications	5.30 %
	Consumer Services	5.10 %
	Energy Minerals	4.51 %

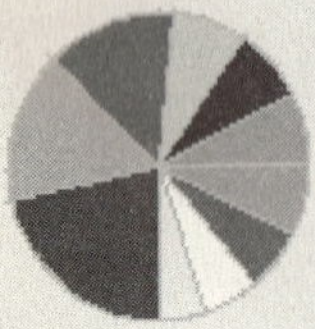

Figure 7.5 (Continued)

VINIX: TOP HOLDINGS **Vanguard Instl Indx**

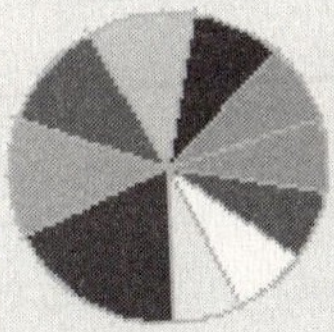

(02/28/2001)	Ticker	Name	Risk Grade	Percentage of Holdings
	GE	GENERAL ELECTRIC COMPANY (USA)	225	4.72 %
	MSFT	MICROSOFT CORP	264	3.19 %
	PFE	PFIZER INC.	175	2.91 %
	XOM	EXXON MOBIL CORP	126	2.90 %
	WMT	WAL-MART STORES INC	187	2.29 %
	C	CITIGROUP, INC	219	2.13 %
	INTC	INTEL CORP	436	1.96 %
	MRK	MERCK & CO (USA)	155	1.89 %
	AIG	AMERICAN INTERNATIONAL GROUP I	151	1.85 %
	IBM	IBM CORP (USA)	248	1.82 %

VINIX: HOLDINGS CATEGORIES **Vanguard Instl Indx**

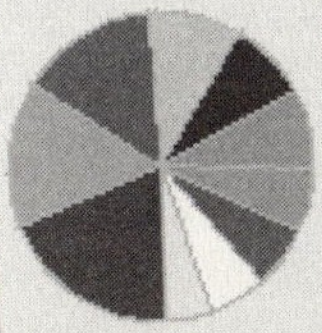

(02/28/2001)	Sector	Percentage in Sector
	Finance	16.93 %
	Electronic Technology	13.73 %
	Health Technology	13.23 %
	Producer Manufacturing	8.80 %
	Consumer Non-Durables	7.31 %
	Retail Trade	7.20 %
	Energy Minerals	6.22 %
	Communications	5.48 %
	Technology Services	5.15 %
	Consumer Services	4.60 %

Source: WealthBench, RiskMetrics Group.

that decrease in value.[3] Some will trade very steadily and others will invariably vacillate more wildly. In short, every asset has a unique temperament. This being the case, whereas a handful of stocks can plausibly trade in tandem (i.e., exhibit positive correlation), the probability that a large number of stocks would move together in synchronous fashion on a day-by-day basis is highly unlikely. Holding a well-diversified portfolio is analogous to being at a roulette table and spreading bits and pieces of our bets across a wide array of numbers rather than placing all our chips on the number seven. The allure of a thirty-five-fold winner-take-all strategy is rationally offset by an expected return that is smaller but more likely to occur. In technical language, a healthy portfolio will generate a final payout that is more predictable because the correlation across a large, balanced group of assets is likely to be low or even negative. Correlation is just a fancy way of measuring similarities in performance patterns between unique assets. A well-diversified portfolio experiences a broad counterbalancing effect between negative and positive moves that leads to steady returns on average as opposed to wild day-to-day swings. Increasing diversification improves the likelihood that the performance will be confined to a narrower set of returns over time. (See Box 7.2.)

Box 7.2 Market Primer: Markowitz Diversification Theorem

The general manner in which we invest today can be attributed to the pioneering research of Harry Markowitz. Known as modern portfolio theory (MPT), it was first introduced in the *Journal of Finance* almost half a century ago and has since revolutionized the way we think about and approach the financial markets.

As a graduate student at the University of Chicago in the early 1950s, while addressing a linear programming problem, Markowitz stumbled onto a simple yet rational idea that would eventually alter the course of financial investing. The basis of modern portfolio theory stems from his assumption that individuals, when given a choice, are risk averse. Contrary to an earlier notion, that "investing is a single-minded process in which the investor bets the ranch" based on chance, Markowitz believed that we behave as creatures of reason. He argued that investors prefer predictability of returns to a winner-take-all strategy. Apart from a small minority of thrill seekers, most of us simply do not yearn for high-risk ventures. "Most investors choose the lower expected return . . . instead of betting the ranch, even when the riskier bet might have a chance of generating a larger payoff."[4]

In Figure 7.6, the vertical axis shows return, and the horizontal axis shows risk, as defined by RiskGrades. For our purposes, we arbitrarily set a 10 percent return as our target performance.

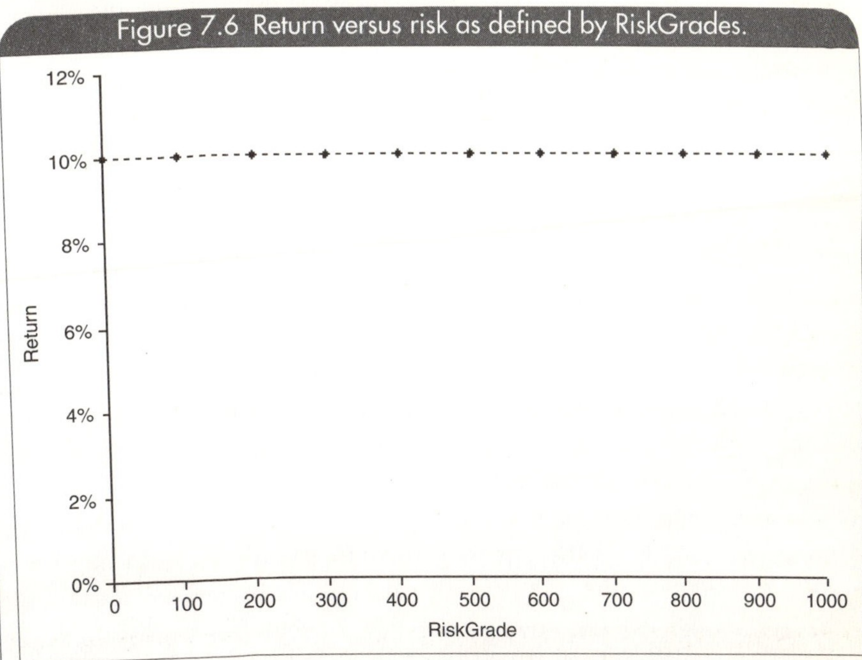

Figure 7.6 Return versus risk as defined by RiskGrades.

As we can see, a return of 10 percent is fixed, but the risk associated with obtaining that return increases from a RiskGrade measurement of 0 to upward of 1,000. The higher the RiskGrade measurement, the greater the risk. For instance, a return of 10 percent with a RiskGrade of 100 is far more attractive than a similar stock or a portfolio with a RiskGrade of 300, which suggests three times as much risk in exchange for an identical return. Given a portfolio return of 10 percent with a RiskGrade of 100 or 300, our rational nature leads us to select the portfolio with the highest return and least amount of risk feasible.

Two Types of Risk

Up until now, we have broached the subject of diversification from a conceptual perspective. We have established what diversification is in principle, why it gained such attention, and how it can help attenuate risk embedded in a portfolio. But our earlier question still remains unanswered: How can we effectively manage diversification to reduce unnecessary risk in our portfolios? Just knowing what, why, and how doesn't address the practical aspect of how-to. How do we gauge whether we have too little or too much diversification? Can we diversify away all our potential returns? In other words, how do we arrive at an optimal level?

As we have suggested throughout the course of this discussion, it is important to understand that diversification is not simply a game of buying more than one stock but less than some unmanageable number. To find a more enduring and foolproof strategy, we need to be able to apply a more systematic approach to managing risk. If we turn to the academic community, one number that is often recommended with respect to optimal diversification is 50,[5] which is arguably a nice round number, but how did we arrive at that? Without going into the quantitative aspect of the analysis, statistical research demonstrates that portfolio risk improves on a marginal basis up to the fiftieth stock. In other words, in a portfolio of domestic equities, diversification benefits effectively accrue to upward of 50, but wane thereafter.[6]

Figure 7.7 provides a graphical illustration. Risk is plotted on the vertical axis and the number of stocks is graphed along the horizontal axis. As the number of stocks in the portfolio increases, diversification increases. This in effect reduces the portfolio's RiskGrade measurement. Company-specific risk, which can be actively massaged through diversification, is the space between the upward-rising arc and the horizontal line. The area below the horizontal line represents the risk of the overall market. Keep in

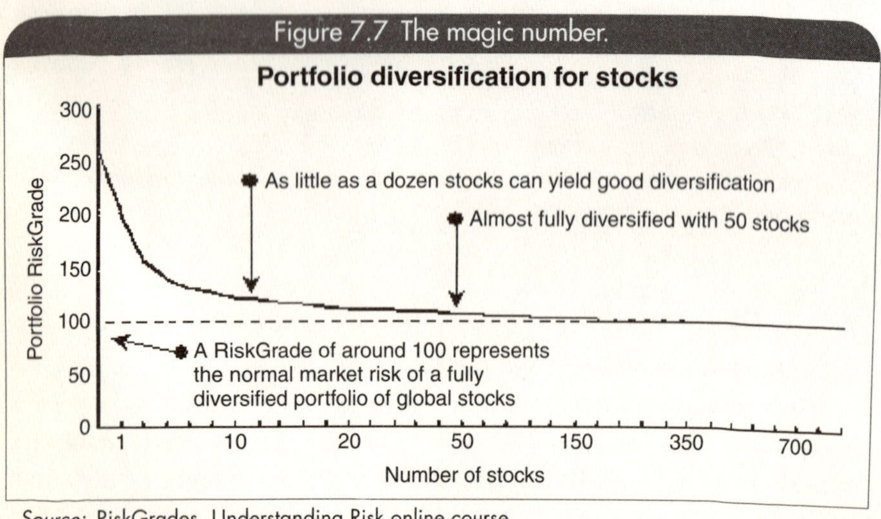

Source: RiskGrades, Understanding Risk online course.

mind that a portfolio that includes assets other than domestic equities, such as bonds and foreign stocks, will see the amount of total market risk fall (i.e., the horizontal line will shift downward).[7] A zero RiskGrade implies no market risk, which is essentially a portfolio made up of short-term Treasury bills and/or cash.

By definition, holding just one stock suggests 100 percent risk, which is tantamount to saying that diversification is nonexistent. In contrast, a well-balanced, diversified portfolio can significantly offset the amount of overall risk. We should note that a portfolio of 50 Internet-related stocks does not qualify as diversified strategy. As the downward-sloping arc indicates, the total risk of a portfolio can precipitously decline to less than one-third the risk of just a single stock (i.e., by almost 70 percent). Notice particularly the dramatic improvement between 1 and 12, reflecting diversification's impact on ameliorating risk within this stretch. Clearly, risk is not additive. But after 50, diversification's effect on total risk fades. This is because some risks associated with a portfolio cannot be entirely eliminated. To wit, there is risk that is avoidable and risk that is unavoidable.

Risk that can be reduced or avoided is known as *unsystematic risk* (or *specific risk*) and can be considered extraneous (see Chapter 2). In simple terms, unsystematic risk is uncertainty or ambiguity attached to investing in a specific company. For example, a new product line, an earnings warning, FDA approval, and accounting irregularities all constitute unsystematic risk. Unsystematic risks can be reduced by diversifying. *Systematic risk* is unavoidable risk. Systematic risks can affect your entire portfolio, not just an individual stock. Examples of systematic risks are natural disasters, wars, and economic factors—events that can influence the entire market. Unsystematic risks can be controlled; systematic risks are left in the hands of nature.

Accordingly, the important question for the dedicated stock investor is, "How much market risk is acceptable and how much is unacceptable?" To eliminate risk altogether would be to eliminate returns as well. How much risk are you willing to take for a given return? We have no uniform solution; it's completely in your hands. Trying to answer this question is the basis for active risk management.

By the laws of physics, a given stock will have a greater impact on a single stream of returns than on a collective stream of prices. Accordingly, the range of returns on individual stocks will be much wider. Evidence of this can be found in any daily stock table. Open a newspaper to the business pages and peruse the top movers of the day. The top-movers list is always populated with stocks that swing much more dramatically than any of the broader market indicators (which has to be the case, given that the major stock composites are averages of individual issues). Let's look at a stock table from the *Interactive Wall Street Journal* from May 9, 2001 (see Figure 7.8). On this day, the top gainer on all U.S. exchanges was Panavision (PVI), jumping 22.8 percent. With a whopping gain of 22.8 percent, an investor whose portfolio held shares of Panavision exclusively is no doubt dancing in the streets. However, the opposite is true for the unfortunate soul with shares in just Katy Industries (KT). In that case, the investor's net worth just evaporated by a devastating −21.5 percent!

Figure 7.8 *Wall Street Journal's* Most Actives.

THE WALL STREET JOURNAL

Price Percentage Gainers – Summary
Wednesday, 4:05 p.m. EDT

NYSE, Price Percentage Gainers				Top 100 list
Issue	**Volume**	**Price**	**Change**	**% Chg**
Panavision (PVI)	18,200	5.65	1.05	22.8
IntgtElec (IEE)	352,500	7.20	1.26	21.2
MutlRisk (MM)	856,300	9.70	1.60	19.8

Price Percentage Losers – Summary
Wednesday, 4:05 p.m. EDT

Nasdaq | Amex

NYSE, Price Percentage Losers				Top 100 list
Issue	**Volume**	**Price**	**Change**	**% Chg**
KatyInd (KT)	74,600	5.77	-1.58	-21.5
WHX Cp pfA (WHX+)	41,600	3.35	-0.64	-16.0
Bombay (BBA)	498,500	2.53	-0.38	-13.1

Source: From the Wall Street Journal Online. Copyright 2001 by Dow Jones & Co. Inc. Reproduced with permission of Dow Jones & Co. Inc. via Copyright Clearance Center.

Holding 50 different stocks can help avert these one-day catastrophes. As we have suggested, a portfolio of just 50 stocks can dramatically reduce the level of risk, simply mirroring the riskiness of the overall market.

Yes, diversification can be achieved with less than 50 stocks. While a portfolio of 50 stocks can offer the same risk characteristics as the total market, the unfortunate reality is that most individuals will find it almost impossible to thoroughly research 50 different companies on a regular basis. Apart from a vast amount of time required to do the initial research, finding 50 stocks that will optimize both returns and diversification benefits is a huge logistical burden. The challenge is to identify 50 good companies in industries that are preferably uncorrelated. It's more difficult than it sounds on paper. According to Peter Lynch, "If you look at ten companies you'll find one interesting. If you look at 20 you'll find two; if you look at 100, you'll find ten. The person who turns over the most rocks wins the game."[8] At Lynch's exhaustive pace, we would have to turn over 500! Whew! Even if money were not an issue, many would balk at the prospects of this project, if for no reason other than time.

We realize this. So let's be clear: We are not advocating that investors go out and purchase an additional 10, 20, 30, 40, or even 48 additional stocks to satisfy the magical diversification number of 50. Fifty is nice in that it narrows diversification into something concrete and provides a reference point. Obviously, your particular situation and lifestyle will determine the way you allocate your assets, and the number of securities you choose will depend on your own tolerance for risk, the types of investments that are most appealing to you, and your time frame for investing. The use of RiskGrades within the context of a portfolio will provide a clearer idea of what the magic number should be for each individual.

Where does this leave investors? Can diversification be achieved with less than 50 stocks? The answer is yes. And in some cases, it's getting easier to do every day. The latest New York Stock Exchange review on share ownership found that the average investor holds just 3.4 different stocks; 15 percent, in fact, hold just one stock. These findings broadcast two problems very loudly. First, investors are in dire need of attaining the benefits of diversification, particularly now that the bull market has abruptly ended and we have entered new, less friendly market conditions. Second, creating a diversified portfolio is time-consuming and expensive.

The following three alternatives can help investors attain their goals for diversified portfolios.

1. *Build a reasonably diversified portfolio with a handful of stocks.* The best way to diversify a portfolio with a small number of holdings is to buy stock in companies in different sectors with diverse product lines. The great benefit of technology is that the exploration phase of narrowing a field of suitable investments can be reduced tremendously. A tool like RiskGrades, for example, can assist with more than simple risk analysis. RiskGrades can filter through mounds and mounds of different stocks to find those that fit the profile of each individual. Moreover, an investment search can be broadened to include not only risk and return metrics, but style and sector information as well.

For example, in only a few minutes we used RiskGrades Stock and Fund screener to create a well-diversified growth portfolio consisting almost exclusively of large, diversified corporations that operate in multiple markets and have the resources to weather cyclical business conditions (see Figure 7.9). We also added a single bond fund to provide us with additional diversification, because during times like these, when stocks perform poorly, an allocation to bonds will help balance your portfolio's overall performance. The portfolio itself is 40 percent less risky due to diversification benefits and, on a relative basis, is 0.66 times less volatile than the S&P 500 Index.

- Automatic Data Processing (ADP) provides paychecks for 29 million workers worldwide, processes securities transactions for clients in 25 countries, delivers computing solutions for auto/truck dealers in 13 countries, and manages 13 million insurance claims estimates annually.
- Berkshire Hathaway (BRK.A and BRK.B) is a holding company primarily involved in the property and casualty insurance business. It is also involved in publishing, manufacturing of confectionery products, cleaning systems, footwear, and retail furnishings.
- Citigroup Inc. (C) provides financial services, including banking, insurance, and investment services, to consumer and corporate customers.
- Exxon Mobil Corporation (XOM) is engaged in the exploration, production, manufacture, transportation, and sale of crude oil, natural gas, and petroleum products. The company manufactures petrochemicals, packaging films, and specialty chemicals.

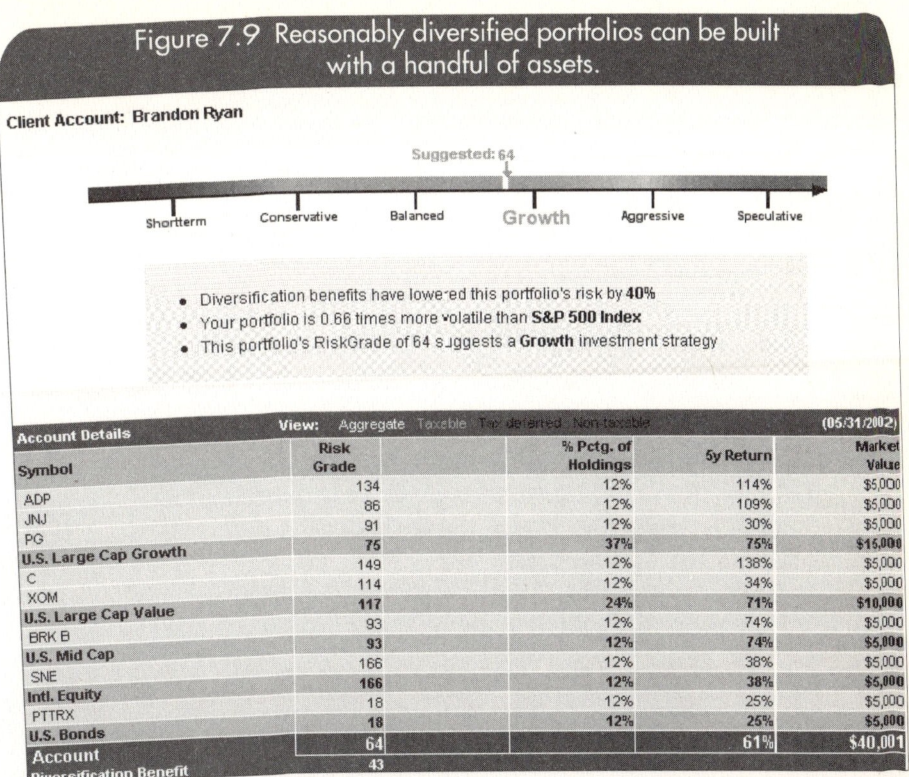

Account Details — View: Aggregate Taxable Tax deferred Non-taxable (05/31/2002)

Symbol	Risk Grade		% Pctg. of Holdings	5y Return	Market Value
ADP	134		12%	114%	$5,000
JNJ	86		12%	109%	$5,000
PG	91		12%	30%	$5,000
U.S. Large Cap Growth	75		37%	75%	$15,000
C	149		12%	138%	$5,000
XOM	114		12%	34%	$5,000
U.S. Large Cap Value	117		24%	71%	$10,000
BRK B	93		12%	74%	$5,000
U.S. Mid Cap	93		12%	74%	$5,000
SNE	166		12%	38%	$5,000
Intl. Equity	166		12%	38%	$5,000
PTTRX	18		12%	25%	$5,000
U.S. Bonds	18		12%	25%	$5,000
Account	64			61%	$40,001
Diversification Benefit	43				

Source: WealthBench, RiskMetrics Group.

- Johnson & Johnson (JNJ) manufactures health care products for worldwide consumer, pharmaceutical, and professional markets.
- Procter & Gamble (PG) markets a broad range of consumer products worldwide in five business segments: (1) laundry and cleaning, (2) paper, (3) beauty care, (4) food and beverage, and (5) health care.
- Sony Corporation (SNE) develops, designs, manufactures, and sells electronic equipment, instruments, and devices. Sony also manufactures and distributes recorded music and image-based software and is engaged in insurance and financing.
- PIMCO Total Return Fund (PTTRX) is a high-quality, well-diversified, intermediate-maturity portfolio that seeks to maintain the value of original investments and to prudently maximize investment earnings. The fund is the largest bond in the United States, and

fund manager William Gross is a two-time winner of Morningstar's Fixed Income Fund Manager of the Year award (1998 and 2000).

2. *Purchase index funds.* An index fund is a mutual fund that mirrors as closely as possible the performance of a stock market index. For example, the Vanguard 500 Index Fund (VFINX) invests to reflect the composition of the market as a whole by matching its investments to the S&P 500 Index. Vanguard purchases all 500 stocks in the same percentages as the S&P 500 Index to ensure that its overall return matches the S&P 500's return stride for stride. Indexing is an investment strategy that is content to match the average performance of a market. The reason? Many research studies have shown that indexing provides greater returns over time with less risk and lower taxes. In any given year, most actively managed funds underperform the markets they set out to beat, especially after fees are subtracted.

Index funds offer the following benefits over mutual funds:

- *Lower fees.* Index funds are passively managed by small staffs without the need for a four-star money manager at the helm. As a result, management fees are small.

- *Diversification.* An investor purchasing an index fund disperses money over the entire market. However purchasing several of the same index funds will actually increase your risk. (See the Sarah Jones example earlier in this chapter.)

- *Tax advantages.* Index funds buy and hold stocks much longer than actively managed funds that buy and sell stocks in hopes of outperforming the market. Capital gains taxes are smaller and are delayed.

3. *Create a personalized basket of stocks.* A personalized basket of stocks (or *folios,* as they're commonly known) offers investors an exciting alternative in attaining a diversified portfolio. Available online, investors and advisors can quickly create diversified portfolios of up to 50 stocks or select from model folios based on sectors, indexes, risk level, or any other user criteria. Sites like FOLIOfn, ShareBuilder, Buy and Hold, and now various online brokerages allow you to pool orders with other traders and buy fractional shares, making the process of buying stocks easier and cheaper for

investors. For example, you could buy all the stocks in the Dow except Philip Morris if you choose not to own a tobacco stock. Because you own the shares, you can even sell a position at a loss to generate taxable losses to offset other income. This type of flexibility allows investors to create or rebalance portfolios specifically to meet long- or short-term investment goals. Folios offer investors more control over their taxes, fees, and knowledge of what they own.

There are some drawbacks to folios. Bookkeeping is required. Because you own the stocks directly, any trading will ultimately be treated as buying and selling events. The sites that offer personalized baskets of stocks do not currently provide professional advisors to help you, so you must research the type of basket that best fits your needs first. The fee structure is reasonable, but may not make sense for everyone. However, don't let these hitches stop you from taking a closer look. In a few years there will be many more synthetic fund services. With the ability to buy up to 50 stocks with a single click of the mouse, these services will go a long way in providing investors with a low-cost, time-effective means to spread their eggs out over many baskets.

A Final Word on Eggs

A funny thing about creating a portfolio: Almost every bit of investment advice circles back to the concept of diversification. Everything—and we mean *everything*—you read about diversification includes a single piece of advice you received as a child: "Don't put all your eggs in one basket." These eight words eloquently summarize one of the most important lessons in investing. As an aside, for those who are curious about where this advice originated (no other book or website that quotes this phrase will tell you), it comes from Miguel de Cervantes' *Don Quixote,* as 400 years ago the noble Spaniard proclaimed, "Do not venture all your eggs in one basket holds." In our minds, those who do not heed these words are chasing windmills in the investment world.

CHAPTER 8

Risk Tolerance

The American International Group (AIG, as it is more popularly known), a global insurance and financial services firm, ran an ad campaign at one time with this slogan: "The Greatest Risk Is Not Taking One." One print ad shows what is presumably the Wright brothers' first flight attempt at Kitty Hawk. Against the backdrop of the Carolina dunes, a following of supporters looks on, enthusiastically cheering on the two brothers. However, intentionally omitted from the frame is the actual flight. Rather than seeing a picture of the successful takeoff, the Wright brothers' plane is erased from the photograph, leaving viewers to contemplate the question, "What if the Wright brothers hadn't taken a risk?" What would the world today be like today without air travel? History owes much to bold adventure seekers who conquer the greatest challenges despite enormous risks. Without the determination of risk takers, the question, "Is it possible?" would repeatedly go unanswered.

For the benefit of soon-to-be risk takers who may have been inspired by the ad, the Wright brothers painstakingly built numerous models to test their theories about flight. The first successful takeoff was the result of an exhaustive number of experiments and simulations run prior to December 17, 1903. Before the Wrights tested their actual flying machines, they often built smaller-scale models to observe what might happen to a larger machine. This same meticulous approach toward investing is essential. In much the same way, RiskGrades is a tool that permits investors to model their portfolios and test assumptions before takeoff. In the markets, investors who consistently take the biggest risks are destined to fail. The most successful investors are those who first consider and measure the risk, then embrace it when warranted.

Much of our discussion until now has centered on reducing unnecessary risk, but we should make it very clear that risk is the essential driver of returns. Risk converts the spirit of opportunity into concrete returns. In *A Random Walk Down Wall Street*, Burton Malkiel sums it best, "Risk, and risk alone, determines the degree to which returns will be above or below average."[1] Our propensity to take risk has a direct influence on whether our financial journey will be met with deep satisfaction or utter disappointment. Put another way, the level of risk determines how far the markets can carry us from where we are today to where we want to be tomorrow. Accepting that risk is in many ways our ticket to financial freedom.

Unfortunately the volatile market swings that come with assuming big risks can be difficult to swallow. We have all experienced our fair share of gut-wrenching moments in the latest bear market that unofficially started in March 2000. While some risk-averse investors have been content to hold on through the storm, many self-proclaimed risk takers have retreated to the safety of the sidelines. Despite Markowitz's supposition that all investors are risk averse, all investors are not created equal. Even among a relatively homogenous group, the capacity to assume risk varies profoundly. Every investor has a unique tolerance for assuming risks, just as every investor has a separate return objective and investment horizon. What one investor considers prudent may very well seem reckless to others, and vice versa. Risk is in the eye of the beholder, and the ability to assume it is a function of our resources and of our propensity to pursue opportunity at a level we deem economical.

With this as a backdrop, we can now reason that the level of risk in a well-constructed portfolio must reflect more than a mere intolerance for risk. We need to learn how to marry a reasonable level of risk with our natural distaste for it. In other words, risk cannot be dictated solely by our emotional impulses but must also reflect sensible foresight. For example, even self-acknowledged risk-averse investors may need to take on more risks than desired in order to meet long-term investment objectives. In this sense, a portfolio can be too safe for its own good. A conservative asset allocation plan or excessive diversification can restrain volatility to such a degree that it diminishes the potential of higher returns and hinders the probability of superior wealth creation over the long term. David Swensen, chief investment officer for Yale University, puts the risk-reward trade-off this way: "Commitment to an equity bias enhances return-generating potential, while pursuit of diversification reduces portfolio risk exposure."[2] More simply, too much diversification can put higher returns in jeopardy. Peter Bernstein suggests in his *Capital Ideas* that one of diversification's many faces is one that reduces the opportunity to attain higher returns.[3] For many, this will pose a larger problem than concentration risk. In the face of this, an appropriate risk level that successfully balances our portfolios between sufficient diversification and adequate return prospects is required.

How Much Risk Can I Afford Not to Take?

Unbeknownst to many risk-averse investors, low-risk strategies also come with high costs. As healthy as an ounce of skepticism may be, an aversion to taking risk can be an investor's greatest failing. While most investors reaped the benefits of extraordinary double-digit gains for a good portion of the 1990s, those who were risk averse found only modest success. With an average annual return of 7 percent, risk-averse portfolios almost doubled over the past decade . . . not bad until we consider that all the while an initial investment in the S&P 500 would have grown fourfold.

The consequences of a long-term conservative strategy are serious in that the symptoms come to light only in the distant future. By then, it's usually too late to remedy the situation. For instance, exchanging long-term potential for short-term predictability appears on the surface to be of little importance, especially from today's perspective. When all is said and done, however, a cautious tone may ultimately prove to be more costly. Many of us may wake up 20 years from now to find that our investment strategies have sorely missed the mark—that, indeed, the admission fee to retirement is much higher than we had calculated. Consider that even if we start with a $100,000 portfolio today and realize 7 percent returns over next three decades that produce a net total of $761,226 (a tidy sum), we may still fall short, given inflation and longer mortality rates. As a frame of reference, *Fortune* magazine estimates that the average 401(k) nest egg for those between 60 and 69 years of age is $130,000.[4] Cast in that light, 7 percent annual returns imply too little risk if the ultimate aim is to secure retirement. (See Box 8.1.)

Box 8.1 Avoiding Risk Is a Sure Path to Failure

Cash is often classified as a riskless investment. After all, $1 is always going to be $1, no matter what happens to the markets. However, things look different from a longer-term perspective because inflation continually erodes the purchasing power of cash. In Figure 8.1, consider the effects of inflation on the value of a $1 bill stuffed in a mattress since 1950. Even though a dollar from 1950 is still worth a dollar today, it now buys 88 percent less than it did 50 years ago. For example, in 1950 a dollar bought lunch and a matinee movie. Fifty years later, the same dollar doesn't buy you more than large fries at a fast-food restaurant.

Figure 8.1 Loss of purchasing power of a U.S. dollar since 1950.

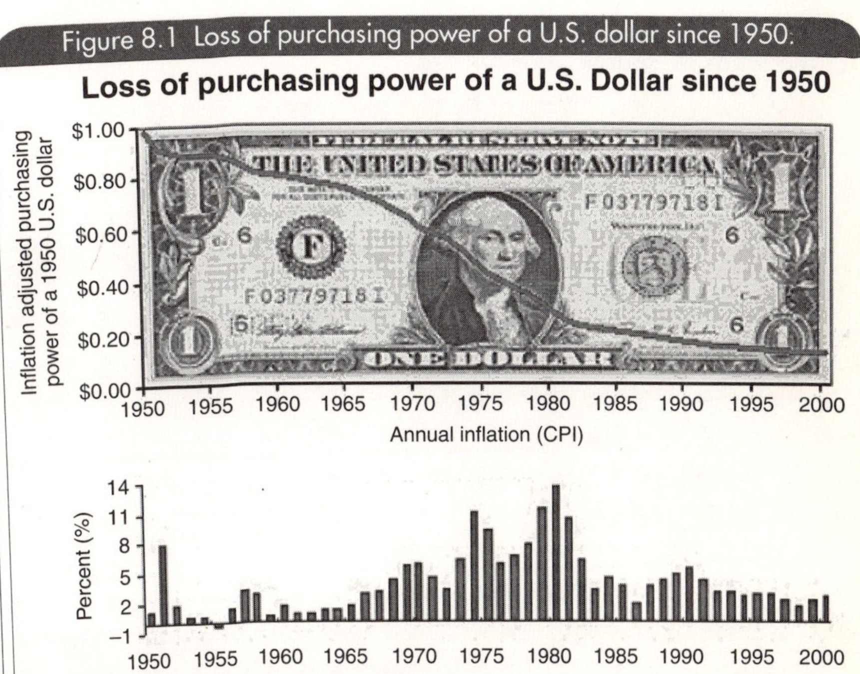

Source: WealthBench, Understanding Risk online course.

Forgoing risk hence only guarantees loss. This is especially true in countries with higher inflation rates (e.g., during the old hyperinflationary periods in Brazil, 100 cruzeiros would have become almost worthless within a year).

The old adage, "nothing ventured, nothing gained," might better be, "nothing ventured, sure to lose."

How long does it take our investments to double? The Rule of 72 is a simple, quick, and easy way to calculate the length of time it takes given a particular interest rate. For example, money doubles every 12 years at 6 percent (72 ÷ 6 = 12). At 9 percent, an investment doubles in eight years. Table 8.1 illustrates the impact of doubling at seven different rates.

What does a higher return on investment really mean to you? By dividing the interest rate into the constant, 72, you can see how long it takes to

Table 8.1 Rule of 72: The Doubling Effect

What does a higher return on investment really mean to you?

By dividing the interest rate into the constant, 72, you can see how long it takes to double your money.

| | **Rate of Return per Year** | | | | | | |
	4%	**6%**	**7%**	**8%**	**10%**	**12%**	**14%**
Start	$100,000	$100,000	$100,000	$100,000	$100,000	$100,000	$ 100,000
1	$104,000	$106,000	$107,000	$108,000	$110,000	$112,000	$ 114,000
2	$108,160	$112,360	$114,490	$116,640	$121,000	$125,440	$ 129,960
3	$112,486	$119,102	$122,504	$125,971	$133,100	$140,493	$ 148,154
4	$116,986	$126,248	$131,080	$136,049	$146,410	$157,352	$ 168,896
5	$121,665	$133,823	$140,255	$146,933	$161,051	$176,234	$ 192,541
6	$126,532	$141,852	$150,073	$158,687	$177,156	$197,382	$ 219,497
7	$131,593	$150,363	$160,578	$171,382	$194,872	$221,068	$ 250,227
8	$136,857	$159,385	$171,819	$185,093	$214,359	$247,596	$ 285,259
9	$142,331	$168,948	$183,846	$199,900	$235,795	$277,308	$ 325,195
10	$148,024	$179,085	$196,715	$215,892	$259,374	$310,585	$ 370,722
11	$153,945	$189,830	$210,485	$233,164	$285,312	$347,855	$ 422,623
12	$160,103	$201,220	$225,219	$251,817	$313,843	$389,598	$ 481,790
13	$166,507	$213,293	$240,985	$271,962	$345,227	$436,349	$ 549,241
14	$173,168	$226,090	$257,853	$293,719	$379,750	$488,711	$ 626,135
15	$180,094	$239,656	$275,903	$317,217	$417,725	$547,357	$ 713,794
16	$187,298	$254,035	$295,216	$342,594	$459,497	$613,039	$ 813,725
17	$194,790	$269,277	$315,882	$370,002	$505,447	$686,604	$ 927,646
18	$202,582	$285,434	$337,993	$399,602	$555,992	$768,997	$1,057,517
19	$210,685	$302,560	$361,653	$431,570	$611,591	$861,276	$1,205,569
20	$219,112	$320,714	$386,968	$466,096	$672,750	$964,629	$1,374,349

Table 8.1 *(Continued)*

Rate of Return per Year

	4%	6%	7%	8%	10%	12%	14%
21	$227,877	$ 339,956	$ 414,056	$ 503,383	$ 740,025	$1,080,385	$ 1,566,758
22	$236,992	$ 360,354	$ 443,040	$ 543,654	$ 814,027	$1,210,031	$ 1,786,104
23	$246,472	$ 381,975	$ 474,053	$ 587,146	$ 895,430	$1,355,235	$ 2,036,158
24	$256,330	$ 404,893	$ 507,237	$ 634,118	$ 984,973	$1,517,863	$ 2,321,221
25	$266,584	$ 429,187	$ 542,743	$ 684,848	$1,083,471	$1,700,006	$ 2,646,192
26	$277,247	$ 454,938	$ 580,735	$ 739,635	$1,191,818	$1,904,007	$ 3,016,658
27	$288,337	$ 482,235	$ 621,387	$ 798,806	$1,310,999	$2,132,488	$ 3,438,991
28	$299,870	$ 511,169	$ 664,884	$ 862,711	$1,442,099	$2,388,387	$ 3,920,449
29	$311,865	$ 541,839	$ 711,426	$ 931,727	$1,586,309	$2,674,993	$ 4,469,312
30	$324,340	$ 574,349	$ 761,226	$1,006,266	$1,744,940	$2,995,992	$ 5,095,016
31	$337,313	$ 608,810	$ 814,511	$1,086,767	$1,919,434	$3,355,511	$ 5,808,318
32	$350,806	$ 645,339	$ 871,527	$1,173,708	$2,111,378	$3,758,173	$ 6,621,483
33	$364,838	$ 684,059	$ 932,534	$1,267,605	$2,322,515	$4,209,153	$ 7,548,490
34	$379,432	$ 725,103	$ 997,811	$1,369,013	$2,554,767	$4,714,252	$ 8,605,279
35	$394,609	$ 768,609	$1,067,658	$1,478,534	$2,810,244	$5,279,962	$ 9,810,018
36	$410,393	$ 814,725	$1,142,394	$1,596,817	$3,091,268	$5,913,557	$11,183,420
37	$426,809	$ 863,609	$1,222,362	$1,724,563	$3,400,395	$6,623,184	$12,749,099
38	$443,881	$ 915,425	$1,307,927	$1,862,528	$3,740,434	$7,417,966	$14,533,973
39	$461,637	$ 970,351	$1,399,482	$2,011,530	$4,114,478	$8,308,122	$16,568,729
40	$480,102	$1,028,572	$1,497,446	$2,172,452	$4,525,926	$9,305,097	$18,888,351

Source: WealthBench, RiskMetrics Group.

double your money. After going over the numbers, making the necessary adjustments to our planned investments, factoring in the rate of inflation, and adjusting for taxes, we should be better prepared to select an investment strategy that is right for us. Figure 8.2 assumes a onetime lump sum of $100,000 in the first year, with an average annual growth rate of 7 percent.

As the Rule of 72 illustrates, investors opting to take the safe path may find that it leads to financial distress. In light of this, it seems clear that harnessing risk is appropriate insofar as it does not jeopardize your ability to meet long-term financial goals. Those with a queasy stomach for risk should stop and ask themselves, "How much risk can I afford not to take?"

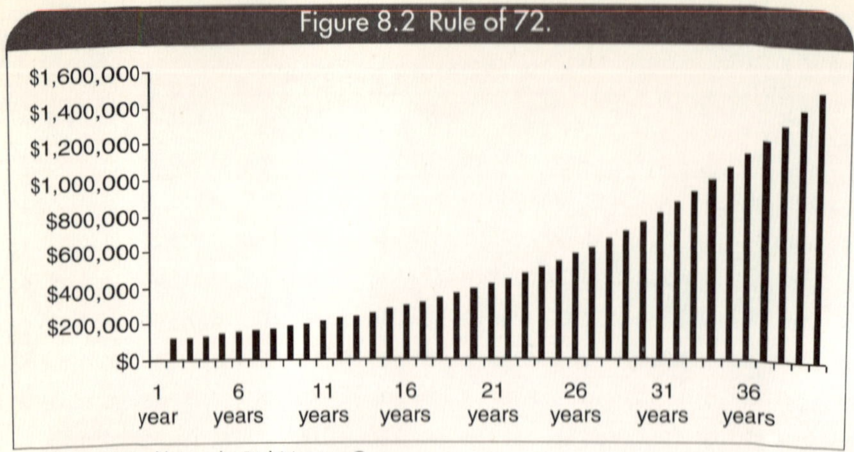

Source: WealthBench, RiskMetrics Group.

This dilemma of finding an appropriate investment schedule strikes at the heart of investing and is common to all segments of the financial community, from individuals to institutions. Getting this equation right, balancing a suitable amount of risk with an agreeable level of return, is the essence of building a thoughtful financial strategy that will steadily enrich us over time. A complementary blend of the two is likely to breed investment results that disappoint on neither the risk nor return front. Yale University's Swensen describes this effort as the trade-off between today and tomorrow:

> **By holding assets that promise low levels of volatility, managers create a stable portfolio allowing budget planners to forecast payouts with reasonable certainty. Unfortunately, low-risk investment portfolios deliver returns insufficient to preserve purchasing power. Exclusive pursuit of stable support for current operations favors today's generation of scholars over tomorrow's beneficiaries.[5]**

Whether you are funding a future generation of scholars or your son's or daughter's education, the problem is basically the same. Unfortunately, the line that separates prudent regulation of risk and adequate exposure to the market is often difficult to define. Truth be told, our financial plans often cause us to toss and turn over uncertainties regarding the future. Most of us know where we want to be, but have little idea how much work—or, more important, risk—it will take to get us there. Some market pundits have argued that in order to reach high investment goals, significant risks must be considered. Others have been more reasonable, suggesting a middle-of-the-road approach. From our perspective, here are the most important issues for today's investor: (1) a reasonable final aim and (2) an adequate level of risk to get there. It is not enough to draw an end line. The road to get there must clearly be established. (An example of the types of comprehensive investment plans constructed on WealthBench has been included in the appendix.)

What's the difference between annual returns of 7 percent and annual returns of 8.2 percent? An additional $300,000 in your portfolio over a 30-year period. Of course, the additional returns will require a portfolio that assumes additional risk. In this case, your portfolio RiskGrade would jump from 30 to 60—a relatively insignificant increase comparable to the difference in risk between a 10-year note and a 30-year bond, on average[6]—a risk most investors should be willing to take. For instance, investors would be surprised by the fact that "long-[dated] corporate bonds have higher returns than long-term Treasury bonds, both *ex post* and *ex ante*."[7] The incremental risk is minor, but the power of compounding certainly works wonders in risk terms as well.

For example, the variability of returns of the constituents in the S&P 500 Index provides a good illustration of how magnitude of risk can create varying degrees of opportunities (see Table 8.2). Since 2000, in regard to the variability of returns, of Philip Morris and Yahoo! represent two distinct ends of the equity market spectrum. Not surprisingly, Yahoo! was the riskiest investment in this selected group. Its average daily volatility was more than four times that of the S&P 500. Regrettably this greater volatility translated into greater losses for Yahoo! investors. For instance, a $10,000 investment in Yahoo! during this period lost 93 percent of it's value, or $9,375. By comparison, a similar investment in Philip Morris gained 144 percent. Over the same time period, the original $10,000 investment is worth $24,427. To suggest that returns are dictated by the amount of risk we take is stating the obvious. However, most of us are in the dark about how much risk is required and how much risk is reckless. Table 8.2 demonstrates how risk, when amplified, opens up the possibility of both higher returns and greater losses. Take a look at Yahoo! and the column labeled Largest Daily Return. How would you like to make 22.61 percent on your investment in a single day? Sounds great! But what's stopping us from putting in a buy order right now? The answer is risk. In the preceding column, we see that Yahoo!'s

Investment	Average Period RiskGrade	Period Return (%)	Largest Daily Decline (%)	Largest Daily Return (%)	$10,000 Invested since 2000
Philip Morris	178	144.27	−8.53	16.27	$24,427
S&P 500 Index	102	−26.67	−5.83	5.01	$7,333
General Electric	185	−37.72	−10.67	12.46	$6,228
Microsoft	230	−56.32	−15.60	19.60	$4,368
Yahoo!	440	−93.25	20.94	22.61	$675

Table 8.2 Comparison of Risk and Return of Popular Investments since 2000*

*Through June 1, 2002.

Source: WealthBench, RiskMetrics Group.

largest daily decline was −20.94 percent. That's a big hit! The riskier the asset, the larger its daily fluctuations, both up and down. As Yahoo! investors who sold their stock prior to 2000 can attest, risk holds tremendous promise for those who are capable of harnessing it. Current shareholders will tell you something completely different.

Targeting Appropriate Levels of Risk

How do you know when you're taking too much risk? Or not enough? To start, define a target risk level that is consistent with your goals, your capacity for taking risk, and your risk tolerance for living with risk. You can begin by putting yourself into one of two broad categories: preserving wealth or growing capital. For those whose main interest is to preserve wealth, the variability of even short-term returns matters. *Steady and stable* are the operative words in this case. On the other hand, if the final objective is to grow capital, short-term market swings should be taken as par for the course. *Higher volatility* is accepted in exchange for (hopefully) ample long-term returns. This concept of preservation over growth, and vice versa, serves as the foundation of portfolio management. (See Box 8.2.)

Reason would suggest that the variability of returns would be high on the list for investors with an abbreviated investment schedule. After all, a significant short-term decline in the value of investments jeopardizes the immediate availability of capital, which goes against the grain of the short-term strategist, who holds liquidity in high regard. In contrast, those with a

Box 8.2 Market Primer: A Hall of Fame Risk Disclosure

The following progressive risk disclosure of the IPS Millennium Fund was profiled by the *Wall Street Journal* in "Read This (and Invest) at Your Peril! Manager Tells Hard Truth in Disclosures" (January 21, 2000). Here are some excerpts:

First of all, stock prices are volatile. Well, duh. If you buy shares in a stock mutual fund, any stock mutual fund, your investment value will change every day. In a recession it will go down, day after day, week after week, month after month, until you are ready to tear your hair out, unless you've already gone bald from worry. It will insist on this even if Gandhi, Jefferson, John Lennon, Jesus and the Apostles, Einstein, Merlin and Golda Meir all manage the thing. . . .

While the long-term bias in stock prices is upward, stocks enter a bear market with amazing regularity, about every 3–4 years. It goes with the territory. Expect it. Live with it. If you can't do that, go bury your money in a jar or put it in the bank and don't bother us about why your investment goes south sometimes or why water runs downhill. It's physics, man. . . .

We buy scary stuff. You know, Internet stocks, small companies. These things go up and down like Pogo Sticks on steroids. . . . Sometimes we get killed . . . when Internet and other tech stocks take a particularly big hit. The "we" is actually a euphemism for you, got it? We also get killed if interest rates go up, because that affects high dividend companies badly. Since rising interest rates affect everything badly, we could get killed even worse if the Fed raises rates, or the economy in general experiences higher interest rates beyond the control of those in control, or gets out of control. . . .

Just so you know. Don't come crying to us if we lose all your money, and you wind up a Dumpster Dude or a Basket Lady rooting for aluminum cans in your old age.

Although such down-to-earth language on risk disclosures is unique to the IPS Millennium Fund, there is a universal trend among funds to make risks more transparent to investors.

Source: RiskGrades, Understanding Risk online course.

long-term agenda are more likely to postpone redemptions until a later date. The biggest concern in this case is not so much a temporary drop in market value, but rather the effects of inflation on future prices.

When the time comes to apply a consistent investment philosophy, many go astray. Our actions regularly prove inconsistent with our outlooks. In practice, we mistakenly mismatch our risk and return priorities. We may adopt a long-term investment horizon but react negatively to short-term swings. The danger of this type of strategy is fairly evident. Consider an investor with a five-year investment term. The investor can opt to pursue a singular approach, taking a five-year outlook to build a portfolio that hopefully averages 10 percent returns per annum, or pursue a discrete tactical strategy, making an effort to achieve 10 percent absolute returns every year by picking stocks for the year. Although the net results may be the same, the subtle difference in the two strategies makes the latter far more risky. An investor who chooses to go in and out of stocks on a short-term basis creates unnecessary reinvestment risk—in this case, doing so five different times by the end of each year. "For longer-term investors, returns on one-year instruments embody significant risk," notes Yale's Swensen.[8] Our attempt to reduce risk by shortening each risk term into annual buckets invariably leads to unintended consequences. Rather than letting the advantages of time free us to assume a riskier long-term view and increase our chance of higher returns, we unduly increase risk absent the safety net of time.

As investment timetables are extended further out into the future, daily market fluctuations are accompanied by anxiety over meeting ultimate financial objectives. Most of this anxiety stems from not knowing what the future will bring. When it comes to long-term investments, the biggest miscalculation on our parts is underestimating what we will eventually require. The ideal scenario for any investment program is to put into action a plan that will generate enough capital to meet future financial needs. Even with thoughtful planning, though, an investor can be led off track if a comprehensive investment picture is not framed. Gerald Loeb, author of *The Battle for Investment Survival*, provides an account of how higher prices can negatively affect our investment strategies over time.

> I remember visiting the Temple of Angkor Vat near Siem Reap in Indo-China, and chatting with the French manager of the hotel in that hot, humid spot. He told me that for years he had been working there in self-chosen exile from his native France, to accumulate a quantity of francs

that would enable him to return home and retire modestly. Needless to say, by the time he reached his goal, devaluation of the franc had wiped out most of the value of his savings. All his sacrifices were in vain. He might just as well have lived at home and spent moderately as he went along, enjoying his life from day to day instead of waiting for his ship which never came in.[9]

Although a long-term investment horizon can work wonders on a portfolio, it can also erode returns to such an extent that performance crumbles under the strain of time. Time is bittersweet in this sense. Many of us may be no better off than Loeb's Frenchman. We need only to leaf through a handful of financial commentaries to get a timely edition of a current profile. The CNNmoney website, for example, dedicates a regular column, *Portfolio Rx,* to personal investment concerns. A recurring theme among the guest participants is the inadequacy of current financial plans. Many of the narratives share an underlying fear that returns will fall short of expectations. Retirement plans will have to be postponed, scaled back, or both.

A deeper probe suggests that our plans for retirement will be thwarted by what we describe as an *underweight risk factor.* The findings may come as a surprise, because for all the things we have done right—diversifying a bit and holding what is presumably a proper allocation—we still seem far off course at times. Even with a well-conceived plan, the investment game is thorny. A common blunder is to defuse the variability of our returns with a variety of safe harbor assets rather than with a well-rounded mix. Consequently, our risk profile is inadvertently mitigated beyond intent. Simply put, we create a safer portfolio than we had intended.

It requires more than a mix of assets and a proclamation of diversification to properly set us on the investment path that will achieve our objectives. "Investment is far more complicated than just getting money value back with interest or at a profit," says Gerald Loeb.[10] As the experts point out, longer-term considerations such as the burden of inflation and a fundamental understanding of risk implications on return must critically factor into our decision-making process. Still others suggest that greater-than-normal risk should be considered as long as time is in our favor. Otherwise, like the Frenchman in Loeb's story, we may critically misread our future returns, which would result in a miscalculation of how much risk should be accepted along the way. If this is our fate, many of our current sacrifices will have been in vain. Know thy risks and embrace them well.

Even if the worst is realized, conscientious investors give themselves ample time to redirect their financial destiny. The key is to determine a suitable level of risk given the time horizon we have set.

How Much Risk for How Much Return?

The dichotomy that exists between what we believe is necessary and what the markets tell us is required to generate ideal returns is the biggest divide separating us from our current position and financial independence. As we have been arguing, to breed longer-term success, every investor needs to map out an appropriate link between a risk level and a consistent long-term economic objective. This should be completed early on and closely adhered to for as long as the final goal we've set for ourselves remains intact.

Perhaps the most convincing way to look at the impact of risk on return is to examine historic risk-return numbers. The most exhaustive research on this subject details the return patterns of various asset classes over much of the modern financial era (1926 to 2000). The data, mined by Roger Ibbotson and Rex Sinquefield, provides most persuasive evidence of the correlation between risk and higher returns. Actual market performance supports what the Wright brothers earlier proved in a different way—that greater returns accompany greater risks.

One way of summarizing the data is through distribution charts like the one offered in Figure 8.3. As we can see, the distribution of return patterns varies widely according to asset type. History provides clear proof that additional risk over time translates into commensurate levels of return. Smaller-capitalization stocks, for example, outpaced large-company stocks by 1.7 percent per annum over the period. This small nominal difference results in an additional $3.64 million over larger-company returns on an initial investment of $1,000. Stated differently, we can argue that small-cap stocks outpaced large-cap stocks by a multiple of 5,477 to 1,833 during this stretch. As expected, concurrent with higher returns, risk (defined as standard deviation) on small-cap stocks ran more than 50 percent higher than on large-cap shares. Simply put, "The long-term benefit of owning equities increases as investments move further out the risk continuum."[11] In this context, it is rather evident that returns come with a price. How much are we willing to pay?

Using empirical data to match risk with return prospects is a good starting point. Seeing the balance between risk and return among various

Figure 8.3 Historic distributions of returns for individual asset classes.

Stocks, Bonds, Bills, and Inflation
Summary Statistics 1926–2000

	Compound Annual Return	Arithmetic Annual Return	Risk (Standard Deviation)	Distribution of Annual Returns
Large Company Stocks	11.0%	13.0%	20.2%	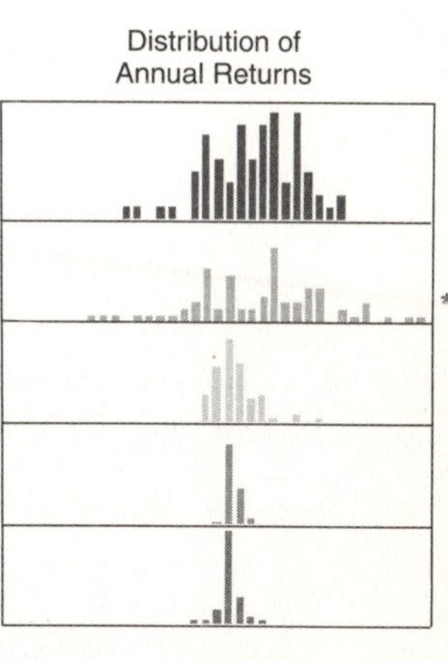
Small Company Stocks	12.4%	17.3%	33.4%	
Government Bonds	5.3%	5.7%	9.4%	
Treasury Bills	3.8%	3.9%	3.2%	
Inflation	3.1%	3.2%	4.4%	

*The 1933 Small Company Stock total return was 142.9%

Source: Stocks, Bonds, Bills, and Inflation ® 2001 Yearbook, © 2001 Ibbotson Associates Inc. Based on copyrighted works by Ibbotson and Sinquefield. All rights reserved. Used with permission.

asset classes should direct us to more appropriate portfolio allocations. Another approach—one favored by WealthBench—relies on sophisticated probability techniques to run return simulations based on current risk weightings and correlations. This quantitative approach is more difficult to perform (requiring either a good financial advisor or knowledge of high finance and access to sophisticated simulation models), but arguably leads to more accurate conclusions.[12] What separates this rigorous statistical approach from a more basic exercise is that the predictability of future returns can be more accurately captured. This is because simulations use historic patterns as an indication of prospective returns.

Using the holdings of the S&P 500 as a proxy portfolio, we provide simulations for a 30-year term as an example (see Figure 8.4). Despite the complexities associated with this iterative process, the final result can be reduced to a simple translation. The two outer bands represent confidence intervals of the best- and worst-case scenarios over the analysis period, 30 years. The middle line is an indication of the most probable stream of returns based on assumptions about risk. As we can see, a $10,000 initial investment should grow to $1,148,041 over the next 30 years, with the

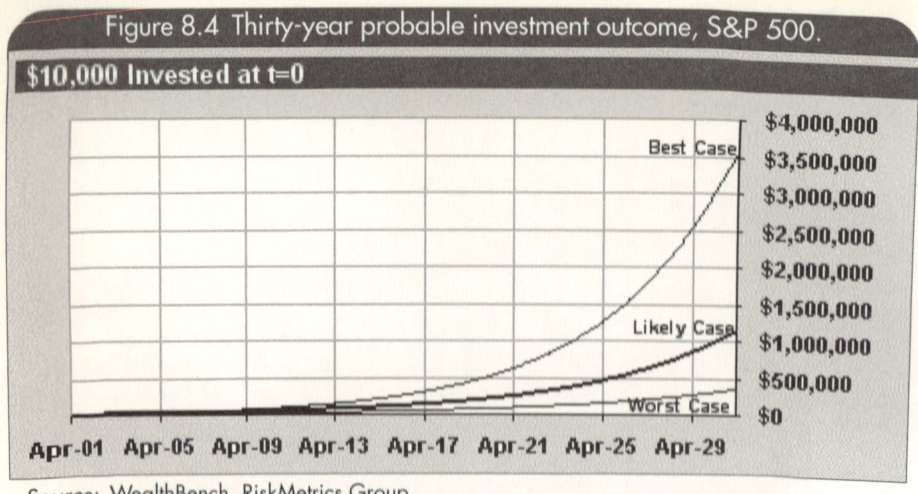

Source: WealthBench, RiskMetrics Group.

worst-case scenario generating $354,678 and the best-case scenario providing $3,538,751. Long-term returns prove consistent with risk parameters insofar as expectations fall between the minimum and maximum bands. Investors should recognize that returns could potentially be more volatile in the interim, as the distribution of probable returns narrows only with time. This supports earlier claims that extended holding periods tend to have a constricting effect on market risk. Additionally, investors should note that the range between the best- and worst-case prospects are quite significant. Given this, we must be prepared to take on more risk or less risk as deemed necessary.

One way to prepare for the future is to look at the past. To help anticipate future volatility we analyzed the historical variability of the S&P 500's RiskGrade. Figure 8.5 is a specialized type of bar chart called a *histogram.* Individual RiskGrade measurements of the S&P 500 are grouped together so that you can determine the frequency with which they occurred since 1970. Higher bars indicate more frequency, and lower bars indicate less frequency. In the histogram we can see that 90 percent of the RiskGrade measurements for the S&P 500 fall between 35 and 109.

Figure 8.6 illustrates the historic rise in value of the S&P 500 index over the past 32 years. The top chart shows the actual price of the index, and the bottom half plots its RiskGrade over the same time period. As significant as the spectacular performance the S&P is, it is only half the story.

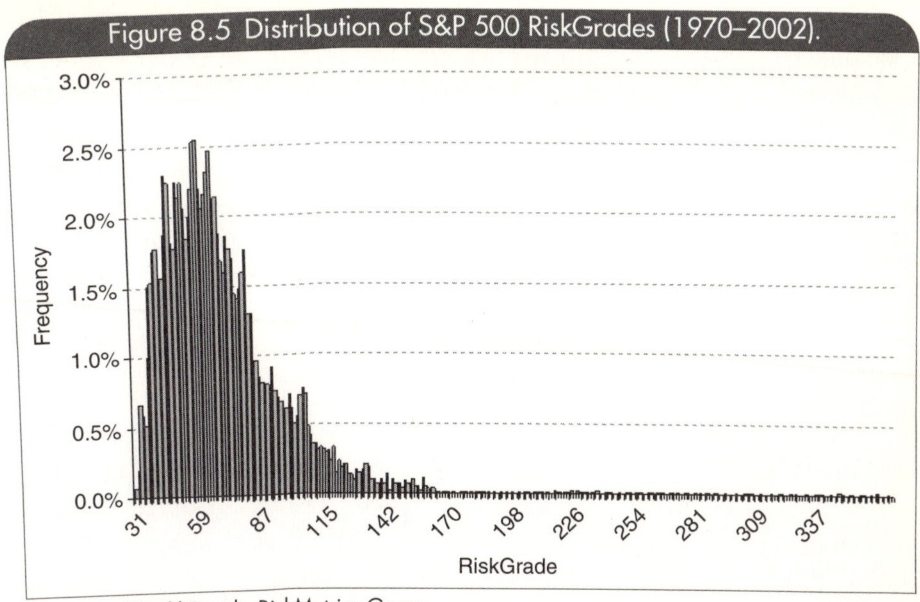

Figure 8.5 Distribution of S&P 500 RiskGrades (1970–2002).

Source: WealthBench, RiskMetrics Group.

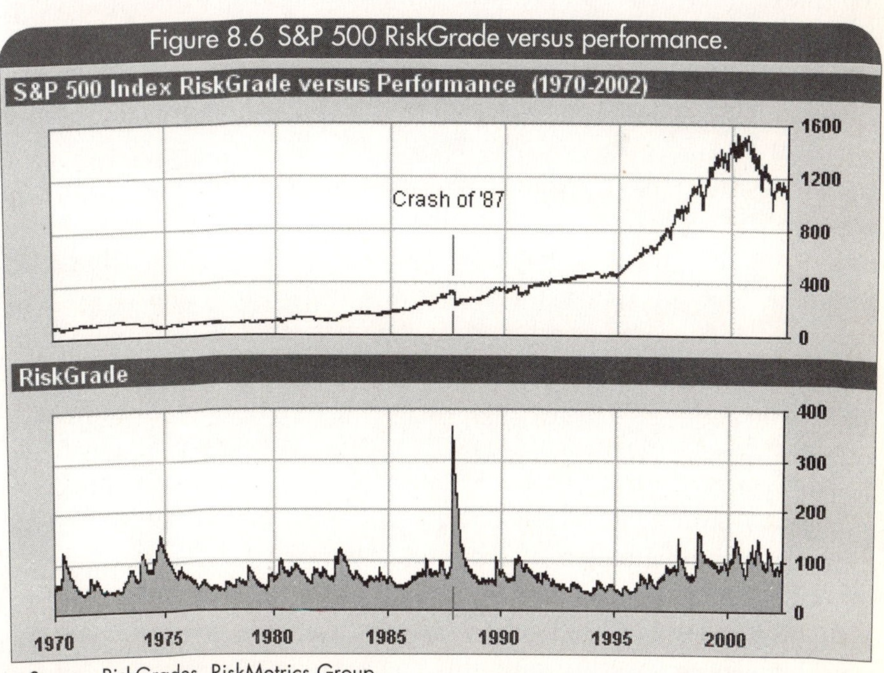

Source: RiskGrades, RiskMetrics Group.

Since 1970, the S&P has risen 1,047, yet its corresponding RiskGrade has risen only 69 percent. Apart from the stunning shock of the 1987 crash, the RiskGrade for the S&P has been consistently bound within a stable range. The average RiskGrade measurement over this period was 72.

The two charts, viewed together, offer a balanced picture of risk and return considerations. Whether you're running return simulations or using a more straightforward estimation, the purpose is to narrow the search for a suitable level of risk that matches your probable returns.

Superior Risk

As we venture out on the risk frontier, it is important to remind ourselves that all returns are not built the same. A premium is warranted for each incremental level of risk. A portfolio that delivers returns of 10 percent with an average RiskGrade of 100 should be considered differently than a similar portfolio that achieves the same 10 percent return but with a RiskGrade of 400. While the return simulation is incredibly helpful in determining a more appropriate risk factor, it fails to tell us whether we are getting paid to take the risk. From the years 1995 through 2000, the S&P 500 Index averaged 20.24 percent annual returns with an average RiskGrade measurement of 79. Is that an appropriate ratio, or could we have done better? In other words, can a portfolio with a similar RiskGrade provide higher returns? At what point should we be indifferent given a level of risk?

Because the risk premium tends to shift with market conditions, it is impossible to settle on one acceptable return that is uniformly applicable for assets with comparable risk characteristics. Instead, we can stipulate a minimum level of return for any investment with a similar level of uncertainty. The logic is a bit tricky, but the rationale of a minimum return makes sense. Those who subscribe to the view that markets are by nature efficient would argue that the return on any risky investment is unpredictable—upside gains share the same probability as downside losses. Common sense tells us that such odds are not a very attractive proposition given that, all else being equal, our expected return is zero. Everyone would be better off accruing guaranteed U.S. Treasury yields. Accordingly, reason guides us to demand a higher level of return to offset a comparable level of variability on the downside. Given a risk-free rate, which implies no volatility in returns, and a standard volatility market for

Table 8.3 Return of Indifference

RiskGrade	0	100	200	300	400	500	1,000
Required return (%)	6.0	9.7	13.4	17.2	20.9	24.6	27.6

Source: WealthBench, RiskMetrics Group, 2002.

each RiskGrade, we can interpolate a level of indifference for every point. Consistent with corporate finance theory, a return of indifference simply suggests that greater unpredictability must reward investors with added incentives. Although the math behind the numbers is a bit arcane, the conclusion is intuitive (see Table 8.3). An acceptable return is one that compensates for the higher degree of uncertainty. Otherwise, the investment is a poor one.

Expectedly, a risk-free asset has a RiskGrade of zero and a 6 percent minimum yield.[13] As we move out along the risk frontier, we see that the minimum required return increases incrementally. Other things being equal, an investor should be indifferent to a 13.4 percent return with a RiskGrade of 200 and a 27.6 percent return with a RiskGrade of 1,000. The additional return of 14.2 percent is the reward for the greater scale of variability.

Do Greater Rewards Require Us to Take Greater Risks?

All investments involve risk. Risk, return, and time are all intertwined. But generally speaking, to achieve greater rewards, such as a higher investment returns, must we always assume greater risk? Conversely, to minimize risk, must we accept lower returns? To answer this question, we're going to look to the market and see if it's possible to find examples of long-term winners that delivered superior returns without excessive risk.

The Cola Wars Redefined

Aaahhh! Nothing beats a nice refreshing cola to quench a heavy thirst on a hot summer day. But the ongoing cola wars make the decision between Coca-Cola and Pepsi very difficult. The proverbial Pepsi Challenge urges us to take a blindfolded taste test. In so doing, we will presumably find Pepsi's "joy of living" to be the winner. Coca-Cola, on the other hand, has campaigned for decades as "the real thing." Devout supporters of Coke will avow that cola in any language always translates into Coca-Cola. Who's right?

From an investment angle, the decision between Coke and Pepsi rests on something other than mere taste. One could certainly argue that taste is instrumental to the bottom line. After all, we are dealing with companies whose primary objective is to sell soft drinks. However, a simple primer in Marketing 101 teaches us that sales volume is about much more than having the best product or, in this case, the best-tasting cola. In addition to the value of its product, a company's success has much to do with its relationships with key vendors, the effectiveness of its brand image, and its reputation for quality control. In other words, our decisions may be influenced less by the flavor of the cola than by customary balance sheet yardsticks. By this token, what should be of interest to us is the cola company that is best projected to sustain high top-line growth, a superior price-to-earnings ratio, and better overall margins. These measures, when carefully considered, should reflect not only taste but, more important, management's ability to successfully execute a focused business strategy that convincingly stimulates sales. In short, these conventional valuation measures have been designed to direct us to the winning formula.

From a sheer performance perspective, Coca-Cola wins hands down over the past decade. In fact, the Atlanta-based beverage company, founded in 1886, started its second century in business on a stronger note than the first. Coca-Cola's 1990s return of 583 percent sizably outpaced Pepsi's 229 percent performance by over a two-to-one margin. In fact, at one point in 1998, Coke was up over 900 percent since 1990. Even with some setbacks as the decade came to a close, Coke's market capitalization stood in the neighborhood of $140 billion on annual sales of $20 billion in 1999. Pepsi, on the other hand, had a market valuation of about a third of Coke's, around $50 billion, despite similar revenue numbers. Presumably, the market had determined that Coke would continue to win the battle for the world's thirsty souls.

Given Coke's lofty performance, we can't help but wonder how much more risk Coke assumed than did Pepsi to achieve its results. Did Coke investors assume a higher degree of risk? Let's find out. During the past decade, Coca-Cola's RiskGrade largely ranged between 100 and 200, averaging 120 for the period (see Figure 8.7), hardly eye-opening given such envious returns. By way of comparison, Pepsi saw its RiskGrade also traverse back and forth between 100 and 200, with a period average of 138 (see Figure

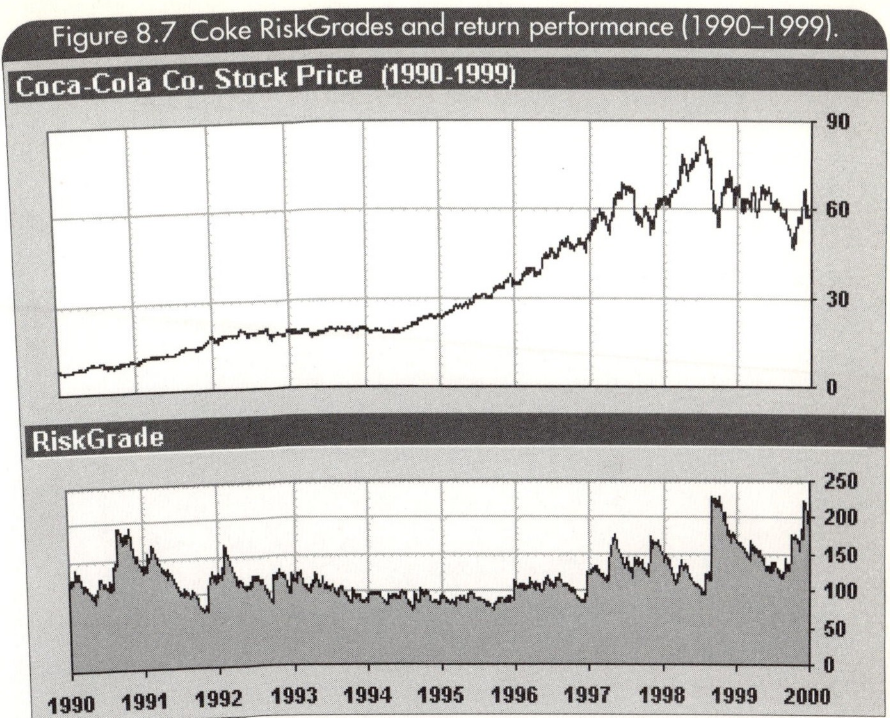

Source: WealthBench, RiskMetrics Group.

8.8). On whole, barring a few isolated events, both cola companies remained fairly stable from the standpoint of risk. Put differently, investors were none the worse for having chosen either Coke or Pepsi. To wit, Coke exhibited a more stable RiskGrade range (155 versus 252). As expected, Coke's performance in the 1990s is that much more impressive—far superior gains with a lower risk profile than Pepsi's. It is very apparent that Coke was the "real thing," particularly on a risk-adjusted basis. This may not come as a big surprise considering that Coca-Cola's brand, built over generations, is second to none. It is certainly one of the most recognizable names in the world.

The value of a stock cannot be attributed solely to a well-distinguished brand or a great-tasting formula. Even final revenue tallies don't tell the whole story, as attested by Coke and Pepsi's comparable numbers. A great deal of credit goes to Coke's management team for capably executing a well-thought-out plan and confidently building a story of growth and confidence that investors clearly bought. While the cola wars are far from over, the 1990s round belonged to the red-and-white swirl of Coca-Cola.

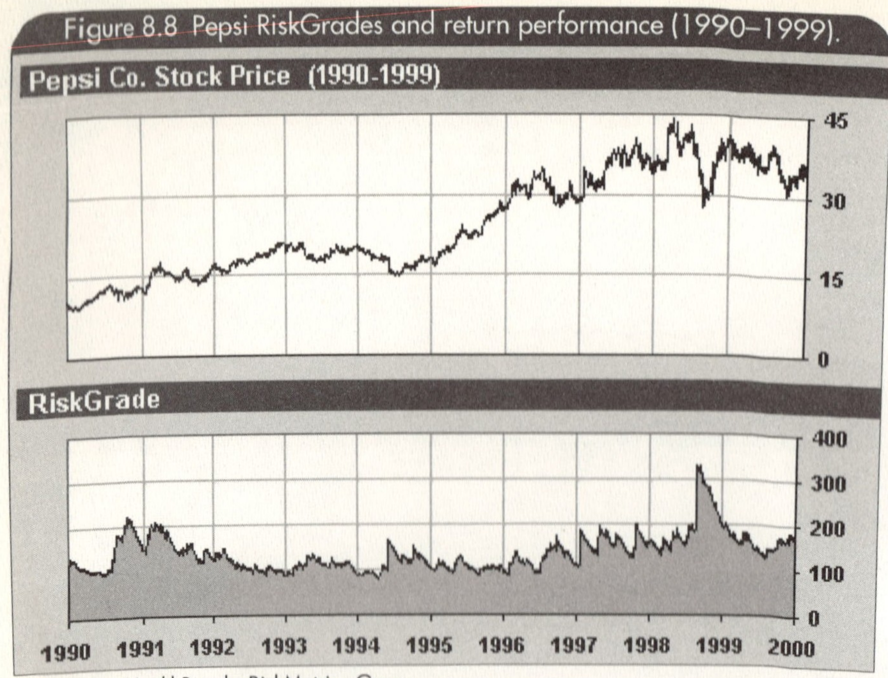

Source: WealthBench, RiskMetrics Group.

Dell versus Hewlett-Packard

Given a fresh perspective on the cola wars, we decided to examine a few other twosomes to see if the same risk-return pattern held. These are summarized in Table 8.4. What becomes clear after running this exercise is that superior stocks often deliver results without significantly higher risk, which points us in the direction of Markowitz's efficient frontier.

The most fantastic comparison is the one between the two computer manufacturers, Dell and Hewlett-Packard (HP). A closer look reveals that this was not even a contest. The amazing story of Dell officially began in 1984 when Michael Dell left college armed with a novel idea (to sell computers directly to the consumer) and $1,000 in start-up capital. Despite taking on established rivals such as Compaq, IBM, and the venerable Hewlett-Packard, Dell's company became the second largest manufacturer of personal computers by 1999, with $18 billion in revenues. For the decade, Dell delivered an unprecedented 88,905 percent! HP's return of 822 percent paled in comparison. To put it in dollar terms, an initial investment of $10,000 in Dell stock at the outset of the decade incredibly guided

Table 8.4 Risk and Return Comparison (1990–1999)

Competitors	10-Year Return	10-Year Average RiskGrade	Maximum RiskGrade	Minimum RiskGrade	$10,000 Invested in 1990–99
Coca-Cola	590%	120	229	74	$69,000
Pepsi	231%	138	329	77	$33,100
Dell	88,905%	286	527	170	$8,900,500
Hewlett Packard	822%	203	403	131	$92,200
New York Times	349%	140	310	73	$44,900
Dow Jones	163%	130	255	68	$26,300
Pfizer	1268%	144	274	84	$136,800
Merck	552%	129	206	75	$65,200

Source: WealthBench, RiskMetrics Group.

an investor to the gateways of retirement with nearly $9 million in terminal value. HP holders were less fortunate, despite accumulating proceeds of over $92,000 during the period. Placed on the same scale, HP's returns barely even register. What is so remarkable about Dell's performance is the manner in which it was accomplished. Dell stock averaged a higher RiskGrade for the period. However, if we throw the stock's RiskGrade range into the analysis, Dell was not substantially riskier than HP.

This pattern, characterized by significantly higher returns but with only slightly greater risk, holds true for the other pairs we examined. That bastion of political liberalism, the *New York Times*, outgunned rival Dow Jones & Company, publisher of the conservatively inclined *Wall Street Journal*, by over two times—349 percent to 163 percent. Merck and Pfizer tell a similar story, with the maker of Viagra stiffing its competitor by a comparable 2:1 margin. Over the 10-year period, Pfizer shareholders were rewarded with an additional $71,600 in market value.

The star performers in our survey bested their peers with only a marginal amount of additional risk. Although far from conclusive, it appears that an incremental increase in risk can lead to a world of difference with respect to returns, especially over time. This conclusion may seem coincidental given the favorable backdrop for stocks during the period. In fact, one could contend that a bull market translated higher risk into higher returns, which is true. During a bear market, the reverse is likely to hold true as well. As we have reiterated throughout, risk cuts both ways. However, the possible implications on asset allocation decisions from our findings are profound. Many have argued that asset allocation is the central determinant of returns. In the face of the evidence presented here, there seems to be plenty of room for stock pickers.

Naturally, drawing firm conclusions on only a decade's worth of data is highly suspect. Moreover, a pool of only four pairs of stocks is far from representative, and we could very likely be left with a slanted perspective. Still, this exercise of evaluating financial assets first from a risk dimension offers a practical look at the impact of risk on return. We can see that it's possible for long-term winners to deliver superior returns with better risk characteristics, pushing the final performance closer to the "efficient frontier" of low risk and high returns. Conversely, we should recognize that a riskier stock is not necessarily one that yields greater dividends over time. Even within the same sector, returns can vary significantly. We need only remind

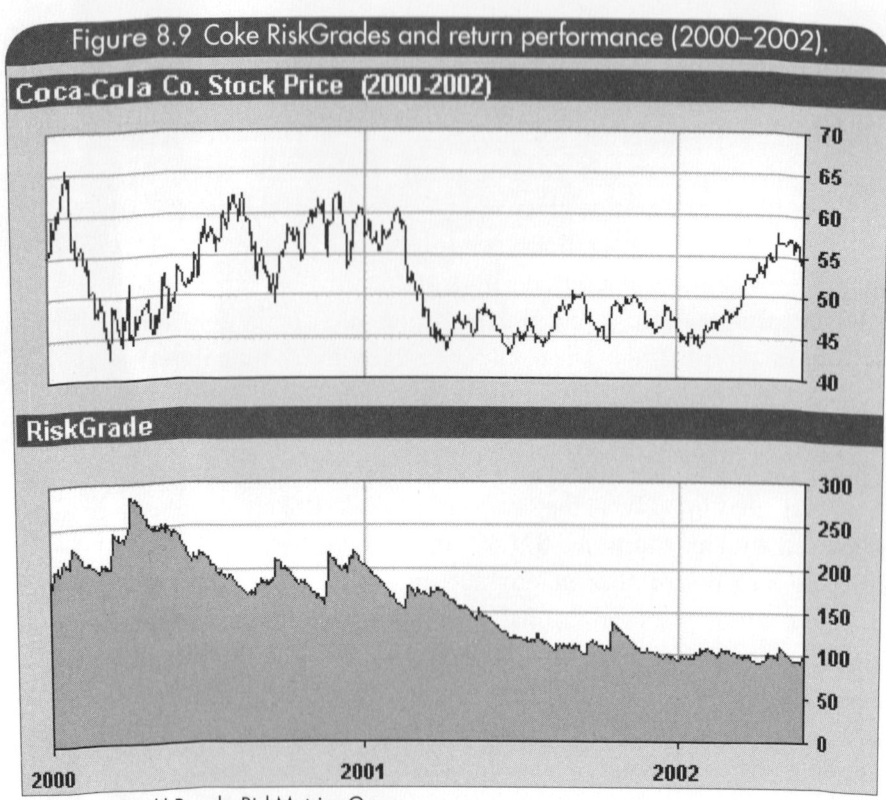

Figure 8.9 Coke RiskGrades and return performance (2000–2002).

Source: WealthBench, RiskMetrics Group.

ourselves of Dell and HP as an extreme example. Choosing the winner in a sector could effectively determine whether you retire in the next decade or many years later. Accordingly, this seems to reinforce our belief that long-term investors should not shy away from smart risk, particularly if the story behind the numbers is really compelling. A fractional difference in risk can go a long way in just 10 years' time.

Risk Is Fluid

Back to the cola wars. It's tough to say whether Coke can maintain its dominance over Pepsi in the years to come. In fact, more recent trends at the time of our analysis suggest that a Pepsi era may be arriving. Although Coke owned the 1990s, Pepsi stock is now outperforming Coke's (see Figures 8.9 and 8.10). From 2000 through the first half of 2002, Pepsi is up 41 percent and Coke is down 1.4 percent. Even after fresh gains, Pepsi stock is still cheaper from a valuation standpoint, but its future prospects look

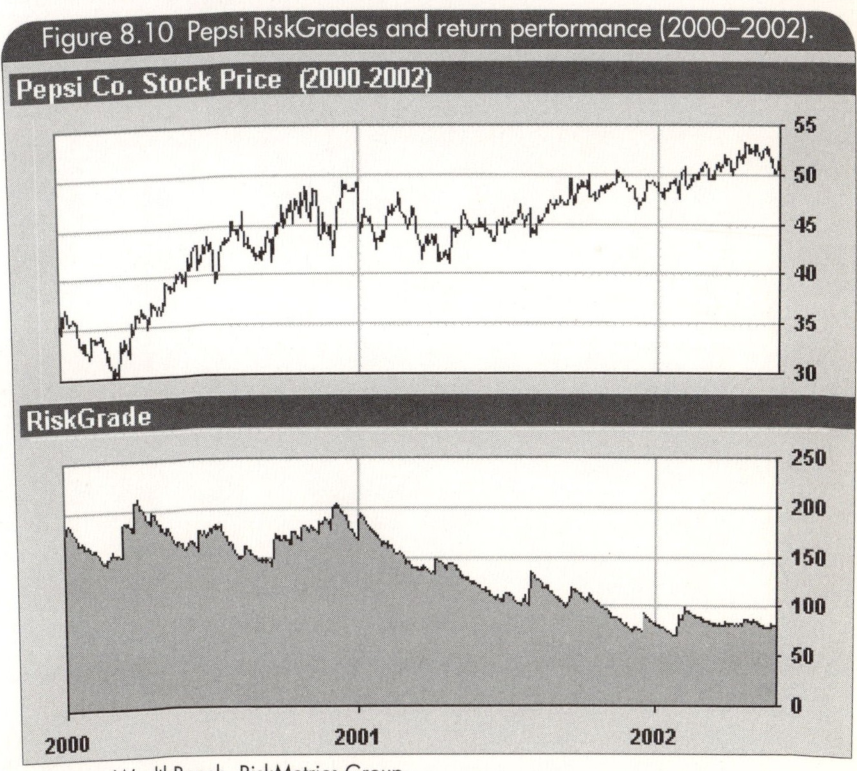

Source: WealthBench, RiskMetrics Group.

bright after successfully diversifying into noncarbonated drinks and snack foods. Coca-Cola's stumbles of late can be partially attributed to some mismanagement and a dated business model that relies too heavily on conventional soft drinks. The one obvious thing we deduce from this is that a change in business cycles impacts companies differently. Yesterday's losers are tomorrow's champions. While many wrote off Pepsi's chances against Coke during the 1990s, Coke's critics are similarly on the attack now. Which cola should we be reaching for now?

CHAPTER 9

Developing Your Portfolio's True Picture of Risk

Seeing is believing. Or is it? In truth, a single frame of reference gives only a partial sense of reality. Absolute clarity from the perspective of one lens may be inconclusive from another, because the camera has the ability to play tricks on our senses. For instance, a photograph is a two-dimensional image of a three-dimensional world; motion is impossible to directly translate onto paper. To compensate, a photographer relies on contrasting angles and degrees of light to inject the appearance of movement and depth onto a print—a technique that promising artists learn early on. The best solution is to piece together several two-dimensional renditions to capture the subtleties of a three-dimensional experience.

Nowhere is more time spent finding the correct angle than in the world of sports. Television coverage of sporting events has grown so vast that a camera can be found positioned almost anywhere on the field. Viewers at home are now offered the richness of a first-row experience without all the hassles of actually being in a ballpark or stadium. In fact, cameras now take us beyond the front-row seats. For example, a miniature camera attached to the catcher's mask in baseball offers a batter's-eye view of every pitch. The power of television now gives us the chance to stand in the batter's box and visualize firsthand how quickly a 95-mile-an-hour fastball crosses the plate. This vantage point presumably gives us the most accurate account of balls and strikes. We can decisively make a call on every pitch. The first pitch looked high and tight—ball one!

Not so fast. From the center-field camera, the same pitch appears to catch the inside corner of home plate. As true to life as the first impression is, the angle of the umpire's stance and, more important, the velocity at which the baseball moves toward the plate, could possibly lend a distorting effect. Did the pitch really cross the plate? Was it lower than we thought we'd seen? Was it a strike? With several different images, the conclusion could be far from clear. As it is, where we are positioned on the field has as much to do with the final verdict as the actual trajectory of the ball. As always, the truth lies somewhere among the many angles of every pitch. Several other cameras, including one overhead looking down at home plate, would lend greater proof, making the final assessment of the situation more reliable. Taking many different perspectives into consideration takes us a step closer to calling a clear-cut ball or strike.

Risk in the financial markets is a matter of angles, too. As we have demonstrated through the course of our discussion, the strength of the RiskGrades service as a tool stems from its ability to synthesize the various components of financial risk and articulate it in a cogent manner. RiskGrades enable investors to make more informed decisions by providing detailed portfolio and investment information from many different perspectives. However, as good as RiskGrades are in depicting these perspectives, we must accept that no one methodology can completely safeguard us from all the various ills that financial markets can toss our way. To wit, Murphy's Law ("anything that can go wrong will go wrong") best characterizes the markets. Risk is fluid. As such, it is difficult to get a sense of how it actively circulates through an entire portfolio. In actuality, risk cuts from all different angles. No service can fully capture the three-dimensional elements of risk that afflict our portfolios. But what the RiskGrades service does very well is to provide a series of two-dimensional snapshots, sensibly cropped, that delivers an accurate representation of how risk behaves in the real world. Our goal is to develop your portfolio's true picture of risk.

One of the central messages up to this point has been that risk is an unavoidable fact of life and investing. Indeed, risk is a natural part of this world and can present great opportunities for those who understand and know how to manage it. To that end, we have explained the need for you to be clear about investment objectives, time horizons, and risk preferences when implementing your investment plan. You should take risk only if you can understand and measure it and are prepared to live with its downside. In Chapters 6, 7, and 8 we presented the basic building blocks of portfolio construction: asset allocation, diversification, and understanding your own tolerance for risk. In the next two chapters we further build on what you have already learned and demonstrate how RiskGrade's portfolio management tools can help you identify, measure, and manage different types of risk so you can decide which ones to take and which ones to avoid. These chapters provide an overview of RiskGrades and illustrate the way in which risk measures are presented. To maintain a degree of consistency in the data, we've created a single theoretical portfolio under the name of Brandon Ryan. The asset base and investment strategy have been selected for illustrative purposes and are not intended to be an endorsement or to imply the future performance of any investments mentioned.

Learn to Be an Intelligent Risk Taker

The naked eye has little ability to discern whether a financial plan is adequately balanced. Even conscientious portfolios contain intricate risks that are not visibly apparent. As we have demonstrated, a basic RiskGrade probe helps to identify the perceptible chinks in our portfolio's armor. However, risks buried below the surface, those that could prove to be quite troublesome, are not easily detectable. A single snapshot of risk is likely to miss such hidden risks altogether. Consequently, a more diligent examination should be taken to safeguard our portfolios against unwanted surprises. For this we need more sophisticated tools that can reveal hidden defects in our investment plans.

With these concerns in mind, RiskMetrics developed the following set of measures as part of the RiskGrades service. They are designed to help you manage your portfolio's exposure to market risk. These additional tools, or lenses, will allow you to see and expose risk from a variety of viewpoints. If they seem complex at times, it is the result of designing tools sophisticated enough to minimize market aberrations in order to gain maximum clarity. Measuring risk on a portfolio basis will show you how well diversified your investments are, where the largest gains and losses are likely

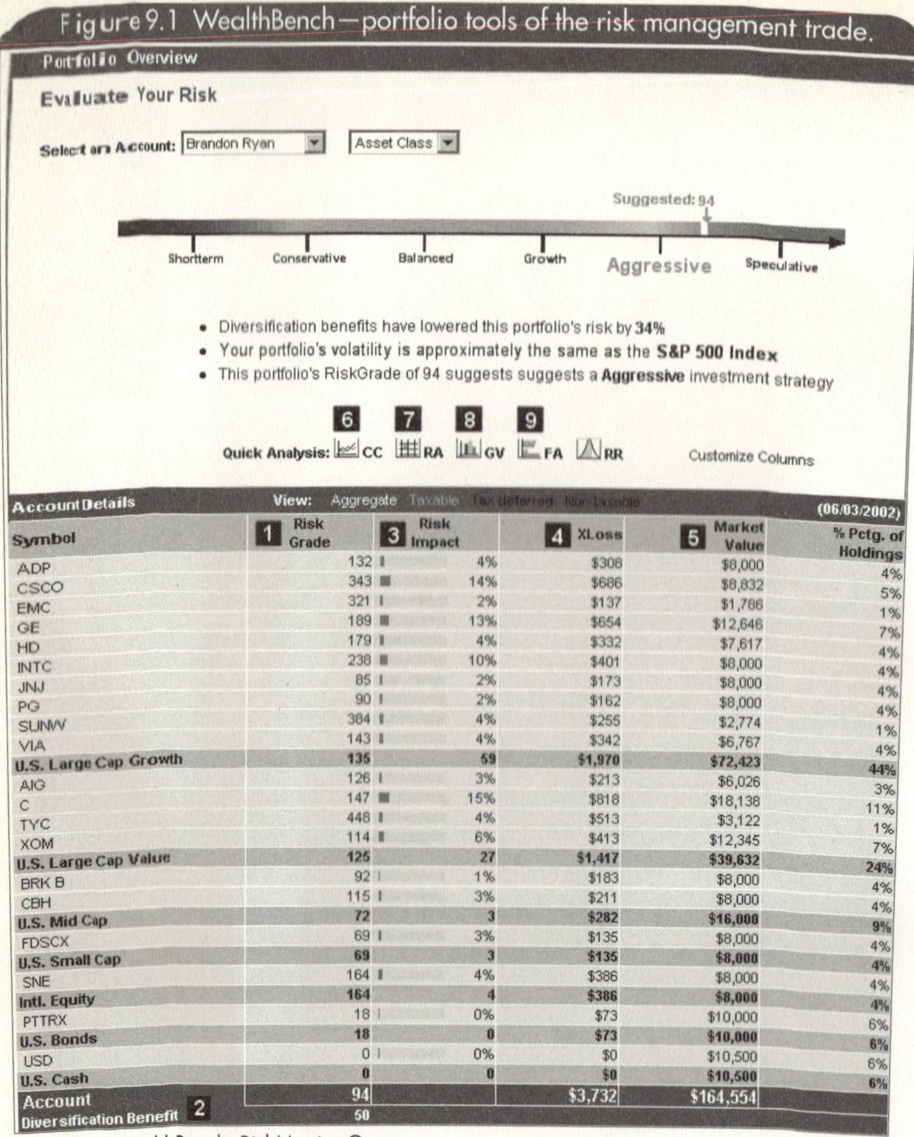

	1 Risk Grade	3 Risk Impact		4 XLoss	5 Market Value	% Pctg. of Holdings
Account Details			View: Aggregate Taxable Tax deferred Non-taxable			(06/03/2002)
Symbol						
ADP	132		4%	$308	$8,000	4%
CSCO	343		14%	$686	$8,832	5%
EMC	321		2%	$137	$1,786	1%
GE	189		13%	$654	$12,646	7%
HD	179		4%	$332	$7,617	4%
INTC	238		10%	$401	$8,000	4%
JNJ	85		2%	$173	$8,000	4%
PG	90		2%	$162	$8,000	4%
SUNW	384		4%	$255	$2,774	1%
VIA	143		4%	$342	$6,767	4%
U.S. Large Cap Growth	**135**		**59**	**$1,970**	**$72,423**	**44%**
AIG	126		3%	$213	$6,026	3%
C	147		15%	$818	$18,138	11%
TYC	448		4%	$513	$3,122	1%
XOM	114		6%	$413	$12,345	7%
U.S. Large Cap Value	**125**		**27**	**$1,417**	**$39,632**	**24%**
BRK B	92		1%	$183	$8,000	4%
CBH	115		3%	$211	$8,000	4%
U.S. Mid Cap	**72**		**3**	**$282**	**$16,000**	**9%**
FDSCX	69		3%	$135	$8,000	4%
U.S. Small Cap	**69**		**3**	**$135**	**$8,000**	**4%**
SNE	164		4%	$386	$8,000	4%
Intl. Equity	**164**		**4**	**$386**	**$8,000**	**4%**
PTTRX	18		0%	$73	$10,000	6%
U.S. Bonds	**18**		**0**	**$73**	**$10,000**	**6%**
USD	0		0%	$0	$10,500	6%
U.S. Cash	**0**		**0**	**$0**	**$10,500**	**6%**
Account	**94**				**$3,732**	**$164,554**
Diversification Benefit 2	**50**					

Source: WealthBench, RiskMetrics Group.

to be concentrated, and how your risk profile compares with that of your peers. Ultimately, the greater transparency achieved through measuring risk will help you make more informed investment decisions. To help introduce the full suite of RiskGrade tools, we refer to Figure 9.1 to illustrate where you can find each measurement tool and explain what each one does.

RiskGrade Measurement

A RiskGrade is a dynamic, quantitative measure of risk.

As depicted in Figure 9.1, the account of Brandon Ryan includes assets with a range of different RiskGrades, from 448 for Tyco International (TYC) down to 18 for PIMCO Total Return Inst (PTTRX). In aggregate, the RiskGrade of the account is 94, indicating an aggressive risk allocation.

The overall RiskGrade for a portfolio is a measure of the account's expected level of volatility. For example, if an investor is planning to take distributions from his or her account in the near future, the participant may target a lower RiskGrade, relative to other investors, in order to decrease the variability of the account's value as retirement income is needed. Alternatively, an investor with a longer time horizon and capital appreciation objectives may target a higher RiskGrade.

As the prices of individual securities and the overall market become more or less volatile, a portfolio RiskGrade will rise and fall, even in the absence of account activity such as balance transfers or changes in the allocation of contributions. Monitoring a portfolio's RiskGrade regularly, even if no transaction has taken place, is important to ensure the portfolio's risk is in line with its target risk allocation. If your investment strategy includes the use of a specific risk target, you may need to adjust your portfolio's risk as the market's level of volatility changes.

As the middle bullet point in Figure 9.1 shows, this portfolio's volatility is approximately the same as that of the S&P 500 Index. Comparing the RiskGrade of an account to that of the S&P 500 Index enables an individual to evaluate the account's risk relative to a broad benchmark index and is generally considered to be an efficient means for investing in the overall U.S. equity market. Since the S&P 500 is a widely tracked equity index, it provides a useful frame of reference for risk. For example, an account might have a RiskGrade that exceeds that of the S&P 500 if the account has a concentrated investment in company stock, or if it has substantial allocations to volatile funds such as emerging markets equities or high yield bond funds. In this case, the investor may wish to consider, among other things, whether he or she is comfortable taking what is considered an *aggressive investment strategy* and whether he or she anticipates returns equal to or in excess of the S&P 500 that would compensate for the elevated level of risk.

Diversification Benefit

Diversification benefit is the risk reduction due to having your funds allocated to multiple investments.

Savvy risk managers continually search out excessive concentrations in order to promote diversification and stable investment growth. Rather than mixing investments randomly, you can assemble investments that collectively perform well under various economic conditions. A portfolio's diversification benefit measures the amount of risk removed from your portfolio by holding multiple investments.

Diversification in one's portfolio is a quality that all investors are encouraged to strive for; however, until recently, few investors have had convenient access to measures that quantify diversification. The diversification benefit score in WealthBench addresses this need. WealthBench's diversification benefit quantifies the extent to which overall risk in the account (as represented by the RiskGrade) has been reduced without lowering the account's overall expected return.

In the example portfolio in Figure 9.1, the portfolio's overall RiskGrade is 94. Had the portfolio not been as well diversified, the portfolio RiskGrade would actually have been 144. The difference is the diversification benefit, which in this case is equal to 50. Another way to measure diversification is in percentage terms. For example, diversification benefits have made this portfolio 34 percent less risky ($50 \div 144 = 34\%$).

As discussed in more detail in Chapter 7, the best way to diversify your portfolio is to spread it across a mix of asset classes. This will significantly increase the likelihood that not all of your investments will fall at the same time, thus preserving the market value of your portfolio.

Computation of the WealthBench Diversification Benefit

The RiskGrade diversification benefit for your portfolio is the difference between the computed portfolio RiskGrade and the market-value-weighted average of the individual asset RiskGrades. The diversification benefit score is computed by regressing the historical returns of an account with the historical returns of the market portfolio. Mathematically, this is expressed as follows:

$$\text{Diversification effect} = \sum_{i=1}^{N} \omega_i \text{RiskGrade of asset } (i)$$

$$= \text{RiskGrade of the portfolio}$$

where N denotes the number of assets in your portfolio and ω_i denotes the weighting of asset i in your portfolio. The RiskGrade measurement of any portfolio will always be less than the weighted-average RiskGrade of its individual holdings, because it is unlikely that all of the assets will perform badly at the same time.

Using the Diversification Benefit Score

By regularly reviewing your diversification benefit score, you can obtain an objective assessment of how broadly diversified your holdings are relative to the overall market. Because a low diversification benefit score is typically associated with concentrated positions in company stock and asset allocations that are significantly different from the market (e.g., a large overweight position in emerging-market equities), the measure can be used to evaluate whether the excess risk from lack of diversification can be reduced or eliminated by diversifying your account holdings in a manner compatible with your overall investment objectives and time horizon. In some cases, it may be perfectly reasonable to maintain concentrated positions in your portfolio and thus have a low diversification benefit score for your account. This could make sense, for example, for young people with long investment horizons and significant financial assets outside of their investment portfolios that diversify their financial assets overall. As with all the measures presented, they are best used in the context of an individual's overall financial profile.

RiskImpact

RiskImpact measures how much risk a given asset is contributing to the portfolio's overall risk.

As discussed, the RiskGrade of individual securities and portfolios overall fluctuate over time in accordance with the markets. Similarly, the diversification benefit score of a portfolio and the risk contribution of each security in the portfolio fluctuate. What happens if one day you check your portfolio's RiskGrade and rather than seeing a target level of 75, you find the RiskGrade has risen to 100 (which represents 33 percent more risk)? Is there a way you can determine how to rebalance your portfolio in order to bring its RiskGrade back in line with your risk allocation target? Or suppose you have a concentrated company stock position in your account and want to know exactly how much risk the position is contributing to the account's overall risk. Is there a way to find out? In both cases, RiskImpact can provide insights.

RiskImpact, a complement to RiskGrade, is a calculation that determines how much each individual asset in the portfolio contributes to the bottom line. Simply put, the RiskImpact of an asset measures how your portfolio RiskGrade would change if the position were removed—that is, if the position were closed out and the proceeds were held in cash. Investors can use RiskImpact to identify concentration risks and measure the change in a portfolio's total RiskGrade if a position were to be sold. The less correlated an asset is to the rest of the portfolio, the lower its RiskImpact and the greater the diversification benefit; the larger the size of the position, the greater the RiskImpact. In general, positions that exceed 10 percent RiskImpact are considered to be concentrated.

Our discussion thus far has put risk on a linear scale. A lower RiskGrade measurement represents a safer substitute, and a higher RiskGrade measurement suggests a riskier alternative. On the surface, this makes perfect intuitive sense. However, within the context of a portfolio, the asset with the highest RiskGrade measurement may not always be your riskiest holding. In a group framework, we must also measure other conspirators that contribute to the portfolio's risk (e.g., the total market size of each position).

Consider a portfolio with 50 shares of Microsoft that have a market value of $3,500 and 500 shares of Coke that have a market value of $22,800. The RiskGrade measurement for Coke is 141, whereas Microsoft's is 252. Which one is riskier? The answer is Coke. Why? Because Coke's market value represents 85 percent of the total portfolio, which points to a concentration risk. In other words, the future of this portfolio is anchored to the market direction of Coke. The relatively small position in Microsoft helps to diversify this portfolio from any losses Coke may suffer. Concentration risk is a critical determinant of overall portfolio behavior, something that a single RiskGrade measure would not point out on its own.

To calculate RiskImpact for asset P, we compare the RiskGrade of the portfolio with and without the asset as follows:

RiskImpact (P) = portfolio RiskGrade (all positions)
        − portfolio RiskGrade (close out P, proceeds in cash)

To report RiskImpact as a percentage of the RiskGrade of the entire portfolio, we simply divide RiskImpact by the portfolio RiskGrade. In a portfolio, the sum of each RiskImpact measurement does not have to total to 100 percent because of the unique correlation of each asset in the portfolio.

How to Use RiskImpact

By quantifying the marginal risk contribution of each position, RiskImpact helps identify potential overconcentrations in particular holdings or asset class categories. For example, referring to Figure 9.1, with RiskImpact, an investor or advisor can immediately determine that Cisco (CSCO) and Tyco (TYC) combined represent 6 percent of total market value of this portfolio but account for 18 percent of the portfolio's volatility. Transferring balances out of Cisco and Tyco and into cash will reduce the portfolio's RiskGrade of 94 by 18 percent, to 81.

XLoss

XLoss quantifies what one could expect to lose on one of the most volatile trading days of the year.

XLoss (loss in extreme markets) was designed to address the effect that severe market conditions have on an investor's performance. XLoss is an approximation of how much money you could lose on an exceptionally bad day in the markets, where the price fluctuations exceed 95 percent of the typical daily price changes. Your portfolio's XLoss is determined by looking at how your current mix of assets would have fared over the previous year. If you are in any way uncomfortable with the overall XLoss of your portfolio, you should be prepared to either reduce risk outright or rebalance your positions. At a glance, investors get a reasonable idea of what a stormy day can bring.

To calculate XLoss for an asset, we first look at the daily performance of the asset on each business day of the previous year, which is, on average, 252 business days. We then rank-order the daily returns from lowest to highest. If you have a long position in the asset, the XLoss is the average of the worst 5 percent of the daily returns, or approximately the worst 13 of the 252 return values. If you have a short position in the asset, the XLoss is the average of the best 5 percent of the daily returns.

Investors should note that although XLoss gives a good approximation of what a sharp down day would look like, the measure does not forecast the absolute worst-case scenario. Because the calculation is based on an average number of down days, some days are naturally going to be worse than XLoss suggests. XLoss is a very good general barometer, not a pinpoint forecast. Investors should also keep in mind that the XLoss statistic is based on observed historical losses, which may or may not come to pass in the future.

Calculating XLoss

To demonstrate how RiskGrades calculates XLoss, let's observe Coke's daily stock price changes over the past 20 years. In Figure 9.2, daily losses and gains are displayed. Price changes above the line are gains and those below are losses.

Next we plot out all gains and losses to draw the Coke return distribution and fit the bell-shaped normal distribution on top of it, as shown in Figure 9.3.

From the roughly equal proportion of daily gains and losses shown in Figures 9.2 and 9.3, we can see that Coke investors stood nearly a 50 percent chance of making or losing money over a one-day horizon. In general,

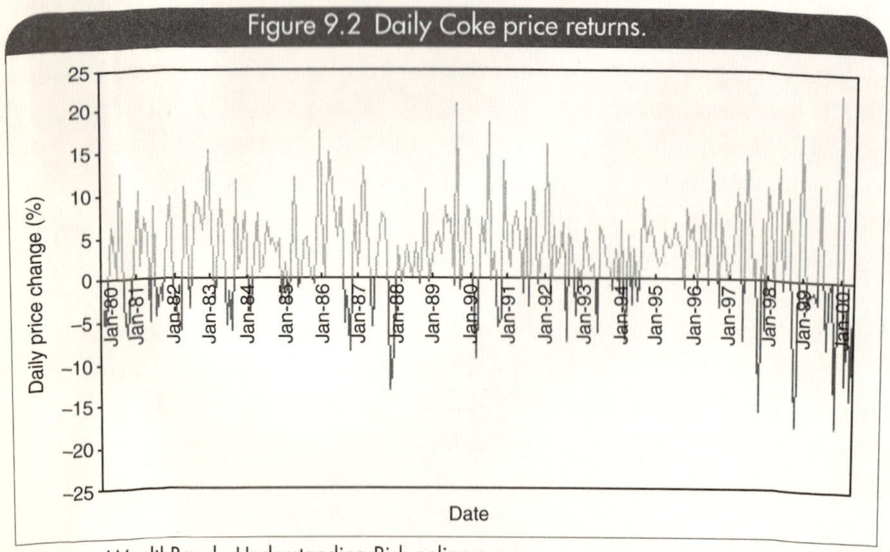

Figure 9.2 Daily Coke price returns.

Source: WealthBench, Understanding Risk online course.

you can expect to earn positive returns on stocks only over a much longer investment horizon (10 years or more).

Now let's focus on the worst 5 percent daily price changes of the Coke return distribution and determine XLoss by averaging of these losses.

In Figure 9.4, the worst-fifth-percentile daily losses, we see that losses have ranged from less than −2.5 percent to more than −10 percent. The XLoss statistic of −3.41 percent is the average of these worst-case daily losses. In other words, on 1 out of 20 trading days, Coke investors could expect a daily loss of −3.41 percent. For example, if an investor has invested $10,000 in Coke, then he or she can expect a loss of $341 under stressed conditions (amount invested times XLoss percentage equals XLoss, or $10,000 × −0.0341 = $341). Savvy investors use XLoss to weigh the short-term loss potential against the expected long-term growth prospects for a stock.

How to Use XLoss

If the potential amount by which your account value can fall in a bad day, as indicated by XLoss, is more than you are willing to risk losing, you may choose to be proactive and rebalance your allocations such that the account's XLoss and other risk measures reflect less overall risk. Even if the

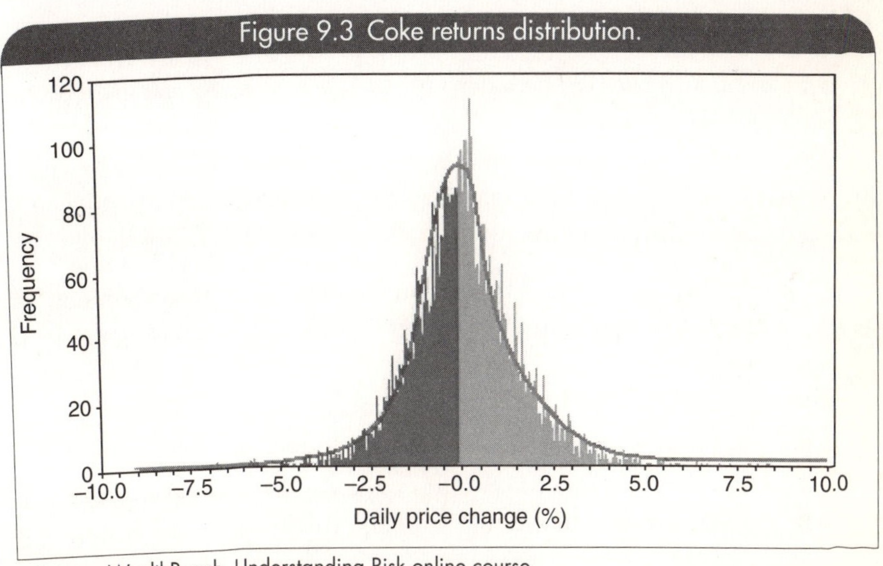

Source: WealthBench, Understanding Risk online course.

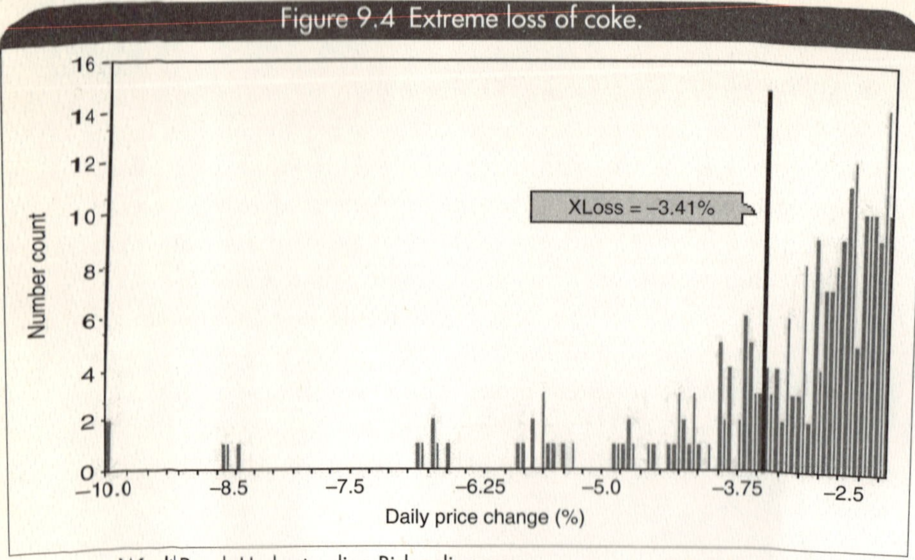

Source: WealthBench Understanding Risk online course.

RiskGrade of the account is at a level that you are generally comfortable with, the account's XLoss may indicate a degree of potential volatility that is undesirable given your time horizon or other preferences. By using RiskGrades and XLoss together, you can obtain a more complete picture of risk.

Market Value

Market value is determined by the number of shares you currently hold multiplied by the most recent close for that asset.

Market value is the amount that a seller can reasonably expect to obtain for securities sold in the open market. The RiskGrades service calculates market value for different types of asset classes in the following ways:

- For equities and mutual funds your market value is determined by the number of shares you hold times the most recent closing price for that asset.
- For bonds, the RiskGrades service determines the value of your holdings from government and corporate yield curves.
- To calculate the value on an option, the RiskGrades service uses the Black-Scholes option pricing model, which considers underlying

stock price, strike price, expiration date, risk-free return, and the standard deviation of the stock's return.

- All cash balances are valued at the exchange rate of your portfolio's base currency.

WealthBench Chart Center

WealthBench charts are stratified into the following four types: risk, price, streak, and range. Investors can see how well their portfolio as a whole or any individual asset has performed historically on both a risk and return basis. It's through charts that we can clearly see how dynamic RiskGrade measurements are and how quickly they adjust to current market conditions.

Risk Chart

In Figure 9.5, we can see the how a portfolio RiskGrade can change over time. Reading the chart from left to right, this portfolio's RiskGrade measurement was at 132 in June 2001 and, after some hesitancy, continually receded throughout the course of the summer close to its low of 78 in early September. Then, on September 11, terrorists attacked America, and in the aftermath of that assault, witness how the portfolio's RiskGrade jumped 74 percent to its high of 132. Subsequently, as order was restored to the market, the RiskGrade of the portfolio peeled back and is now below its one-year average of 103. As the chart illustrates, during turbulent times, a portfolio's RiskGrade measurement can easily double or triple to reflect periods of higher risk and uncertainty in the market.

Risk and Price Chart

Generally, the focus of most investors has been on tracking returns—while neglecting the amount of risk taken to generate those returns. However, in order to judge investment performance, we cannot ignore the risk factor required to generate those returns. To help in this regard, the chart in Figure 9.6 illustrates the risk/price relationship by showing the historical risk of an asset or portfolio as a dotted line and the return performance as a solid line.

This ability to include risk analysis in investment decisions allows investors to change their asset allocation in a way that enhances their

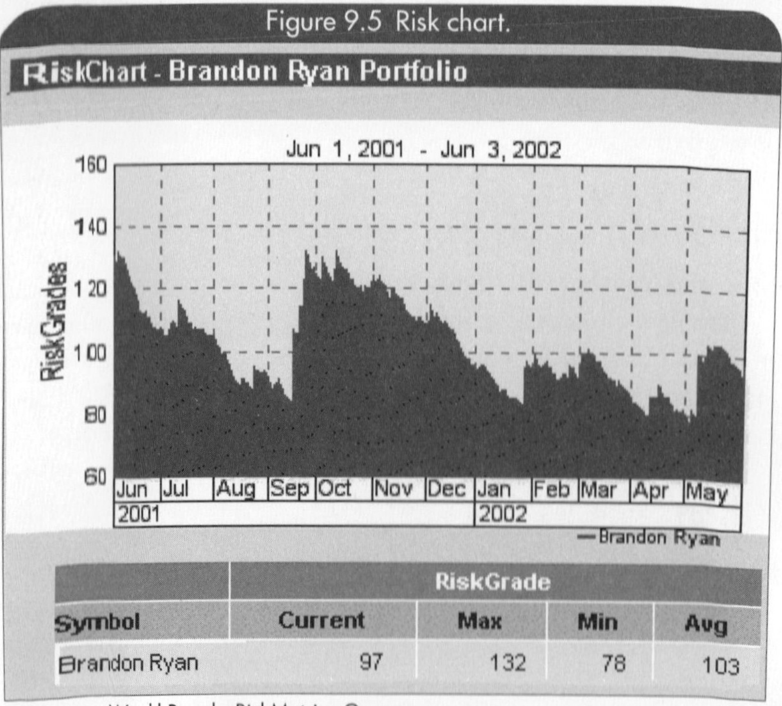

Figure 9.5 Risk chart.

Symbol	RiskGrade			
	Current	Max	Min	Avg
Brandon Ryan	97	132	78	103

Source: WealthBench, RiskMetrics Group.

return on risk. As we demonstrated in Chapter 8, rather than focusing on maximizing returns, the smart investor selects opportunities that are attractive based on their return on risk. This is important because sometimes the promise of a big return may not be worth the risk.

In Figure 9.6, the line chart represents the market value of your portfolio, and the drop lines or mountaintops reflect your portfolio risk. Note how sizable increases in RiskGrades tend to precede declines in a portfolio's market value, and visa versa.

Streak Chart

Are rising RiskGrades always bad news? The answer is no, not necessarily. RiskGrade measurements are indicators of risk based on the volatility of returns. Higher volatility of returns, regardless of whether it's positive or negative, will result in a higher RiskGrade measurement. As we explained

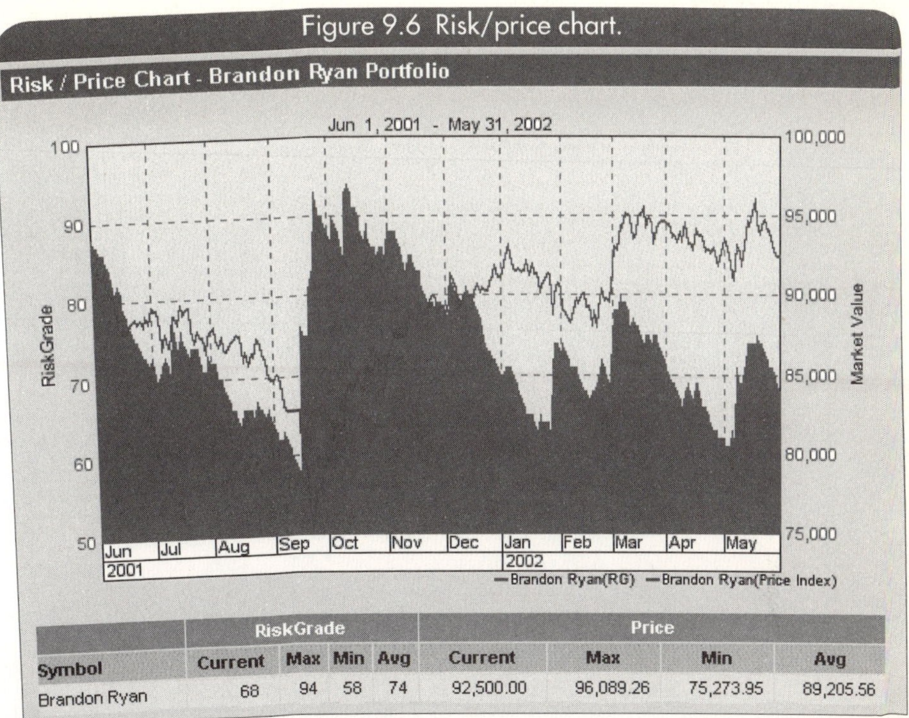

Symbol	RiskGrade				Price			
	Current	Max	Min	Avg	Current	Max	Min	Avg
Brandon Ryan	68	94	58	74	92,500.00	96,089.26	75,273.95	89,205.56

Source: WealthBench, RiskMetrics Group.

in Chapter 8 (remember the cola wars?), some risks are definitely worth taking.

In the wake of September 11, we have all witnessed extreme and unexpected market movements, which can give rise to large short-term fluctuations in market values. The results may run counter to the long-term risk trends indicated by the RiskGrade of your portfolio. To provide individuals with a measure of how risky the market can be during its most volatile months, streaks charts measure the largest historical three-month, six-month, and one-year increases and decreases in value of an account (see Figure 9.7).

Range Chart

The final graph in our Chart Center is a range chart (see Figure 9.8). The range chart can help investors monitor their assets' ongoing exposure to

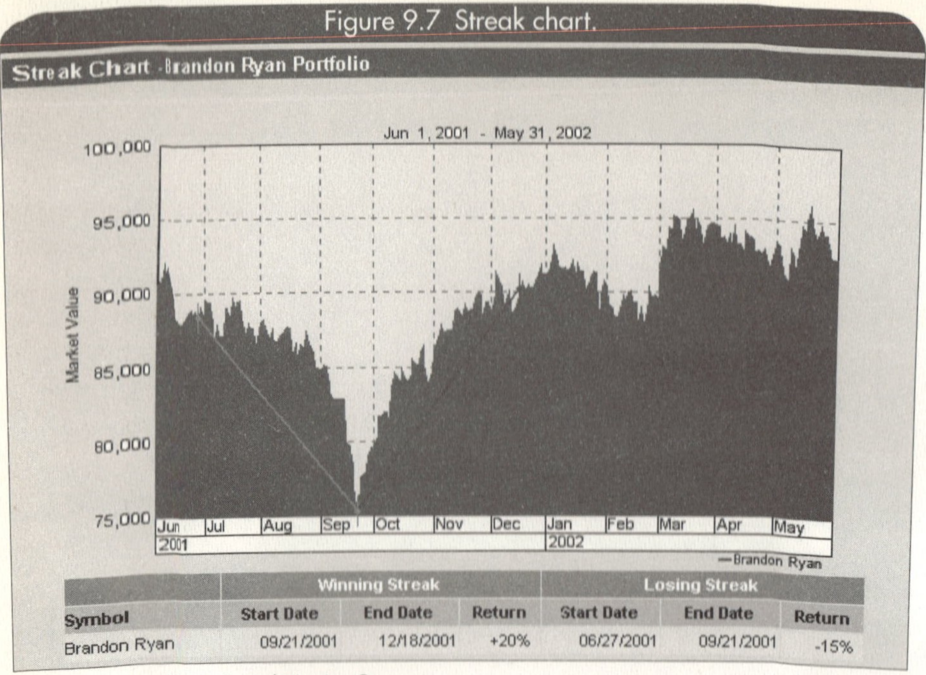

Figure 9.7 Streak chart.

Symbol	Winning Streak			Losing Streak		
	Start Date	End Date	Return	Start Date	End Date	Return
Brandon Ryan	09/21/2001	12/18/2001	+20%	06/27/2001	09/21/2001	-15%

Source: WealthBench, RiskMetrics Group.

market risk, which is always changing. The gray bars depict the extent to which our portfolio RiskGrade measurement varied over the course of a selected period. The darker gray bars within the range denote the frequency of the RiskGrade in that area. In general the majority of the darker bars will be in the vicinity of the average RiskGrade for the range period. In Figure 9.8, the average RiskGrade of the portfolio is 74. The darker bars indicate an increased number of RiskGrade measurements in the mid-70s.

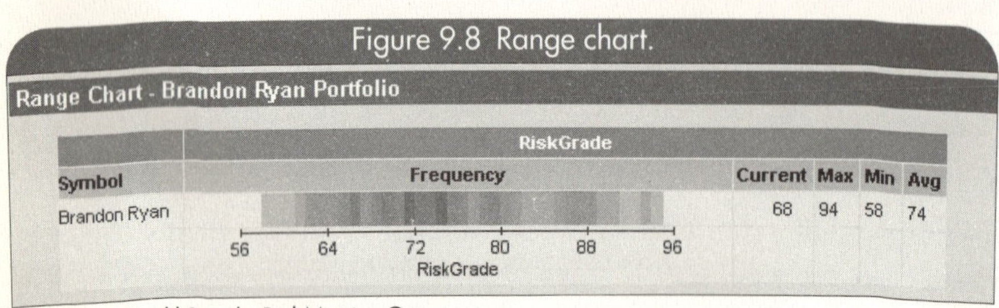

Figure 9.8 Range chart.

Symbol	Frequency	Current	Max	Min	Avg
Brandon Ryan		68	94	58	74

Source: WealthBench, RiskMetrics Group.

Risk-versus-Return Analysis of Portfolio Assets

The risk-versus-return chart shown in Figure 9.9 helps investors select opportunities that are attractive based on their risk-adjusted return. As investors, we can't expect to get anywhere if we avoid risk. Rather than avoiding risk entirely, we need to avoid taking poorly understood risks. The return analysis tools embedded in the RiskGrades service are designed to help you understand the risk-return trade-offs inherent in investment decisions.

Risk versus Return: The Basics

Assets that have a greater probability of loss are categorized as more risky than those with a lesser chance of loss. The objective of an advisor is to obtain the largest possible rate of return without placing a client's invested funds at more risk than is bearable. A common approach to evaluating a portfolio involves plotting its individual holdings on a risk and return basis. Each asset in the portfolio is placed with respect to its RiskGrade (x-axis) and return (y-axis) over a user-defined period of time. As a result, each asset falls into one of the four quadrants shown in Figure 9.9.

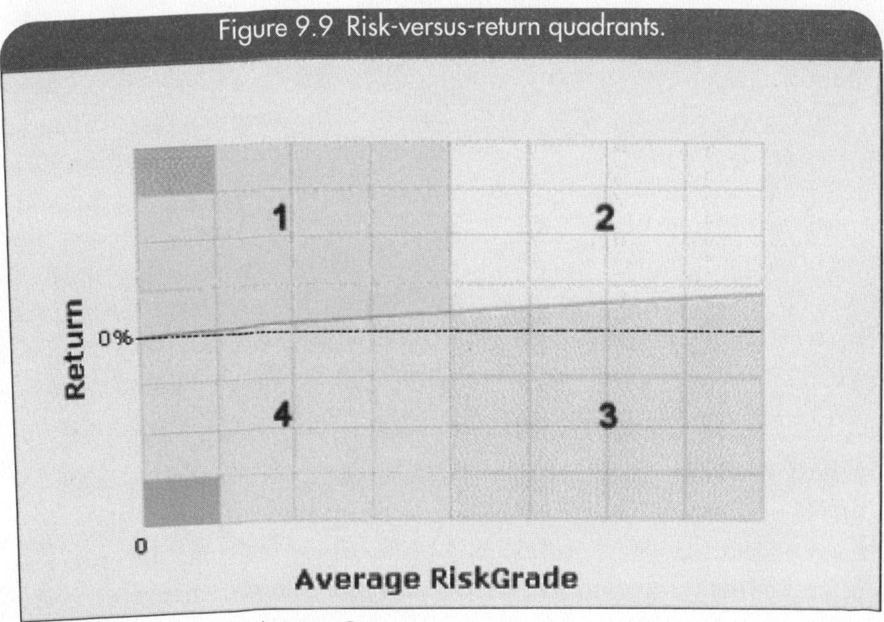

Source: WealthBench, RiskMetrics Group.

- Assets that fall into quadrants 1 and 2, or above the dotted line, are offering superior returns given the level of risk.

- Assets that fall below the dotted line, quadrants 3 and 4, are offering inferior returns given their level of risk.

- The most advantageous point on the chart is the dark rectangle in quadrant 1. This point represents maximum return for the minimum amount of risk.

- The most unfavorable point on the chart is the dark rectangle in quadrant 4. Assets in this space have such low volatility that they stand little chance of moving above the dotted line into positive returns (low return and low risk).

- The area between the horizontal dotted line and the angled solid line represents the risk premium demanded by investors as compensation for investing in assets with a higher RiskGrade measurement. As the incremental risk of an asset increases, investors should expect a corresponding increase in returns.

Risk-versus-Return Chart

Figure 9.10 plots each asset in a portfolio and highlights whether you're being offered superior or inferior returns for its given level of risk. Investors should keep in mind that an asset with a higher level of risk should always provide a greater amount of return.

In Figure 9.10, the area above the solid line implies that sufficient returns are being generated for the amount of risk taken. The area below the dotted line implies the opposite—that return is inadequate for the level of risk. At the time of our analysis, we saw that Commerce Bancorp, Inc. (CBH) was performing magnificently, up 28 percent for the year compared to the Citigroup (C), which was down −9 percent for the year. Cisco Systems (CSCO), on the other hand, was a double offender, as it had the highest RiskGrade measurement (341) and the lowest return (−22 percent).

ReturnGrade

Until now, we've focused on RiskGrade measurements, which show the degree of risk for your portfolio as a whole or for individual investments within it. Now it's time to take a look at another measurement that treats

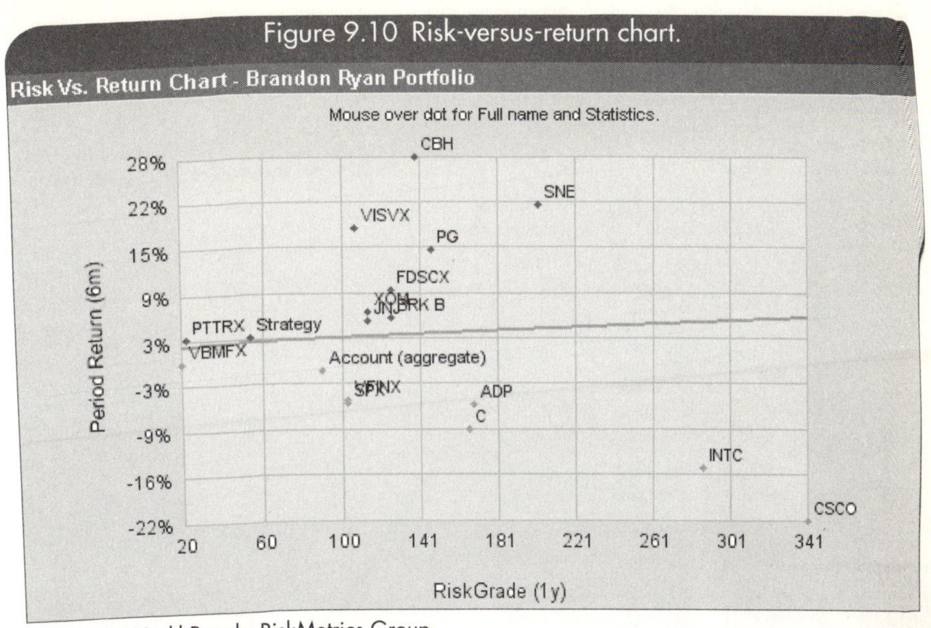

Figure 9.10 Risk-versus-return chart.

Source: WealthBench, RiskMetrics Group.

performance and risk together. It's called a ReturnGrade. A ReturnGrade is a risk-adjusted performance measure that helps you compare investments on both a risk and return basis.

As a case in point, open up just about any business publication today and you're likely to find an article ranking the top 10 mutual funds based solely on the returns they generated. Say, for example, that Fund A produced a 25 percent return and Fund B generated a 20 percent return. Most publications draw the errant conclusion that Fund A outperformed Fund B. But in order to judge any fund or asset properly, it's not enough to examine raw investment returns. Instead, we need to evaluate funds by taking into account the risks an investor may be exposed to and then measure the return. That's why we introduced ReturnGrade, a return measure adjusted for risk. ReturnGrade is a coefficient that reflects an asset's performance scaled for risk. As you can see in Table 9.1, a higher ReturnGrade implies a higher quality of return. No surprises in this portfolio. However, take a look at the leaders and laggards mutual fund table on our site and see how rankings based on ReturnGrades can really change the way you view some of your own mutual funds.

Table 9.1 ReturnGrade Table

Year-to-Date 25 Highest ReturnGrades in Small-Cap Value Funds (06/04/2002)

Rank	Return Rank	Ticker	Name	RiskGrade	ReturnGrade	Year-to-Date Return
1	2	RYSEX	Royce Fund: Royce Special Equity Fund; Investment Class	43	43.7	20.5
2	1	NISVX	RBB Fund, Inc: n/i Numeric Investors Small Cap Value Fund	71	40.0	21.3
3	3	PSCVX	Wells Fargo Funds Trust: Small Cap Value Fund; Institutional Class Shares	70	36.2	18.8
4	4	BRSIX	Bridgeway Fund, Inc: Ultra-Small Company Tax Advantage Portfolio	53	35.8	17.9
5	6	BRUSX	Bridgeway Fund Inc.: Bridgeway Ultra-Small Company Portfolio	60	32.3	16.3
6	10	FRMCX	Franklin Value Investors Trust: Franklin MicroCap Value Fund; Class A Shares	38	32.3	15.3
7	9	BABEX	Babson Enterprise Fund Inc.	53	31.0	15.8
8	5	HSCSX	Homestead Funds, Inc: Small Company Stock Fund	78	30.3	16.9
9	8	FMIWX	FMI Mutual Funds, Inc: FMI Woodland Small Capitalization Value Fund	70	29.9	15.9
10	7	SKSEX	Skyline Funds: Skyline Special Equities Portfolio	72	29.4	16.1

Source: WealthBench, RiskMetrics Group.

Look at the number 2 ranked fund on the list in Table 9.1, RBB Fund, Inc: n/i Numeric Investors Small Cap Value Fund (NISVX). This fund, with its 21.3 percent year-to-date return would have been ranked at the *top* of every list published by the traditional media. Not here. Our approach is to factor in risk as well as return. Taking a closer look at RBB Fund we see that the fund's RiskGrade is 71. On a return basis, RBB Fund surpassed our number 1 ranked fund (RYSEX) by 8 basis points, which is great, but after doing the math, you realize the fund took 40 percent more risk to achieve only a marginal difference in returns. With that type of risk premium attached to such a small incremental gain, it's clear why the Royce Fund is the top-rated fund.

A Graphical View of Portfolio Risk Measures

At the graphical view level, investors can observe their portfolios in a series of interactive charts—portfolio level, asset class level (Figure 9.11), and sector level (Figure 9.12).

Factor Analysis

Analyze your investment style against benchmark indices. Perform a factor analysis to explore your sector weightings and risk levels as well as your asset class weightings and risk levels.

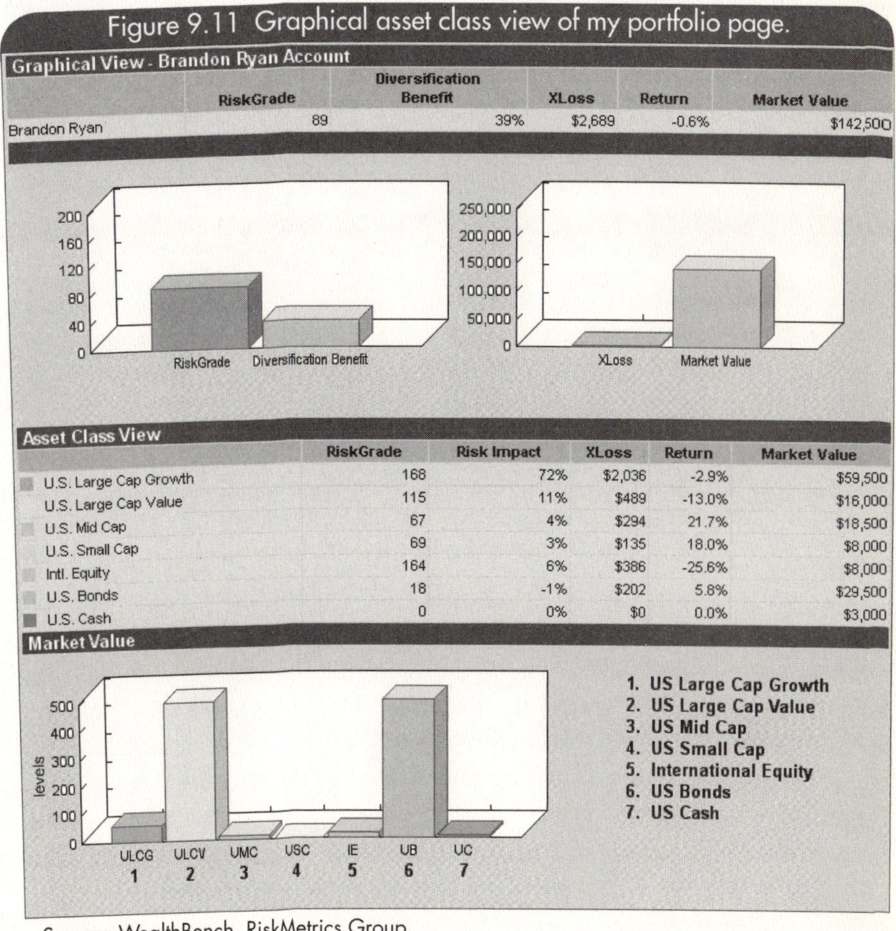

Asset Class View	RiskGrade	Risk Impact	XLoss	Return	Market Value
U.S. Large Cap Growth	168	72%	$2,036	-2.9%	$59,500
U.S. Large Cap Value	115	11%	$489	-13.0%	$16,000
U.S. Mid Cap	67	4%	$294	21.7%	$18,500
U.S. Small Cap	69	3%	$135	18.0%	$8,000
Intl. Equity	164	6%	$386	-25.6%	$8,000
U.S. Bonds	18	-1%	$202	5.8%	$29,500
U.S. Cash	0	0%	$0	0.0%	$3,000

Source: WealthBench, RiskMetrics Group.

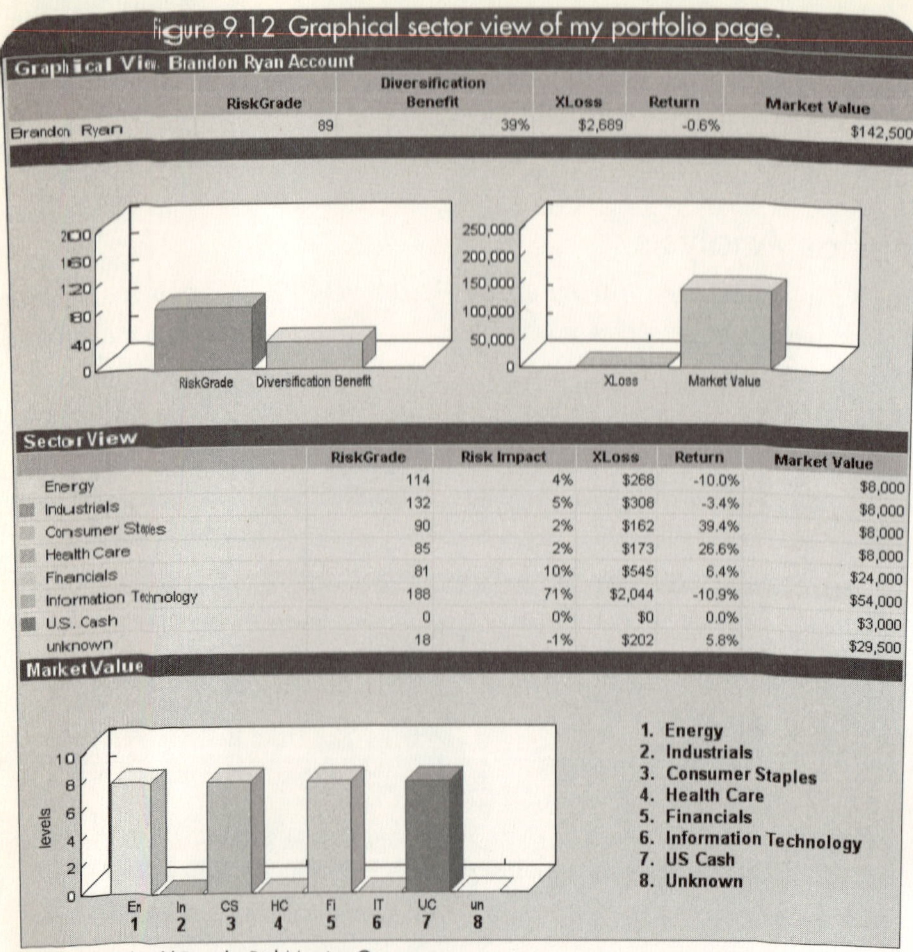

Sector View	RiskGrade	Risk Impact	XLoss	Return	Market Value
Energy	114	4%	$268	-10.0%	$8,000
Industrials	132	5%	$308	-3.4%	$8,000
Consumer Staples	90	2%	$162	39.4%	$8,000
Health Care	85	2%	$173	26.6%	$8,000
Financials	81	10%	$545	6.4%	$24,000
Information Technology	188	71%	$2,044	-10.9%	$54,000
U.S. Cash	0	0%	$0	0.0%	$3,000
unknown	18	-1%	$202	5.8%	$29,500

Source: WealthBench, RiskMetrics Group.

One question we're asked from time to time by mutual fund investors is, "How can I build a diversified portfolio when I don't know exactly where the fund managers are investing my money?"

It's a great question, and for those who don't know, the mutual fund industry is clouded in a veil of secrecy when it comes to disclosing current investments. As a result, scrutinizing fund-holding data is often very difficult. Current SEC rules mandate that mutual funds disclose holdings information only on a semiannual basis. The point in time when the data is released is not the most recent snapshot of the portfolio holdings. As a result, fund shareholders never receive the complete data that would help them adjust their own allocations to reduce overlap and maximize portfolio diversification.

Fund managers, on the other hand, contend that more frequent release of data will actually harm fund investors because it would spawn dishonest investment strategies like *front running* and *piggybacking*. According to the Investment Company Institute, in one scenario front-runners use advance knowledge to increase their position in a fund, thus driving up share prices. Conversely, front-runners can drive down the prices by selling their shares ahead of funds managers and clearing out the best bids.

To help resolve this investor dilemma, RiskMetrics has developed a pair of factor analysis tools—*sector analysis* and *asset class analysis*—based on the variance decomposition technique of econometrics.

Sector analysis is a simple method that explains the movement of your portfolio through the average value movement of each sector in the market. Sector analysis breaks down your portfolio into sectors and compares the holdings to a designated benchmark with respect to sector concentration and corresponding risk. Although designed for funds, sector analysis proves quite useful in analyzing individual equity portfolios as well. It is worth noting that the purpose of sector analysis is not to duplicate the actual sector weights, but rather to capture the relative impact of each sector in terms of risk and return on the fund (see Figure 9.13).

Later in the chapter, we explore sector analysis in more detail, including how to interpret the chart. For now we'll just include a quick breakdown analysis of Brandon Ryan's portfolio:

- *Consumer staples* is the most overweight sector compared to the S&P500 Index.
- *Consumer discretionary* is the most underweight sector compared to the S&P500 Index.
- *Information technology* is the most overexposed sector compared to the S&P 500 Index.
- *Consumer discretionary* is the most underexposed sector compared to the S&P 500 Index

The sector data used in RiskGrades and WealthBench service is the Global Industry Classification Standard (GICS)^{SM} developed by MSCI and Standard & Poor's to enable global and regional equity managers to ana-

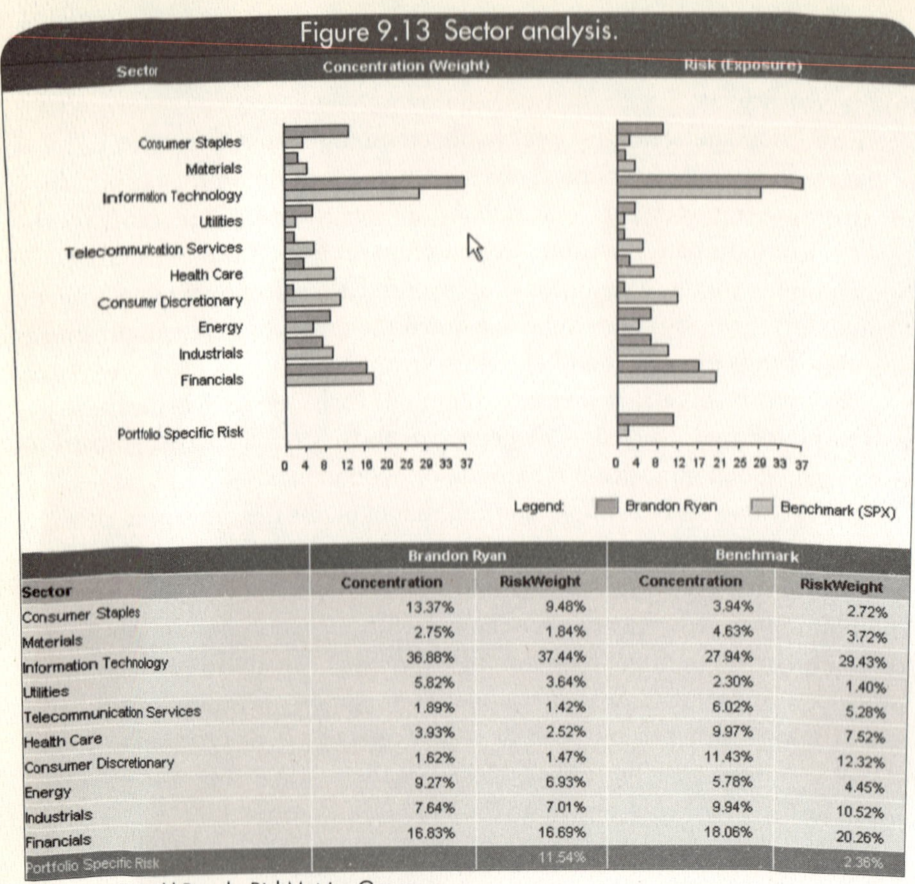

Sector	Brandon Ryan		Benchmark	
	Concentration	RiskWeight	Concentration	RiskWeight
Consumer Staples	13.37%	9.48%	3.94%	2.72%
Materials	2.75%	1.84%	4.63%	3.72%
Information Technology	36.88%	37.44%	27.94%	29.43%
Utilities	5.82%	3.64%	2.30%	1.40%
Telecommunication Services	1.89%	1.42%	6.02%	5.28%
Health Care	3.93%	2.52%	9.97%	7.52%
Consumer Discretionary	1.62%	1.47%	11.43%	12.32%
Energy	9.27%	6.93%	5.78%	4.45%
Industrials	7.64%	7.01%	9.94%	10.52%
Financials	16.83%	16.69%	18.06%	20.26%
Portfolio Specific Risk		11.54%		2.36%

Source: WealthBench, RiskMetrics Group.

lyze portfolio performance and test investment strategies based on sector measurement.[1] Following is a definition for each of the 10 GICS sectors:

Global Industry Classification Standard

Energy Sector. The GICS Energy Sector comprises companies whose businesses are dominated by the following activities: the construction or provision of oil rigs, drilling equipment, and other energy-related service and equipment, including seismic data collection; companies engaged in the exploration, production, marketing, refining, and/or transportation of oil or gas products.

Materials Sector. The GICS Materials Sector encompasses a wide range of commodity-related manufacturing industries. Included in this sector are companies that manufacture chemicals, construction materials, glass, paper, forest products, and related packaging products, and metals, minerals, and mining companies, including producers of steel.

Industrials Sector. The GICS Industrials Sector includes companies whose businesses are dominated by one of the following activities: the manufacture and distribution of capital goods, including aerospace and defense, construction, engineering and building products, electrical equipment, and industrial machinery; the provision of commercial services and supplies, including printing, data processing, employment, environmental, and office services. The provision of transportation services, including airlines, couriers, marine, road and rail, and transportation infrastructure.

Consumer Discretionary Sector. The GICS Consumer Discretionary Sector encompasses those industries that tend to be most sensitive to economic cycles. Its manufacturing segment includes automotive, household durable goods, textiles and apparel, and leisure equipment. The services segment includes hotels, restaurants, and other leisure facilities, media production and services, and consumer retailing.

Consumer Staples Sector. The GICS Consumer Staples Sector comprises companies whose businesses are less sensitive to economic cycles. It includes manufacturers and distributors of food, beverages, and tobacco and producers of nondurable household goods and personal products. It also includes food and drug retailing companies.

Health Care Sector. The GICS Health Care Sector encompasses two main industry groups. The first includes companies who manufacture health care equipment and supplies or provide health care–related services, including distributors of health care products, providers of basic health care services, and owners and operators of health care facilities and organizations. The second regroups companies primarily involved in the research, development, production, and marketing of pharmaceuticals and biotechnology products.

Financials Sector. The GICS Financials Sector contains companies involved in activities such as banking, consumer finance, investment banking and brokerage, asset management, insurance and investment, and real estate, including REITs.

Information Technology Sector. The GICS Information Technology Sector covers the following general areas: first, technology software and services, including companies that primarily develop software in various fields such as the Internet, applications, systems, and/or database management and companies that provide information technology consulting and services; second, technology hardware and equipment, including manufacturers and distributors of communications equipment, computers and peripherals, electronic equipment and related instruments, and semiconductor equipment and products.

Telecommunications Services Sector. The GICS Telecommunications Services Sector contains companies that provide communications services primarily through a fixed-line, cellular, wireless, high-bandwidth and/or fiber-optic cable network.

Utilities Sector. The GICS Utilities Sector encompasses those companies considered electric, gas, or water utilities or companies that operate as independent producers and/or distributors of power. This sector includes both nuclear and nonnuclear facilities.

Sector Spotlight Chart

Analyze risk in industrial sectors from around the world.

The sector spotlight offers international investors a flexible, easy-to-use tool for equity allocation and risk measurement. Based on MSCI's All Country Sectors data, the sector spotlight helps investors and advisors analyze what has or has not contributed to a portfolio's performance so that you can evaluate and refine the investment strategies.

Figure 9.14 illustrates the range of RiskGrades for each equity sector in the United States. Users have an option of viewing 10 different countries. The gray bars in the sector spotlight highlight the distribution of RiskGrades over the time period across individual sectors. The individual bars within the range will become darker each time a specific RiskGrade is repeated. The darker area of the box indicates more time spent at that RiskGrade level by a given sector.

MSCI Data Model

The methodology is as follows: MSCI All Country Sectors provides an index-level breakdown of the MSCI indices into sectors. To construct an

Figure 9.14 Sector spotlight for the United States.

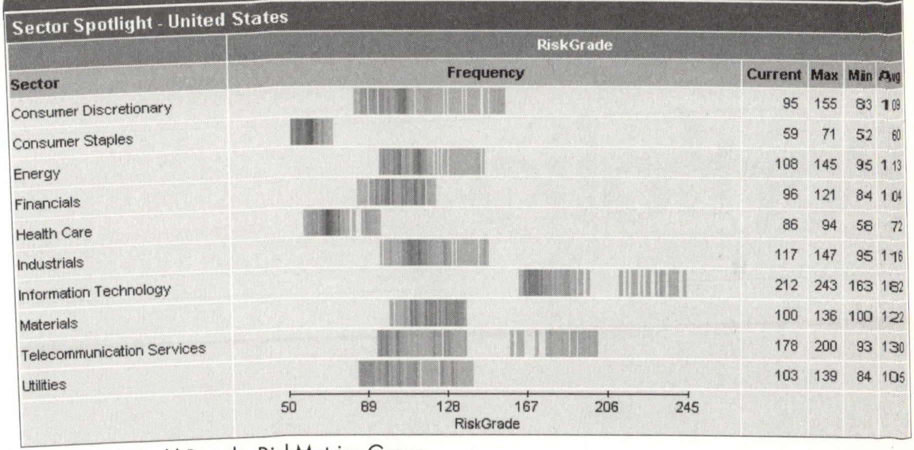

Sector	RiskGrade Frequency	Current	Max	Min	Avg
Consumer Discretionary		95	155	83	109
Consumer Staples		59	71	52	60
Energy		108	145	95	113
Financials		96	121	84	104
Health Care		86	94	58	72
Industrials		117	147	95	116
Information Technology		212	243	163	182
Materials		100	136	100	122
Telecommunication Services		178	200	93	130
Utilities		103	139	84	105

RiskGrade: 50   89   128   167   206   245

Source: WealthBench, RiskMetrics Group.

MSCI Country Index, every listed security in the market is identified, and data on its price, outstanding shares, significant owners, free float, and monthly trading volume are collected. The securities are then sorted by industry group, and stocks are selected, targeting 60 percent coverage of market capitalization.

Summary: The Importance of Portfolio Risk Analysis

Risk measurement is an essential step in the cycle of investing. The RiskGrades' features highlighted in this chapter teach investors how to quantify risk. Without this capacity, you cannot be fully aware of potential outcomes and the likelihood of winning or losing. Even though you may have an intuition about individual stocks, it is difficult to visualize how different investments are likely to move together without portfolio risk analysis. The RiskGrades service synthesizes vast amounts of historical information to help you make better decisions about the future.

CHAPTER 10

This Old Portfolio

Television today is populated by numerous do-it-yourself help programs. The programs cover a wide spectrum of human interest. Wave the remote control, and Martha Stewart is waiting to offer help in the garden. Interested in gourmet? Let's check on the *Iron Chefs* of Japan. Our favorite is the classic *This Old House*, which dedicates every episode to a variety of home improvement repairs. The show tackles house restorations, both large and small, from a Georgian Revival in Massachusetts to a Mediterranean bungalow in West Palm Beach. The appeal of the show stems from host Steve Thomas's role as the ultimate home enthusiast. His good nature, coupled with his ability to demystify the complex technical, financial, and often-emotional aspects of home renovation has endeared him to homeowners across America. Each week the viewer sees the newest products and tools, receives tips from the pros, and learns the latest techniques for doing the job right. Even a large project like renovating a kitchen is made to look fairly trouble-free. Using a reciprocating saw, a belt sander, and a pipe wrench never looked so easy. In fact, an entire bathroom is thoroughly overhauled in less than 30 minutes. Avid viewers have learned many lessons over the years, gaining valuable insights into craftsmanship, fine design, and home restoration. Successful restorations do not start with a hammer, but with a pencil and eraser during the planning stage ... just like investing.

Like most old homes, our old and existing portfolios also require attention or we risk having them fall into a state of disrepair. Some portfolios
will be in worse shape than others, but it's likely that everyone's would benefit from a proper inspection and a little preventive maintenance. However,
without the right tools and guidance, even the most experienced investors
will find it difficult to locate all the problem areas. To be successful, you
first need to know where to look, which diagnostic tools to use, what to be
on the lookout for and, of course, how to react if trouble is spotted. In this
chapter, we're going to address each of these points by introducing you to
a series of sophisticated portfolio simulation tools available within the
WealthBench service.

Portfolio Simulations: Stress Testing and What-If Analysis

First we're going to look at stress testing, a process of determining the
potential vulnerability of a portfolio when confronted with extreme or
abnormal market conditions.

Stress Testing

Stress testing consists of generating worst-case scenarios and then revaluing the portfolio under those stressed conditions. We recommend stress
testing because risk measurements, RiskGrades and XLoss included, work
well for estimating risk during normal market conditions but cannot predict the occasional unexpected crises that result in an extreme market
shock. Events such as natural disasters, wars, and political crises still lie
beyond the reach of statistical forecasting. To address this issue, we've
developed a series of stress-testing scenarios to run against your portfolio.

An easy way to grasp the concept of stress testing is to conjure up the
image of stress-testing a home you're contemplating buying. As part of the
due diligence of buying a home, you as the prospective buyer hire a certi-
fied engineer to perform a top-to-bottom assessment of the structural
soundness of the home. The engineer thoroughly evaluates everything—
inspecting the plumbing, heating, air-conditioning, and electrical systems,
checking for wood-destroying insects, searching for underground storage
tanks. After spending most of the day at the house, your inspector provides
a report.

Is that report 100 percent accurate? Does it include everything you need to know about the house?

The answer is no. In almost all cases, the inspection is performed under normal weather conditions. In reality, the best time to inspect a home (for the benefit of the prospective homeowner) is during a state of emergency. And not just one emergency or disaster but a succession of them. Let's see how the foundation and roof hold up through historical weather events: the blizzard of 1968, the flood of 1973, and the Mount Saint Helens volcano eruption of 1980. Running a stress test would measure and report the damage to the home caused by each of these events and recalculate the home's value accordingly.

In WealthBench, if none of the predefined historical events satisfy what you're looking for, you can create your own scenario by individually adjusting the parameters. In the preceding examples, a home buyer could adjust the severity of the weather conditions by increasing "feet of snow" or "velocity of the hurricane" or "proximity to Mount Saint Helens volcano." The challenge with stress testing is to run your portfolio against a probabilistic scenario. Otherwise, you may react defensively to a condition that is not likely to affect your portfolio in any meaningful way. For example, if you live in New York City, stress-testing your home against volcanic eruptions would be of no real benefit.

Now that you understand the basics behind stress testing, let's draw our attention back to our portfolios and the markets. The home inspection is the equivalent to the WealthBench tools explained in Chapter 9. In normal market conditions, or 95 percent of the time, RiskGrades will provide you with a very reliable approximation of your portfolio's risk. Stress tests are designed to estimate potential monetary losses in abnormal markets the other 5 percent of the time. But don't be lulled into complacency. Historical analysis of the markets shows that extreme market moves, beyond 3 standard deviations, occur far more frequently than we would like to believe. For this reason, professional risk managers and banking regulators like the Federal Reserve view regular stress testing as an indispensable tool. On the RiskGrades event risk simulations page (Figure 10.1), we offer investors the option of two stress-test simulation tools: *historical events* and *user-defined events*.

In an event risk simulation, investors can gauge how the values of their current portfolios would likely change under distressed financial conditions. This in turn allows investment advisors to determine whether a portfolio's exposure to risk is in line with their client's tolerance for risk. Select

Figure 10.1 Select a historical event against which to stress-test.

Historical Event Risk							As of 06/07/02
Shock Names	Select	S&P	NASDAQ	FTSE	NIKKEI	JPY	GBP
Black Monday	⊙	-20.5%	-13.4%	-10.8%	-2.4%	0.0%	-0.5%
Gulf War	○	-10.4%	-13.1%	-7.9%	-16.8%	-2.1%	-3.4%
Euro Crisis	○	-2%	-0.6%	7.8%	-3.2%	-4.5%	8.1%
Mexican Peso Crisis	○	1.9%	4.3%	-3.4%	-8.4%	-0.4%	-2.2%
Asian Crisis	○	-6.9%	-7.2%	-2.6%	-1.9%	-0.2%	-1.8%
Russian Crisis	○	-12.9%	-23.5%	-16.8%	-13.5%	-17.6%	-5.5%
Tech-Wreck	○	-11.2%	-33.1%	-8.3%	2.4%	-2.2%	0.3%
September 11th	○	-11.7%	-16.1%	-11.9%	-6.3%	3.7%	-0.1%

Source: WealthBench, RiskMetrics Group.

an event from the list of major financial crises shown in Figure 10.1, and, in effect, your portfolio will relive the traumatic experience. RiskGrades will calculate the results in only a few seconds, as shown in Figure 10.2.

As you would expect, the extreme volatility inherent in reliving Black Monday ravages our portfolio. Were you prepared for the results? Our portfolio suffered a −12 percent loss. Although our original portfolio XLoss measurement provided a reasonable indication of a bad day (−$1,533), a stress test offers a more complete picture of how our portfolios can be devastated by a crash on the magnitude of Black Monday 1987. In this case, the owner of the Brandon Ryan portfolio can expect to lose $10,974.

In the user-defined simulation feature, event risk can be personalized to reflect specific assumptions about individual stock prices, interest rates, and foreign currency rates. For example, investors may be curious about how a sudden shock in the equity markets and a simultaneous flight-to-safety rally in long-term Treasury yields would ripple through a portfolio. With event risk, investors have the ability to modify key market indicators like the S&P 500 Index and the 10-year Treasury note to replicate a distressed or even a more favorable financial environment. Given the changes to the market backdrop, the application simulates how our current holdings would react.

Equity Shocks

To simulate how a shock in the equity markets would affect your portfolio, investors have the option of creating a personalized "equity stress" event by shocking an individual stock or stock indices. In WealthBench, equity shocks are expressed in percentages. In Figure 10.3, a user can input a negative number and it will simulate the impact on your portfolio's profit and

Figure 10.2 Historical event risk results.

Black Monday (Oct.16, 1987 - Oct.19,1987) **As of 06/07/02**

Assumptions:

- S&P500 index depreciated by 20.5%
- Nasdaq index depreciated by 13.4%
- FTSE 100 index depreciated by 10.8%
- Nikei index depreciated by 2.4%
- JPY appreciated by 0.0%
- GBP depreciated by 0.5%

Results:

- The "Brandon Ryan-taxable" Portfolio would have decreased by $10,974.79 (-12%)

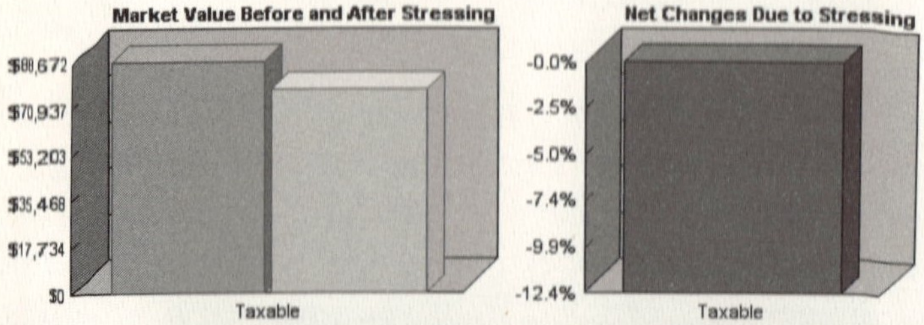

Detail View By Instrument

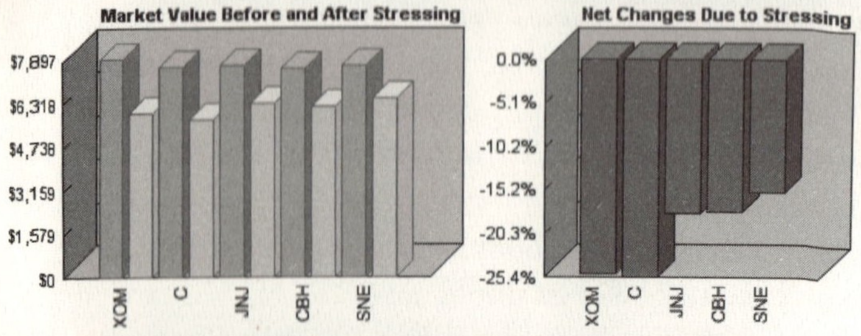

	Before	After		
Name	**Market Value**	**Change**	**Market Value**	**% Change**
XOM	$7,897	-$1,980	$5,917	-25%
C	$7,596	-$1,929	$5,666	-25%
JNJ	$7,603	-$1,366	$6,236	-17%
CBH	$7,498	-$1,345	$6,152	-17%
SNE	$7,640	-$1,196	$6,444	-15%
PG	$7,981	-$1,166	$6,814	-14%
FDSCX	$7,717	-$1,105	$6,612	-14%
ADP	$7,858	-$675	$7,183	-8%
BRK B	$8,016	-$315	$7,700	-3%
INTC	$6,372	-$23	$6,348	0%
USD	$2,500	$0	$2,500	0%
PTTRX	$9,990	$129	$10,119	1%
TOTAL:	$88,668	(-$10,974)	$77,691	(-12%)

Source: WealthBench, RiskMetrics Group.

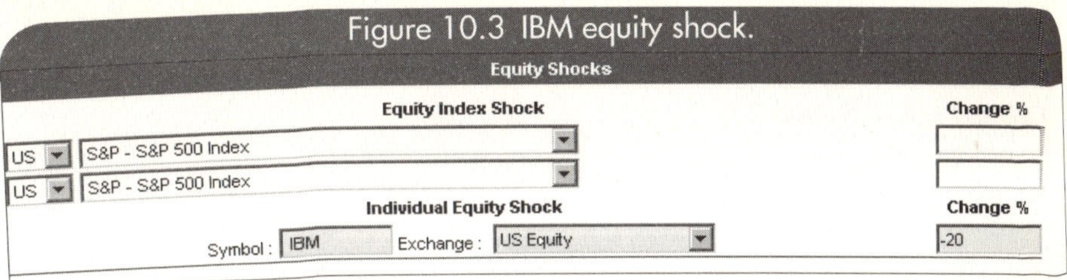

Figure 10.3 IBM equity shock.

Source: WealthBench, RiskMetrics Group.

loss due to the adverse move in the specific stock or the index. In this stress test we're going to gauge the impact of a 20 percent drop in value of IBM stock on our portfolio.

For an individual equity shock to be informative, it's not a necessity that your portfolio holds the security you are shocking. RiskGrades calculates how the negative move in that security will correlate with your other holdings. For example, because our test portfolio is relatively overweighted in the information technology sector, an announcement from IBM that it will miss its earning estimates by a wide margin will have a significant impact on the portfolio. By how much?—That is the question.

In Figure 10.4, we can see the dramatic impact on our portfolio's profit and loss when IBM falls 20 percent. Our information technology sector fell 23 percent as a whole. Our total portfolio fell 8 percent. Can you live with

Figure 10.4 IBM equity shock results.

	Before		After	
Sector	**Market Value**	**Change**	**Market Value**	**% Change**
Information Technology	$21,730	-$5,179	$16,551	-23%
Industrials	$7,858	-$1,334	$6,523	-16%
Financials	$23,110	-$993	$22,116	-4%
U.S. Cash	$2,500	$0	$2,500	0%
Energy	$7,897	$117	$8,015	1%
Unclassified	$9,990	$187	$10,178	1%
Consumer Staples	$7,981	$200	$8,181	2%
Health Care	$7,603	$236	$7,840	3%
Total	**$88,669**	**(-$6,766)**	**$81,904**	**8%**

Source: WealthBench, RiskMetrics Group.

that? Or should you contemplate making a change? Later in this chapter we will test several ways to potentially mitigate some of your simulated losses using the what-if analysis.

Interest Rate Shocks

In addition to moves in the equity markets, investors can use stress testing to gauge the vulnerability of their portfolios to interest rate risk. Doing this will help investors structure immunization strategies to changes in rates.

When interest rates rise, the price of a bond falls. Issuers of new bonds will have to pay higher coupon rates or issue the bonds at a discount. Existing bonds will fall in price, and the *yield* (the interest rate adjusted for changes in the price) will rise until it becomes competitive.

Perhaps a simple example can clarify this process. Suppose you have a one-year bond with a face value of $100 that pays one coupon of 5 percent interest, or $5, in one year. This bond has a yield of 5 percent. If the general rate of interest rises to, say, to 6 percent, no one could issue a bond with a 5 percent coupon at its full face value. Not only that, but the price of the existing bond must fall. Otherwise, the investor could sell it at face value and buy a new bond that gives him or her $6 instead of $5 at the end of one year. The existing bond's price must fall to about $99 so it, too, yields 6 percent.

The rise in interest rates means that any bond investor who currently owns a bond suffers a capital loss (i.e., a loss in the market value of the security), because he or she owns a security that yields 5 percent rather than 6 percent.

By the same logic, bond prices rise if interest rates fall. Investors with bonds yielding 5 percent will benefit if rates fall to 4 percent because they now own an investment that yields 1 percent above the market rates. Therefore, we can say that interest rates and bonds have an inverse relationship: When one goes up, the other goes down, and vice versa.

In Figure 10.5 investors can manipulate yield curves to create stress scenarios that will help them determine suitable portfolio immunization strategies to avoid being stung by changing interest rates.

Currency Rate Shocks

As more investors invest internationally, currency risk is a major factor to consider. What would be the consequences to your portfolio if the value of the yen falls against the dollar? When you invest in a foreign market, and

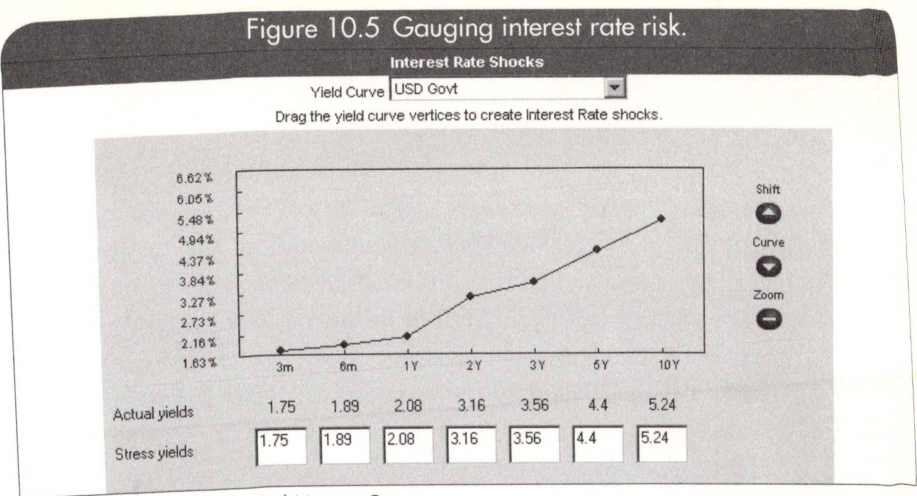

Source: WealthBench, RiskMetrics Group.

your investment is denominated in a foreign currency, changes in the value of that currency against the U.S. dollar could add to the volatility of your investment.

In Figure 10.6, when the U.S. dollar strengthens 20 percent against the yen, our investment in Sony potentially decreases in value by 23 percent. As a result, even if our Sony investment performs well, currency fluctuations

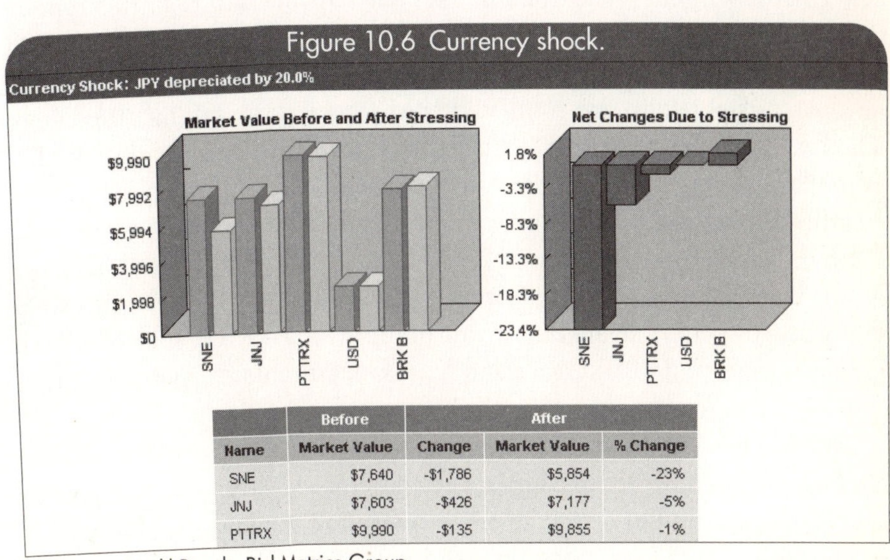

Name	Before		After	
	Market Value	Change	Market Value	% Change
SNE	$7,640	-$1,786	$5,854	-23%
JNJ	$7,603	-$426	$7,177	-5%
PTTRX	$9,990	-$135	$9,855	-1%

Source: WealthBench, RiskMetrics Group.

can have a negative effect on stock prices. To monitor your exposure to foreign exchange risk, create similar currency rate shocks.

What-If Analysis

As the term implies, *what-if analysis* is intended to illustrate how specific decisions actually affect the performance of our portfolios. The what-if functionality is similar to event risk in that potential consequences of changes to a portfolio can be crystallized even without following through with the real decision. Whereas event risk makes it possible to stress external market factors on current holdings, what-if analysis permits investors to see the implications of changes made to current positions. As such, it's a valuable tool to screen potential new positions. We can picture the impact of changes before actually making a trade. In effect, this functionality permits users to take a portfolio out for a spin before actually taking it out of the showroom.

Apart from employing what-if analysis to test for current imbalances, investors can also use it to analyze the effectiveness of new positions. What-if analysis can be particularly useful as a safeguard against anticipated events. Consider our earlier equity shock simulation (Figure 10.4). CNBC reports on speculation that IBM is unexpectedly about to announce changes in its first-quarter earnings estimates—it appears the company will report a loss rather than a gain and miss the quarter by 35 cents. If the rumor is true, then market participants will read this type of earnings surprise very negatively, not only on the future prospects of IBM but on the technology sector as a whole. To gauge the effect of this bad news on our portfolio, we simulated IBM's stock price falling 20 percent. The results of the stress test indicated our portfolio could potentially fall as much as 8 percent, or $6,766. Uncomfortable with a sudden loss of this magnitude, we contemplate preventive steps. In the what-if scenario in Figure 10.7, we consider minimizing our exposure to the tech sector by selling half our most volatile position, Intel (RiskGrade 370), and investing the proceeds into a diversified giant, Philip Morris (MO). Our goal is to reduce our portfolio RiskGrade and XLoss measurements, maintain diversification, and increase our portfolio's expected return.

As the charts in Figure 10.7 illustrate, selling 145 shares of Intel and purchasing 57 shares of Philip Morris with the proceeds decreases our portfolio's RiskGrade by 14 percent, to 63. As a result of removing volatility from our portfolio, our XLoss measurement drops 10 percent, or −$153, to a new

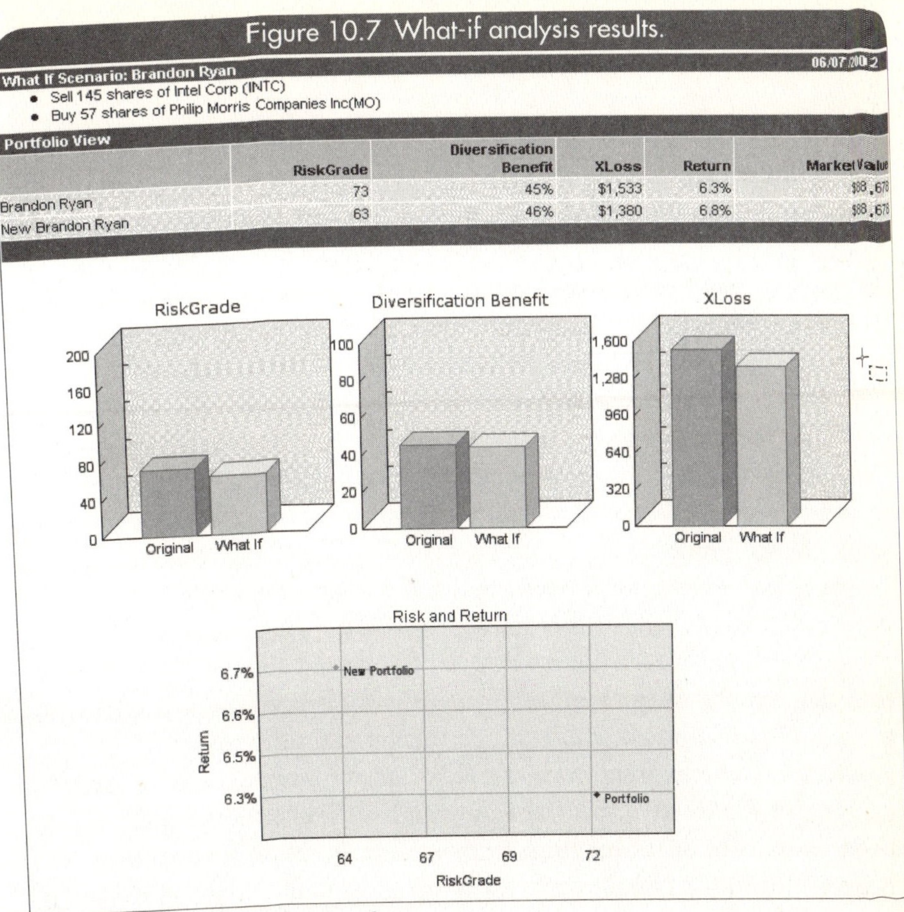

Source: WealthBench, RiskMetrics Group.

total of $1,380. We have also slightly increased our diversification benefit and our expected return. It's feasible to believe that adding Philip Morris to the new asset mix will achieve a greater portfolio return with less risk.

What if an investor doesn't know how to best rebalance his or her existing assets to reduce risk? In the preceding case, to reduce our risk we sold off half our Intel position in favor of Philip Morris. But what if an investor isn't quite sure which securities to retain, or even how many? Since launching RiskGrades in May of 2000, the majority of investors we speak with share these feelings of uncertainty. After all, these are not easy questions. To help answer them, we've developed a series of WealthBench tools that use quantitative measures to obtain a balance between risk and reward suitable for each individual investor. Before we demonstrate some of the tools that will help you rebalance your portfolio, let's demonstrate why it's important you rebalance your portfolio.

Rebalancing Your Portfolio

Successful investing starts with a sound, diversified asset allocation plan—one that balances your long-term financial goals and tolerance for assuming risk. As we learned in Chapter 6, studies have shown that asset allocation is the single most important factor in determining your portfolio's future returns. The reason being, investors who carefully allocate their holdings across stocks, bonds, and cash reduce their portfolio volatility and receive the benefits of diversification in the form of stabilized returns.

However, it's important to remember that creating an allocation strategy is not a one-time event, but rather an ongoing process. That's because things change—market fluctuations, economic conditions, your financial objectives, and even your attitude about risk. Left unattended, your original risk allocations will drift from your carefully constructed plan for the future. Over time, asset allocations can become unbalanced, as some grow faster than others. Assets that perform very well become overweight, while others that perform less well become underweight. Investors who do not rebalance may be exposed to more risk than they are willing to take. For example, in Figure 10.8, we trace how market fluctuations cause an asset allocation plan to drift over time. In this example, the investor started with an asset allocation of 80 percent stocks and 20 percent bonds on December 31, 1992. Assuming the investor did not rebalance, the portfolio would have an asset allocation four years later of 85 percent stocks and 15 percent bonds; by the end of 1999 the allocation would be 91 percent stocks and only 9 percent bonds due to sharp increases in stock returns after 1996. Then, at just the wrong time, while the portfolio risk was at its highest, the

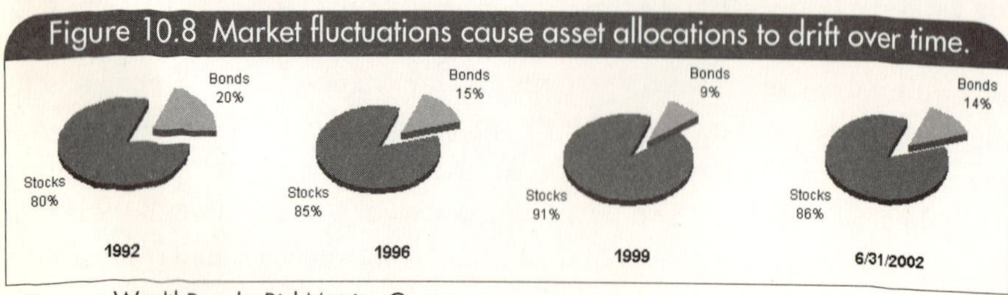

Source: WealthBench, RiskMetrics Group.

stock market imploded, and our investor was blitzed by double-digit negative returns in 2000, 2001, and 2002—precisely the period when the bond market was returning solid annual returns. In the short run, these changes may not significantly impact your plan, but over the long run, changes in asset allocation can leave your plan significantly overexposed to risk that could potentially derail your plans for the future.

Onward

Portfolio simulation tools like event risk and what-if analysis relieve some of the headaches that come with financial planning, but they cannot eliminate the pains altogether. Accordingly, we see the primary purpose of these tools as a frame of reference and not as an end solution. The value added comes in the form of a relative appraisal that responds scientifically to the market rather than to the noise it generates.

Much progress has been made on the frontier of risk analysis. As we have demonstrated, putting sophisticated tools like RiskGrades and WealthBench in the hands of the public allows advisors and investors to intelligently align personal return objectives with tolerance for risk. Although risk factors have long been available in some format, it is only recently that investors have been offered tools as practical and robust. Previously deprived of these tools, investors have been largely kept in the dark about the extent to which they can control and improve their overall risk-return profiles. As a result, investors have been unable to size up risk on a timely basis, which has caused them to be more reactive than forward-thinking. We believe that regularly monitoring risk can divulge unusual shifts in the foundation of your portfolio and, if read correctly, foretell dramatic events ahead. With RiskGrades, and now the WealthBench service, early warnings can caution investors before the actual storm hits.

Now that you are well versed on the full suite of tools comprising our services, we invite you to log on to the site and begin managing your risk and creating wealth today. We have included for your reference a complete strategic investment analysis to demonstrate how effective the two are when planning for your financial futures. Please see the appendix.

CHAPTER 11

The Final Frontier

In late 1999, critics of Warren Buffett were labeling him a dinosaur. As technology companies soared, giddy investors were seeing the value of their portfolios reach new highs on a weekly, if not daily, basis. Meanwhile, holders of Berkshire Hathaway were seeing red. From a high of $80,900 per share set in June 1998, Berkshire Hathaway steadily fell, to as low as $40,800 by March 2000.

Even as shares in his conglomerate holding company were being shunned in favor of new-economy stocks, Buffett adamantly refused to participate in the technology game. In his customary plain language, he admitted he didn't "get" technology and would not be goaded into something he didn't understand. The future cash flows of these new era companies, he claimed, were just too difficult to predict. He remained steadfastly focused on value, even as many of his long-standing fans suggested his time in the sun had elapsed. Surely he was missing a fundamental shift in the economic landscape: the birth of the Internet and the wondrous implications of technology. Forget the fact that his Berkshire Hathaway had provided long-term investors with astounding average annual gains of 23 percent for almost three and a half decades, beating the S&P 500 in all but four years during this period (1965 to 2001). The Oracle of Omaha, with one of the finest investment records in history, had apparently lost his Midas touch.

Fast-forward to early 2001. Buffett himself acknowledges that his stock was a short-seller's dream at the time. As it turns out, however, the decline in Berkshire shares was a grand opportunity to buy into one of the premier U.S. companies on the cheap. Berkshire Hathaway stormed back in late 2000, up nearly 27 percent in a year when the three major equity indices, S&P, Dow, and the Nasdaq, fell −6.18, −10.15, and −39.29 percent, respectively. Ironically, the cruel spring of 2000 had given way to a prosperous autumn and winter. Buffett's resilience and insistence on sticking with his value-oriented investment style had proven his critics wrong.

Reviewing Warren Buffett's fabled investment success is a lot like stargazing. It is easy to sit back and be awestruck by the wonders of Berkshire Hathaway's incredible performance over the years. After all, during the period 1964 through 2000, the company outperformed the S&P 500 by 190,194 percent![1] When examining Buffett's record, it's natural to ponder, "If only I had ..." But let us look at the keys to his success. First, he has a clearly defined objective. His stated goal is to produce superior long-term returns. He is undeterred by short-term losses such as those he saw in early 2000, and he painstakingly sticks to his overall goal of long-term performance. Second, he remains disciplined in his investing style. He has long espoused "value investing," and despite the incredible underperformance of so-called value stocks during the dot-com frenzy and significant pressure from peers, shareholders, and the media, he has stuck to his approach. Third, he invests in what he understands and avoids what he doesn't. Even as technology stocks soared, he avoided the stock market darlings because, as he himself said, he "didn't understand them." Fourth, he continues to manage a well-diversified portfolio made up of everything from lessors of private jets to candy stores, insurance, soda pop, furniture, newspapers, and cartoons. Finally, he understands not only the potential return of his assets, but also their risk. In fact his holding company, Berkshire Hathaway, is primarily an insurance company whose main line of business is the accurate assessment of risk.

In the end, we find ourselves with the same principles we outlined in the beginning: Define your objectives; remain disciplined; understand diversification and risk. These are the keys to successful financial investing.

Next Steps

By this time you have surely noticed that this book does not include an optimal portfolio of stocks, funds, and bonds designed especially for you and your financial situation. We have not picked 10 stocks to hold in 2003 or outlined an option trading strategy to guarantee financial success. We will leave that to the monthly magazines, the Wall Street analysts, and the TV prognosticators. Instead, we have given you a guide for building and monitoring your own investment portfolio. Much of the discussion has been at a high level, describing the workings of financial markets, the power of diversification, and the tools like RiskGrades and WealthBench that give you, the individual investor, access to the same technology and information used by the professionals. In conclusion, we would like to outline a few practical steps that will allow you to close this book and become your own successful investor.

Step 1

Decide what you are trying to get out of investing. This is the personal side of setting an objective. Sure, we all want to become rich. But investing is not about becoming wealthy. It is about achieving your financial goals. Are you investing for fun? For a short-term gain? To be part of the action? Are you investing to have money for your children's education? A second house? To retire two years earlier? The answer to these questions should lead you to an investment strategy. This is the hardest part of investing and should not be taken lightly. Take the time to think through your financial goals, to evaluate your current and expected financial situation, and perhaps to talk to a financial professional. This strategy should guide every investment decision you make.

Step 2

Once you have a strategy, stick to it. Follow it. Write it down. Don't let the market, the media, or your friends coax you into straying from a prudent strategy. Think about what kind of investments are appropriate for your particular strategy. If you are investing for short-term gains, then IPOs, momentum stocks, and options may be investments you should examine. On the other hand, if you are investing for the long term, then established mutual funds, index funds, and a mix of well-established individual stocks and high-grade bonds may make sense. Long-term investors should not be checking up on their portfolios every hour of every day, whereas short-term investors should monitor their portfolios often.

Step 3

Once you have determined the kinds of investments you should be considering, learn about the different choices among those investments. If you are
looking at funds, understand the fund's investment strategy, its benchmark,
its track record, and its fees. If you are looking at individual stocks, invest
only in companies whose business you understand—factors that might make
them successful and risks that might make them fail. Some of the best investments are companies that you (or your company or your family) do business
with, businesses that you have been pleased and satisfied with. All too often
we hear that investors don't even know what the companies they have
invested in do, let alone what might make them successful. Don't fall into the
investment trap of buying recommended funds or stocks without a thorough
understanding of their fundamentals. If you don't have the time or interest to
learn about various investment opportunities, perhaps you should turn to a
financial advisor or to a group of well-managed mutual funds.

Step 4

As you start to choose particular investments, make sure that you diversify.
A well-diversified portfolio experiences a broad counterbalancing effect
between negative and positive moves that leads to steady returns, on average, as opposed to wild day-to-day swings. We can't overemphasize how
important this is to your investment success. Because creating a well-
diversified portfolio is often difficult to achieve, especially if you invest
only in assets you fully understand (as suggested in step 3), we often suggest professional help, either by consulting a financial planner or by investing in mutual funds. Although it might be appropriate for you to invest in a
handful of individual equities you understand from a sector you know,
consider balancing those investments with a group of mutual funds that
specialize in alternative sectors or industries. The optimal level of diversification is difficult to measure, though you can use RiskGrades and
WealthBench tools to measure the diversification of your own portfolio of
investments and to determine how a new investment may potentially affect
that diversification. You may be surprised to learn which investments add
risk to a portfolio and which ones subtract risk. In addition, it is important
to note that diversification changes over time and that you need to monitor
your portfolio on a regular basis.

Step 5

As your portfolio begins to take shape, know how much risk you are taking. Before you make your first purchase, use RiskGrades to accurately measure and monitor the potential risk of those investments. Make sure that your expected returns are appropriate for the risks you are about to take and that the pleasure of this year's returns will not be wiped out by next year's losses. Before making investment decisions based on historical returns or recommended lists, know the risk of the investment, on both a stand-alone and a portfolio basis. An attractive investment for one person's portfolio may not be for another's. Make sure you can stomach the risks of the investments that you are making. Look at the XLoss of your portfolio. You do not want to be forced to sell during a down market because the portfolio has lost more money than you can afford to lose. Markets do not go straight up. In all probability, you will lose money in the short term, because no one buys at the lowest price every time. Knowing at the outset how much money you can expect to lose will enhance the chances of your weathering short-term losses and achieving long-term gains.

A Final Word

Finally, it is important to realize that financial investing is an ongoing process. It is not an activity to be taken up and completed in one weekend, like your tax return. Instead, it needs careful nurturing and monitoring. It is, as we say at RiskMetrics, a living plan. Although your overall strategy should rarely change, many other aspects of your investments (e.g., your risk, your diversification) will definitely move as the markets move. The frequency of your active involvement should reflect your investment horizon, your goals, and the markets themselves. As we have noted, the overall risk of the Nasdaq increased almost fivefold in the past five years, clearly impacting even the longest-term investors. There is no single correct answer to how often you should rebalance an investment portfolio, but you need to have the information to understand the changes that occur with the natural ups and downs of market performance—and to marry that with the changes naturally occurring in your own financial situation.

These are the keys to creating wealth in financial markets. As financial investing becomes more important in all of our lives, we believe it is more vital than ever to follow these ideas and to get the information necessary to make wise investment decisions. At RiskMetrics, we are committed to promoting sound financial ideas, to educating individuals, and to providing the tools and information necessary to support a growing world of independent investors. We hope this book, combined with our website (www.riskmetrics.com) and our other tools and services (found at www.wealthbench.com), will help you establish your own financial goals and provide you with the insights and con-fidence necessary to achieve them.

Client Report

Strategic Investment Analysis for Thurston Howell & Lena Howell

This is an example of a client report. It is divided into three sections: (1) client profile, (2) portfolio analysis, and (3) investment strategy.

Client Profile

This section summarizes your profile based on information that you provided. Since your profile is the basis for constructing your investment plan, please verify that the information is correct.

Name: **Thurston Howell**
Birthday: 05/01/1960
Salary: $275,000.00
Retirement age: 65
IRA/401(k) disbursements start: 70
Life expectancy: 85
Name: **Lena Howell**
Birthday: 06/01/1962
Salary: $125,000.00
Retirement age: 65

The analysis in this report is based solely on the portion of your assets for which you have provided information. It is recommended that any analysis be conducted on an investor's entire portfolio in order to generate a more complete investment strategy.

Prepared by Paul Dettor, MSM Capital Management.

Financial Assets Under Analysis
$1,470,037.00
Investment Plan Objective
Maximize the probability of meeting goals
Tax Status
Average Federal Tax Rate: 25%
Average State/Local Tax Rate: 5%
Marginal Federal Tax Rate: 39%
Marginal State/Local Tax Rate: 6%
Long Term Capital Gains Tax Rate: 20%
Economic Assumptions
Inflation: 2.3%

Investment Policy

Your responses to the investment policy questionnaire are summarized below. Our investment analysis uses the responses to estimate your risk tolerance and capacity to bear investment-related market risk.

1. Investment time horizon refers to the number of years you expect the portfolio to be invested before you must dip into principal. When do you anticipate the need for money from this portfolio?
   A. Less than 1 year (or already doing so)
   B. Between 1 and 5 years
   C. Between 5 and 10 years
   D. More than 10 years
2. Which of the following best describes your purpose for investing? Please select the most important one.
   A. I expect to use these funds for a large purchase or expenses within five years.
   B. I want to be certain that my capital is secure and that I have regular income now.
   C. I place dual emphasis on capital growth and income, with moderate fluctuation in year-to-year returns.
   D. I would like long-term growth and I am less concerned about income and return volatility at this time.
   E. I'm only interested in aggressive growth over the long run, and accept significant short-term fluctuations in returns.

3. Which of the following best describes your current stage of life?
   A. Single with few financial burdens. I am eager to accumulate wealth for the future. However some funds must be kept available for enjoyment such as cars, travel and entertainment.
   B. A couple without children. Life is grand. With dual incomes, my spouse and I are well off financially and preparing for the future by establishing a home, careers, and retirement accounts.
   C. Young family. This is the peak home purchasing stage. I have a mortgage and maintain only small cash balances (bank savings, money markets, etc.) equal to 3 or 6 months of living expenses to cover emergencies. Saving for my children's education is top priority.
   D. Mature family. I am in the peak earning years and have the mortgage under control. My children are growing up and have either left home or require less supervision. I am starting to think about retirement, although it may be many years away.
   E. **Preparing for retirement. I own my home and have few financial burdens. My primary concern is ensuring that I can afford a comfortable retirement. I am interested in pursuing other interests such as travel, recreation and self-education.**
   F. Retired. No longer working, I rely on existing funds and income from investments to maintain my lifestyle. I am keen to enjoy life and maintain my health.

4. Which of the following statements best describes your current investment experience? (If you don't currently have any investments, choose the response that best describes how you think you would manage your investments.)
   A. All of my investments to date have been in Treasury Bills because I need the security of capital.
   B. Most of my investments were made to generate income and preserve capital, but I now need some capital growth.
   C. Most of my investments tend to be mutual funds or trusts, although they are generally not aggressive funds.
   D. **Most of my investments tend to be moderately aggressive. My objectives are long-term, therefore I don't often make changes unless my reasons for investing have changed.**
   E. I tend to choose aggressive investments for long term growth.
   F. I currently do not have any investments; this is my initial attempt at long-term investment planning.

5. Over what period of time do you judge the performance of an investment?
   A. Monthly
   B. Quarterly
   C. **Annually**
   D. Between 2 and 5 years

6. Excluding short-term money market securities, how long do you typically hold a security?
   A. Less than 3 months
   B. 3 months to 1 year
   C. Between 1 and 3 years
   D. **Between 3 and 5 years**
   E. More than 5 years

7. How would you describe your portfolio allocations (i.e., the relative amount held in each asset class) over time?
   A. My portfolio allocations have remained fairly consistent over time.
   B. **My portfolio allocations have changed, but not dramatically, over time.**
   C. My portfolio allocations have changed significantly over time.

8. Which of the following statements best describes your investment philosophy?
   A. I am not comfortable taking risks with my capital, but I am prepared to do so with a small portion of my assets as I need some capital appreciation to offset inflation.
   B. I understand that the opportunity for greater returns comes with taking greater risks, but I am only prepared to do so with less than half of my assets.
   C. **I understand that the opportunity for greater returns comes with taking greater risks, and I am prepared to do so with more than half of my assets.**
   D. I have an aggressive investment approach and I am investing for the long term. Therefore, I want to invest the majority or even all of my assets in the stock markets, as this is the best way to ensure higher returns over the long term.

9. If an investment offers the opportunity for higher long-term returns but also carries the chance of going down in the short term, how comfortable with it would you be?
   A. Very comfortable
   B. **Not bothered**

C. Uncomfortable but prepared to try it
D. Very uncomfortable with the prospect of any loss

10. How long would you be prepared to see your investment performing poorly before you cashed
    A. I would sell it immediately if there was any loss in value.
    B. Less than one year
    C. Between 1 and 3 years
    D. Between 3 and 5 years
    E. Between 5 and 10 years
    F. 0 years or more

11. On Black Monday, October 1987, stocks declined more than 22% in a single day. If this happened again, how would you react?
    A. Sell all of my investments. Security of capital is critical to me and I do not intend to take risks.
    B. Sell some of my investments. It's time to cut my losses and transfer my funds into more secure investments.
    C. Do nothing. This was a calculated risk and I will leave the investments in place, expecting performance to improve.
    D. Buy more. I am a long-term investor and consider this sudden market correction as an opportunity to purchase additional shares at a lower cost basis.

12. Listed below are four different investments of $100,000 after one year. Which investment would you be most comfortable owning?
    A. $73,000–$127,000
    B. $84,000–$116,000
    C. $90,000–$110,000
    D. $96,000–$104,000

Income

Below is a summary of your sources of income (in today's dollars):

Salary Source	Amount	Nominal Growth
Client Salary	$275,000.00	3%
Spouse Salary	$125,000.00	3%

Retirement Income

Source	Description	Amount	Start	End
Pension	Thurston	$ 12,000.00	2025	
Pension	Lena	$ 12,000.00	2025	
Social Security	Lena	$ 16,000.00	2025	
Social Security	Thurston	$ 20,000.00	2025	

Other Recurring Income

Source	Description	Amount	Start	End
Rental	Rental	$ 24,000.00	2002	2002

One-Time Income

Source	Description	Amount	Date
Inheritance	Inheritance	$200,000.00	

Savings Deductions

Below is a summary of your sources of savings deductions (in today's dollars):

Contributions to Tax-Deferred Savings

Source	Amount
My 401(k)	$11,000.00
Spouse 401(k)	$10,000.00
My Employer	$ 2,500.00
Spouse Employer	$ 2,000.00

Expenses and Goals

Below is a summary of your projected living expenses and goals (in today's dollars):

Recurring Expenses

Source	Description	Amount	Start	End	Nominal Growth
Living expenses	Living expenses	$ 150,000.00	2002	2025	0%

Financial Goals

Retirement

Source	Description	Amount	Start	End	Nominal Growth
Expense in retirement	Expense in retirement	$ 135,000.00	2026	2045	0%

Wedding

Source	Description	Amount	Start	End	Nominal Growth
Joan wedding	Joan wedding	$ 75,000.00	2007	2007	0%

Bequest

Source	Description	Amount	Start	End	Nominal Growth
Princeton Univ	Princeton Univ	$ 500,000.00	2015	2015	0%

Education

Source	Description	Amount	Start	End	Nominal Growth
Med School	Med School	$ 40,000.00	2002	2006	0%

Major Purchases

Source	Description	Amount	Start	End	Nominal Growth
Sailboat	Sailboat	$ 125,000.00	2010	2010	0%

Leave Estate

Source	Description	Amount	Start	End	Nominal Growth
Estate to kids	Estate to kids	$2,000,000.00	2045	2045	0%

Cash Flow Map

Based on the income, expense, and goals information you provided, the chart below depicts your anticipated cash flows, in today's dollars. Note that this chart does not include any investment-related cash flows. A net positive cash flow in any given year is assumed to generate funds that will be invested in taxable financial assets. A net negative cash flow in any given year is assumed to result in the drawdown of your savings.

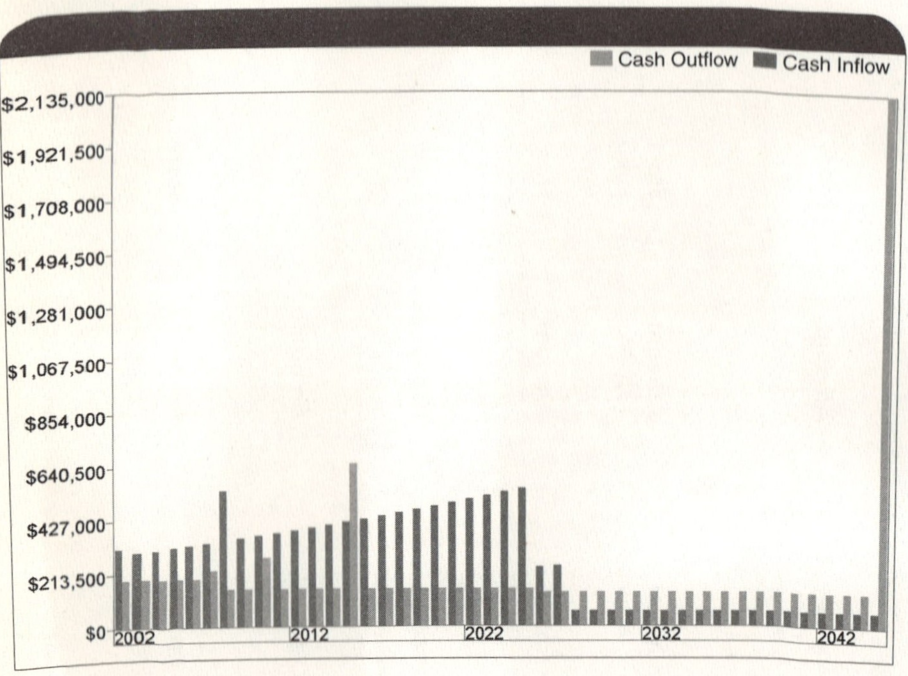

Portfolio Analysis

This section of the report provides a summary and analysis of your portfolio of financial assets. With a clear understanding of the risk and return characteristics of your investments, you can better evaluate how well your current investment approach will enable you to meet your financial objectives.

The portfolio analysis includes:

- Asset allocation
- Allocation by tax status

- Distribution by account
- Industry sector distribution
- RiskGrade
- Risk versus return
- Asset value projection
- Market shocks
- Account holdings

Asset Allocation

The risk and return characteristics of your current asset allocation are similar to those of an *aggressive* investment strategy.

An aggressive asset mix is generally suitable for investors who seek long-term capital appreciation and can accept substantial year-to-year volatility in the value of their assets.

Below is an overview of the total value, asset allocation, and RiskGrade™ of your assets, based on the information you provided.

Asset Allocation	Percent	Market Value
U.S. Large Cap Growth	17.0%	$249,647.82
U.S. Large Cap Value	64.3%	$945,370.00
U.S. Mid Cap	--	--
U.S. Small Cap	0.9%	$13,248.76
Intl. Equity	--	--
U.S. Bonds	11.0%	$161,773.75
U.S. Munis	--	--
Intl. Bonds	--	--
U.S. Cash	6.8%	$100,000.00
Total		**$1,470,040.33**
Estimated Annual Return	5.9%	
Portfolio RiskGrade	119	

Allocation by Tax Status

The assets in your portfolio are distributed across taxable, tax-deferred, and nontaxable account as follows:

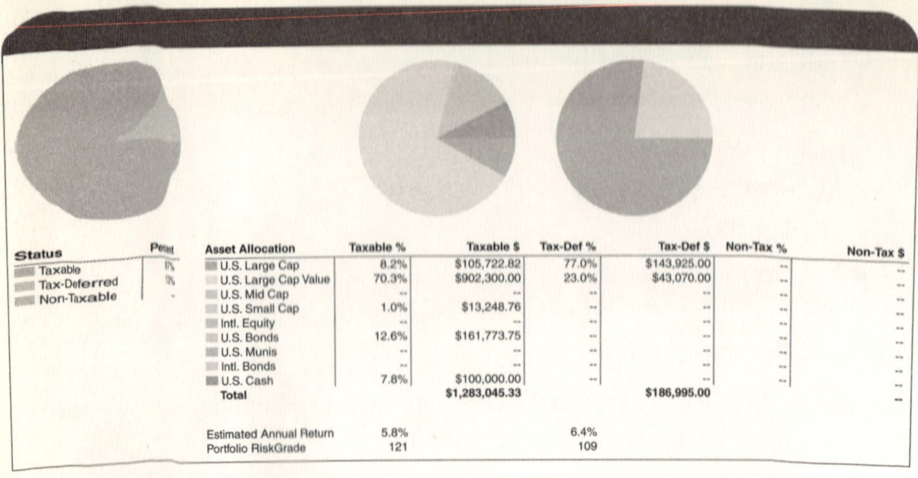

Status	Percent	Asset Allocation	Taxable %	Taxable $	Tax-Def %	Tax-Def $	Non-Tax %	Non-Tax $
Taxable	87%	U.S. Large Cap	8.2%	$105,722.82	77.0%	$143,925.00	--	--
Tax-Deferred	13%	U.S. Large Cap Value	70.3%	$902,300.00	23.0%	$43,070.00	--	--
Non-Taxable	-	U.S. Mid Cap	--	--	--	--	--	--
		U.S. Small Cap	1.0%	$13,248.76	--	--	--	--
		Intl. Equity	--	--	--	--	--	--
		U.S. Bonds	12.6%	$161,773.75	--	--	--	--
		U.S. Munis	--	--	--	--	--	--
		Intl. Bonds	--	--	--	--	--	--
		U.S. Cash	7.8%	$100,000.00	--	--	--	--
		Total		$1,283,045.33		$186,995.00		--
		Estimated Annual Return	5.8%		6.4%			
		Portfolio RiskGrade	121		109			

Distribution by Account

Below is a listing of your accounts with a summary of each account's tax status and value:

Account	Status	Market Value	Percent
Brokerage	Taxable	$1,283,045.33	87.3%
401(k)	Tax deferred	$ 186,995.00	12.7%
Total		$1,470,040.33	

Industry Sector Distribution

Investing across multiple industry sectors helps increase the overall diversification of your portfolio.

For the portion of your assets allocated to equities and equity mutual funds, it is important to consider diversifying your investments across industry sectors. Below is an equity style analysis that details the industry sector exposure of your current portfolio relative to the composition of the S&P 500.

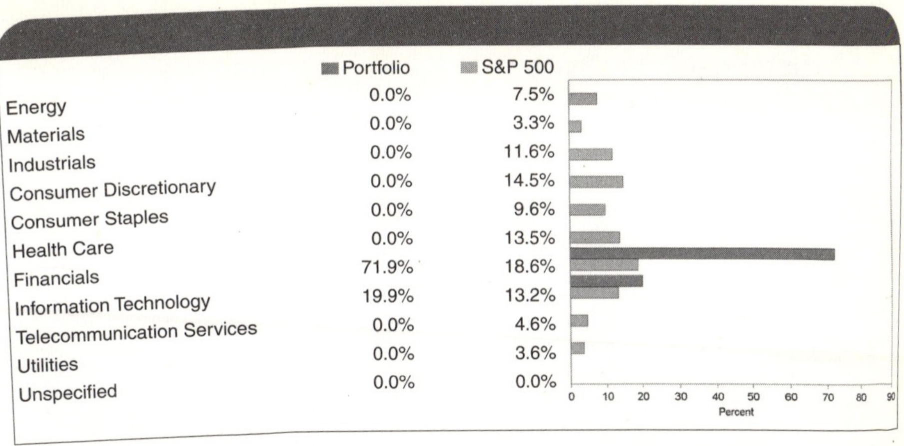

RiskGrade

RiskGrades is a market-standard for quantifying the risk of a portfolio. Below is a summary of the RiskGrade analysis of your portfolio:

Highlights

- Your portfolio's RiskGrade of 119 suggests an aggressive investment strategy.
- The diversification benefit indicates that your portfolio is 7.8% less risky than a portfolio with holdings that move in lockstep with each other.
- Your portfolio's XLoss value is $47,909. This means your portfolio's value could fall by 3.3% or more during extreme market conditions.
- Your portfolio's RiskGrade is 22.7% higher than the S&P 500.

Risk	Portfolio	S&P 500
RiskGrade	119	97
Diversification Benefit	10	—
XLoss	$47,909	$33,558

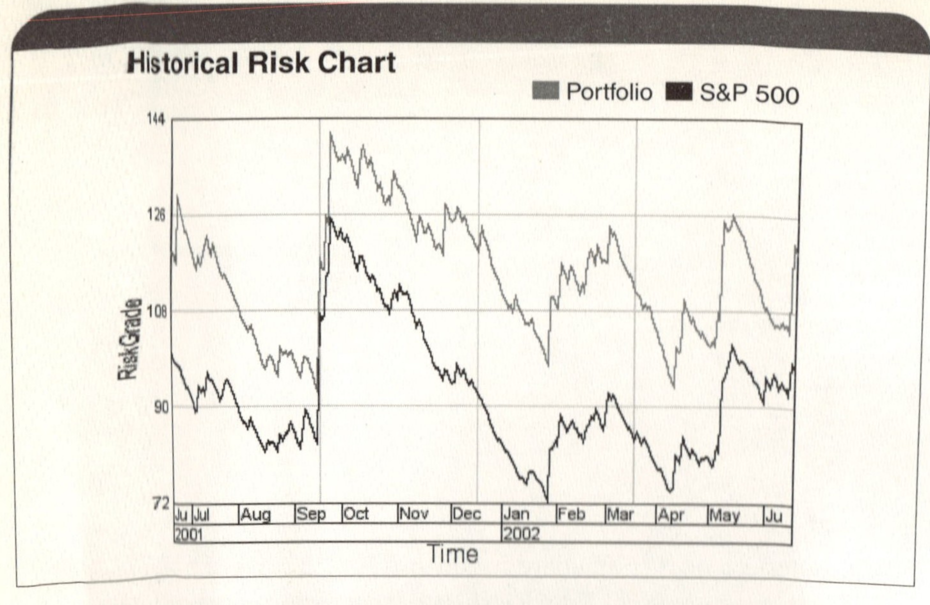

Top 5 by RiskImpact	RiskGrade	RiskImpact	Market Value
Citigroup Inc	164	82%	$904,470.00
Vanguard Index Trust: Vanguard	98	12%	$239,875.00
Merrill Lynch&Co Inc	196	3%	$ 40,900.00
Texas Instruments	230	1%	$ 7,827.00
CSCO 04/2003 $20 C	1012	1%	$ 1,952.00

Asset Value Projection

Based on the assets in your portfolio, we have run a Monte Carlo simulation to project the future value of the portfolio, ignoring any potential future additions to or drawdown of funds from the portfolio. This analysis is designed to illustrate the growth potential of your financial assets in the absence of non-investment-related cash flows.

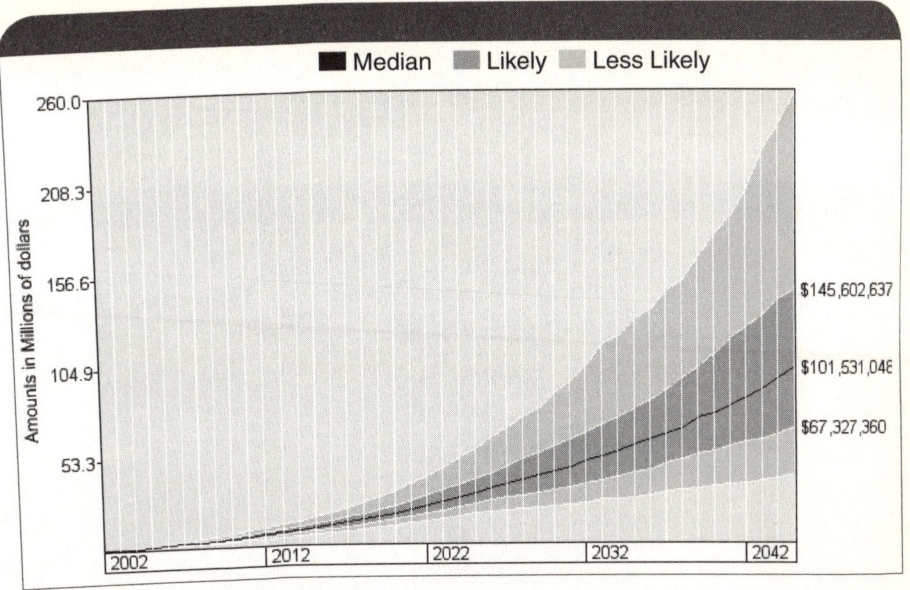

The estimated value of your portfolio in 2046 is $101,531,048 based on long-term average returns. There is a 25% chance your wealth could be below $67,327,360, and there is a 25% chance your wealth could be above $145,602,637.

Market Shocks

Market shock analysis enables you to assess the degree of exposure you may have to events that are outside of the expected norm. Looking at how your portfolio could behave due to an extreme move in the markets is an important component in determining the overall level risk with which you are comfortable. While the timing and likelihood of market shocks are unpredictable, it is possible to estimate the potential impact of a scenario that is based on history or constructed based on educated guesses. Below is an analysis of a hypothetical market shock and its estimated impact on your portfolio.

Market Shock Assumptions: Black Monday

Nasdaq down −13.4%	S&P 500 down −20.5%
Nikkei down −2.4%	FTSE 100 down −10.8%
GBP down −0.5%	JPY down 0%

Appendix

Estimated Impact

Your portfolio's value would change by −23.1% due to the above market shock.

Details		
Holding	**Current Market Value**	**Estimated Change**
C	$904,470.00	−31.1%
VFINX	$239,875.00	−20.6%
MER	$ 40,900.00	−30.8%
TXN	$ 7,827.00	−13.4%
CSCO (C) 20 04/21	$ 1,951.58	−26.6%
USD	$100,000.00	0.0%
BGNMX	$107,800.00	0.6%
05/15 5.75%	$ 53,965.03	3.2%
9984	$ 13,248.76	27.0%

Holdings

Below is a listing of your accounts with a summary of each account's tax status and value:

Taxable Account Holdings

Name	Ticker	RiskGrade	Quantity	Price	Market Value	% Total	Return (1y)
Texas Instruments	TXN	230	300	$ 26.09	$ 7,827.00	0.8%	−16.2%
Softbank Corp	9984	276	1,000	$ 13.25	$ 13,249.00	1.4%	−58.6%
Citigroup Inc	C	164	20,000	$ 43.07	$ 861,400.00	93.3%	−13.5%
Merrill Lynch&Co Inc	MER	196	1,000	$ 40.90	$ 40,900.00	4.4%	−34.0%
Total Equities		160			$ 923,376.00	72.0%	
Vanguard Index Trust:	VFINX	98	1,000	$ 95.95	$ 95,950.00	47.1%	−13.1%
American Century	BGNMX	12	10,000	$ 10.78	$ 107,800.00	52.9%	7.6%
Total Funds		44			$ 203,750.00	15.9%	
CSCO 04/2003 $20 C	CSCO	1012	1,000	$ 1.95	$ 1,952.00	100.0%	−31.4%
Total Options		1012			$ 1,952.00	0.2%	
Aaa Corp 5.75 05/2012		34	50,000	$107.95	$ 53,965.00	100.0%	3.4%
Total Bonds		34			$ 53,965.00	4.2%	
Cash					$ 100,000.00	100.0%	0.0%
Total Cash					$ 100,000.00	7.8%	
Total		121			$1,283,042.00	−12.4%	

Tax Deferred Account Holdings

Name	Ticker	RiskGrade	Quantity	Price	Market Value	% Total	Return (1y)
Citigroup Inc	C	164	1,000	$ 43.07	$ 43,070.00	100.0%	−13.5%
Total Equities		164			$ 43,070.00	23.0%	
Vanguard Index Trust:	VFINX	98	1,500	$ 95.95	$ 143,925.00	100.0%	−13.1%
Total Funds		98			$ 143,925.00	77.0%	
Total		109			$ 186,995.00		−13.2%

Investment Strategy

An investment strategy acts as the guide for your investment plan, taking into account your financial objectives and risk tolerance.

An investment strategy is the focal point of an investment plan. The purpose of an investment strategy is to help you achieve your financial objectives with a level of risk with which you are comfortable. The investment strategy articulates the action steps for your plan by identifying the asset classes into which you will invest and the percentage allocations to each.

Different asset classes carry different levels of market risk and estimated returns. By dividing your investments across asset classes, your investment strategy mitigates risk through diversification. This diversification across asset classes helps you avoid putting all your eggs in one basket.

An investment strategy has been prepared for you based upon an assessment of your financial needs and risk tolerance.

A summary of both your current asset allocation and an optimized investment strategy is detailed below for your consideration.

Assumptions: Estimated Returns

Estimated returns data are used to forecast the long term potential value of your investments.

In order to assess the investment performance of both your current asset allocation and the target investment strategy, the asset allocation model uses the following annual return assumptions:

Asset Class	Estimated Annual Return
U.S. Large Cap Growth	6.4%
U.S. Large Cap Value	6.3%
U.S. Mid Cap	6.7%
U.S. Small Cap	6.7%
Intl. Equity	6.1%
U.S. Bonds	4.6%
U.S. Munis	2.2%
Intl. Bonds	4.9%
U.S. Cash	3.1%

The above returns assumptions are based on the Black-Litterman asset allocation model, which is an established approach for estimating returns. For more information, please see www.wealthbench.com. Past performance is no guarantee of future results.

Assumptions: Asset Constraints

Asset class constraints may be specified in order to ensure a particular degree or type of diversification in your investment strategy.

The following customized constraints have been taken into consideration in order to determine your target investment strategy:

Asset Class	Min	Max
U.S. Large Cap Growth	20%	20%
U.S. Large Cap Value	25%	25%
U.S. Mid Cap	5%	5%
U.S. Small Cap	5%	5%
Intl. Equity	15%	15%
U.S. Bonds	10%	10%
U.S. Munis	15%	15%
Intl. Bonds	5%	5%
U.S. Cash	—	—

Suggested Strategy: Taxable

The risk and return characteristics of your suggested asset allocation are similar to those of a *balanced* investment strategy.

A balanced asset mix is generally suitable for portfolios that emphasize relatively stable investment growth over the long term.

As a result of an analysis of the information you provided, a personalized target investment strategy has been selected for you, as shown below.

Asset Allocation	Percent	Market Value
U.S. Large Cap Growth	6%	$79,023.33
U.S. Large Cap Value	29%	$373,466.16
U.S. Mid Cap	0%	$6,114.48
U.S. Small Cap	26%	$337,085.71
Intl. Equity	19%	$239,092.84
U.S. Bonds	4%	$55,803.48
U.S. Munis	0%	$0.00
Intl. Bonds	15%	$192,456.35
U.S. Cash	0%	$0.00
Total		**$1,283,042.36**

Estimated Annual Return	6.1%	
Portfolio RiskGrade	68	

Suggested Strategy: Tax Deferred

The risk and return characteristics of your suggested asset allocation are similar to those of a *balanced* investment strategy.

A balanced asset mix is generally suitable for portfolios that emphasize relatively stable investment growth over the long term.

As a result of an analysis of the information you provided, a personalized target investment strategy has been selected for you, as shown below.

Asset Allocation	Percent	Market Value
U.S. Large Cap Growth	13%	$24,350.50
U.S. Large Cap Value	32%	$60,579.91
U.S. Mid Cap	13%	$23,943.43
U.S. Small Cap	31%	$58,474.34
Intl. Equity	11%	$19,646.81
U.S. Bonds	0%	$0.00
U.S. Munis	0%	$0.00
Intl. Bonds	0%	$0.00
U.S. Cash	0%	$0.00
Total		**$186,995.00**

Estimated Annual Return	6.4%
Portfolio RiskGrade	87

Strategy: Performance

By implementing your personalized target investment strategy, the estimated value of your future wealth is $52,965,670. Past performance is no guarantee of future results.

In determining a personalized investment strategy for you, we have taken into account your investment policy questionnaire and financial objectives. Shown below is a Monte Carlo simulation–based projection of your future wealth, assuming you were to implement the suggested investment strategy.

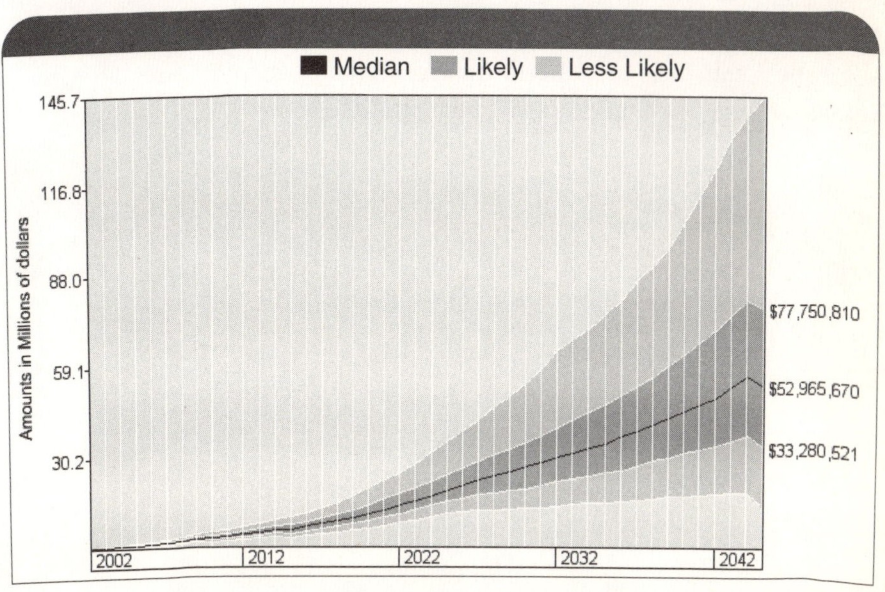

The estimated value of your wealth in 2046 is $52,965,670, based on long-term average returns. There is a 25 percent chance your wealth could be below $33,280,521, and there is a 25 percent chance your wealth could be above $77,750,810.

Note that the likelihood of achieving goals is affected by your savings rate, estimated return on investment, and the size and timing of your goals.

The table below summarizes your financial goals and the likelihood of achieving the goals, assuming you were to implement the suggested investment strategy.

Goal	Amount	Start	End	Likelihood
Med school	$ 40,000	2002	2006	95+%
Expense in retirement	$ 135,000	2026	2045	95+%
Joan wedding	$ 75,000	2007	2007	95+%
Sailboat	$ 125,000	2010	2010	95+%
Estate to kids	$2,000,000	2045	2045	95+%
Princeton Univ	$ 500,000	2015	2015	95+%

Comparison of Strategies

Below is a comparison of the allocation percentages, risk and return characteristics, and estimated performance for your current asset allocation versus the suggested target investment strategy.

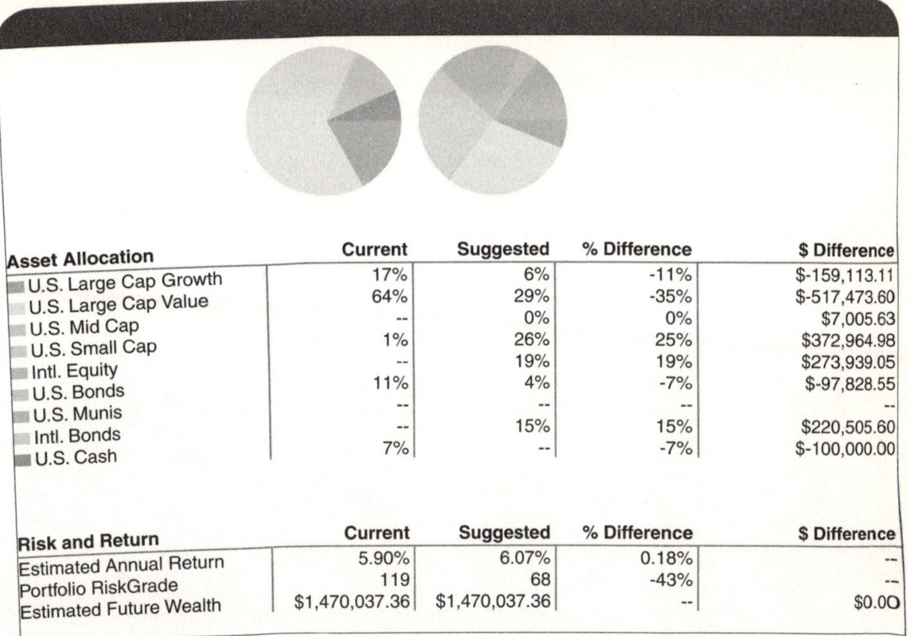

Asset Allocation	Current	Suggested	% Difference	$ Difference
U.S. Large Cap Growth	17%	6%	-11%	$-159,113.11
U.S. Large Cap Value	64%	29%	-35%	$-517,473.60
U.S. Mid Cap	--	0%	0%	$7,005.63
U.S. Small Cap	1%	26%	25%	$372,964.98
Intl. Equity	--	19%	19%	$273,939.05
U.S. Bonds	11%	4%	-7%	$-97,828.55
U.S. Munis	--	--	--	--
Intl. Bonds	--	15%	15%	$220,505.60
U.S. Cash	7%	--	-7%	$-100,000.00

Risk and Return	Current	Suggested	% Difference	$ Difference
Estimated Annual Return	5.90%	6.07%	0.18%	--
Portfolio RiskGrade	119	68	-43%	--
Estimated Future Wealth	$1,470,037.36	$1,470,037.36	--	$0.00

The table below compares the likelihoods of success for achieving your financial goals of your current and suggested investment strategies.

Financial Goals: Likelihood of Success			
Goal	Current	Suggested	Difference
Med school	95+%	95+%	—
Expense in retirement	95+%	95+%	—
Joan wedding	95+%	95+%	—
Sailboat	95+%	95+%	—
Estate to kids	95+%	95+%	—
Princeton Univ	95+%	95+%	—

Wealth Projection

Below is a comparison of how your wealth is projected to grow under the two different investment strategies.

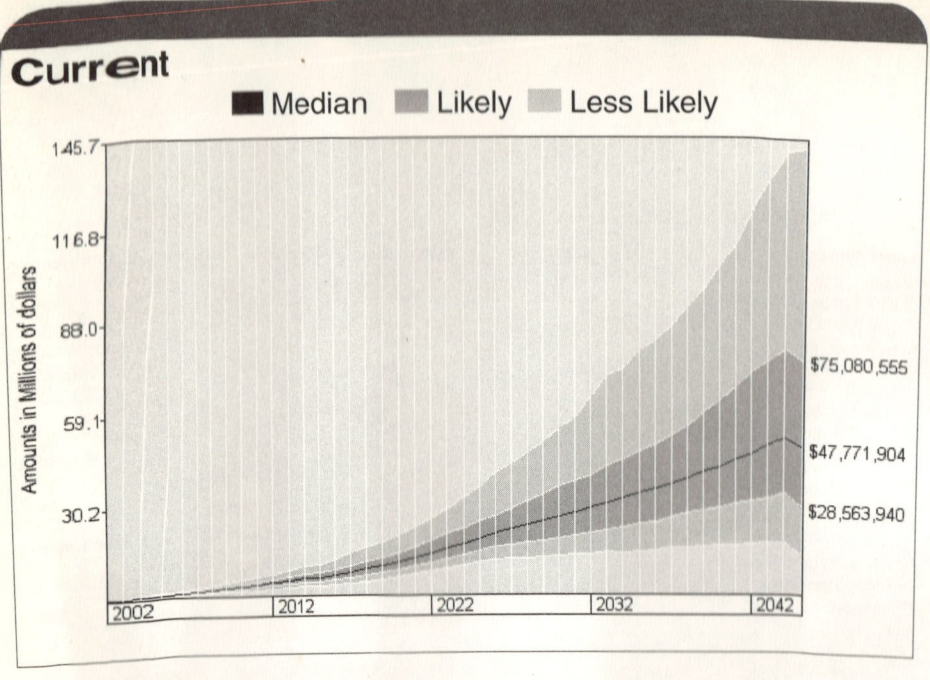

Current
Median
Likely
Less Likely
Amounts in Millions of dollars
145.7
116.8
88.0
59.1
30.2
2002
2012
2022
2032
2042
$75,080,555
$47,771,904
$28,563,940

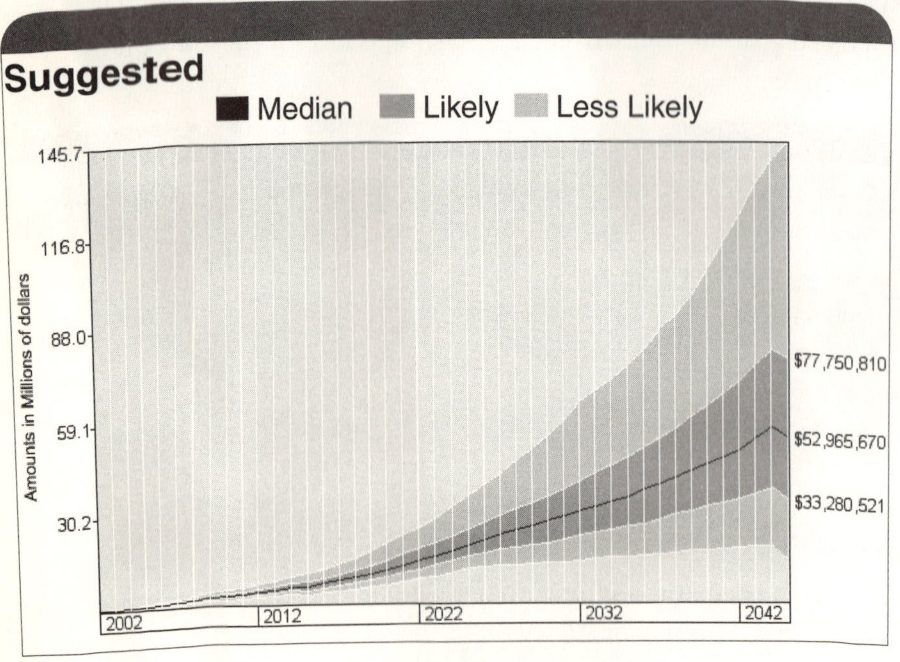

Suggested
Median
Likely
Less Likely
Amounts in Millions of dollars
145.7
116.8
88.0
59.1
30.2
2002
2012
2022
2032
2042
$77,750,810
$52,965,670
$33,280,521

RiskGrades

A RiskGrade is a standard way to measure the risk of individual securities, mutual funds, and portfolios.

RiskGrades, developed by the RiskMetrics Group, address an investor's need for a consistent and reliable way to measure market risk. The RiskGrade is a standardized measure of volatility and therefore allows an "apples to apples" comparison of investment risk across all asset classes and regions.

RiskGrades can range from 0 to 1000 or more, where 100 corresponds to the long-term average risk level of the equity markets. Using Risk-Grades, you can:

- Compare the risk of one asset against the risk of another asset, or
- Compare the RiskGrade of your portfolio against the RiskGrade of an index or investment strategy that you use as a benchmark.

RiskGrades are also dynamic and vary over time to reflect asset-specific events (e.g., the price of a stock reacting to an earnings release) and changing market conditions.

The RiskGrade of a portfolio measures the volatility of a portfolio's market value. The portfolio RiskGrade provides a convenient way for you to understand how the risks of the various assets in your portfolio combine with each other, taking into account the effect of diversification. The portfolio RiskGrade is a function of each asset's RiskGrade, the correlation of the assets with each other, and the size of the position in each holding.

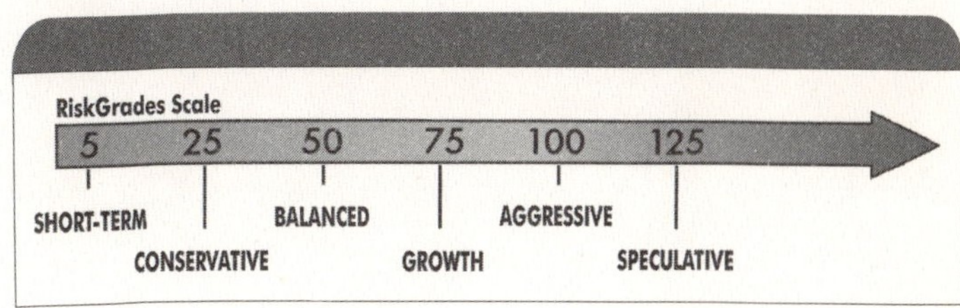

Your portfolio's overall RiskGrade enables you to characterize the overall risk level of your investments. The RiskGrades Scale shows the level of risk that corresponds to a range of different investment strategies.

For more information, please see www.wealthbench.com.

RiskMetrics Group Disclaimer

The data and information contained herein: (1) include proprietary information of RiskMetrics Group and may not be copied or redistributed, (2) are not guaranteed to be complete or accurate, and (3) are not intended to be and do not constitute investment or tax advice by RiskMetrics Group or an opinion or recommendation by RiskMetrics Group regarding the appropriateness of any investment. All express and implied warranties and representations are hereby disclaimed, including that the data and information are in any way guidance for any investor or investors in general to determine the suitability or desirability of an investment in a particular security or securities in general. RiskMetrics Group is not responsible for any losses or damages resulting from use of this data and information. Results are calculated based on historical observations and should not be relied on to predict future market movements; past performance is no guarantee of future results. The data and information contained herein are provided for informational and discussion purposes only and are not intended to be and should not be relied on or acted upon without consulting with and obtaining specific advice from your financial or tax advisor.

Glossary

absolute market risk   Risk associated with the change in value of a position or a portfolio resulting from changes in market conditions (e.g., yield levels or prices).

absolute return   Measure of net economic return. Takes into account all costs (e.g., cost of funding, balance sheet charges, administrative expenses).

asset   Any possession that has value.

asset allocation   The decision regarding how an investor's funds should be distributed among the major assets (e.g., equities, bonds, money markets, commodities).

base currency   Your local currency. For example, an American's base currency is the U.S. dollar.

benchmarks   The performance of a predetermined set of securities, used for comparison purposes. Such sets may be based on published indexes or may be customized to suit an investment strategy.

beta   The measure of a fund's or stock's risk in relation to the market or an alternative benchmark. A beta of 1.5 means that a stock's excess return is expected to move 1.5 times the market excess returns. For example, if market excess return is 10 percent, then we expect, on average, the stock return to be 15 percent. Beta is referred to as an index of the systematic risk due to general market conditions that cannot be diversified away.

Black-Scholes option pricing model   Model developed by Fischer Black and Myron Scholes to gauge whether option contracts are fairly valued. It incorporates such factors as the volatility of a security's return, the level of interest rates, the relationship of the underlying stock's price to the strike price of the option, and the time remaining until the option expires.

bonds   A bond is debt issued for a period of more than one year. The U.S. government, local governments, water districts, companies, and many other types of institutions sell bonds. When an investor buys bonds, he or she is lending money. The seller of the bond agrees to repay the principal amount of the loan at a specified time. Interest-bearing bonds pay interest periodically.

call option   A call option is the right, but not the obligation, to buy an asset at a prespecified price on or before a prespecified date in the future.

CAPM   Capital asset pricing model. A model that relates the expected return on an asset to the expected return on the market portfolio.

caps and floors   Interest rate options. Caps are an upper limit on interest rates (if you buy a cap, you make money if interest rates move above cap strike level). Floors are a lower limit on interest rates (if you buy a floor, you make money if interest rates move below floor strike level).

concentration risk   Portfolio risk resulting from increased exposure to one risk category or groups of correlated risk factors.

correlation   A linear statistical measure of the degree to which two random variables are related. A correlation will range from +1.0 to −1.0. For market risk, international equity markets rising and falling together show positive correlation. In credit risk, clumps of firms defaulting together by industry or geographically show positive correlation of default events.

country risk   Developments in a national economy that can affect the outcome of an international financial transaction.

coupon   The periodic interest payment made to the bondholders during the life of a bond.

cross-market correlations   Correlations across different markets—for example, correlation between the U.S. and Japanese stock markets.

current exposure   For market-driven instruments, the amount it would cost to replace a transaction today should a counterparty default. If there is an enforceable netting agreement with the counterparty, then the current exposure would be the net replacement cost; otherwise, it would be the gross amount.

currency risk   Risk of loss due to movements in currency rates.

decision theory   Theory of making rational decisions given a set of defined outcomes and probabilities.

default   Failure of a debtor to make timely payments of principal and interest or to meet other provisions of a bond indenture.

derivatives   Securities, such as options, futures, and swaps, whose value is derived in part from the value and characteristics of another underlying security.

discount (1) The difference between a bond's current market price and its face or redemption value; (2) a manner of selling securities such as Treasury bills issued at less than face value and redeemed at face value.

diversification Holding a large collection of independent assets to reduce overall risk.

diversification benefit Measures risk reduction that arises from holding a collection of assets that are not perfectly correlated. The diversification benefit for your portfolio RiskGrade is the difference between the computed portfolio RiskGrade and the market-value-weighted average of the individual asset RiskGrades. The portfolio diversification benefit for XLoss is the difference between the computed portfolio XLoss and the sum of the individual asset XLoss values.

economic exposures Or *strategic exposures.* Market exposures that consider how changes in foreign exchange rates, interest rates, or commodity can affect the overall operating environment of a firm (e.g., level of demand for products and services).

efficient frontier Refers to the maximum return you can expect for any given level of risk based on historical returns of major asset classes.

equity Ownership interest possessed by shareholders in a corporation (i.e., stocks as opposed to bonds).

equity risk Risk due to fluctuations in stock prices, a component of market risk.

event risk The risk that some unexpected event (natural disasters, technology failures, human error, political upheavals, war) will cause a substantial decline in the market value of a security.

exponential weighting A method of applying weights to a set of data points (returns), with the weights declining exponentially over time. In a time series context, this results in weighting recent data more heavily than past data.

foreign exchange risk Risk of loss due to movements in foreign exchange rates.

futures A term used to designate contracts covering the sale of financial instruments or physical commodities for future delivery on an exchange.

global equity markets World stock markets, which are composed of publicly listed companies that the general public can buy or sell on exchanges.

hedge fund A fund targeted to sophisticated investors that may use a wide range of strategies to earn returns, such as taking long and short positions based on statistical models.

Glossary

hedging   Eliminating an exposure by entering into an offsetting position. For example, a gold mine can hedge exposure to falling prices by selling gold futures. When hedging, we look for highly correlated substitute securities.

historical simulation   A nonparametric method of using past data to make inferences about the future. One application of this technique is to take today's portfolio and revalue it using past historical price and rates data.

independent   Implies no correlation (no relationship) between variables.

inflation   The rate at which the price that consumers pay for goods and services rises over time.

interest   The cost of using money, expressed as a rate per period of time, usually one year.

interest rate   Cost of using money, expressed as a percentage rate per annum.

interest rate risk   Risk arising from fluctuating interest rates. For example, a bond's price drops as interest rates rise.

investment manager   A manager of a portfolio of investments.

liquidity   There are two separate meanings: *At the enterprise level,* the ability to meet current liabilities as they fall due; often measured as the ratio of current assets to current liabilities. *At the security level,* the ability to trade in volume without directly moving the market price; often measured as bid/ask spread and daily turnover.

long   When you buy an asset, you are *long* the asset. You will benefit if the price goes up.

long position   Opposite of short position—a bet that prices will rise. For example, you have a long position when you buy a stock and will benefit from prices rising.

market-cap weighted   Refers to a market-value-weighted index. Market value is computed as shares times current market price, converted to a standard currency (e.g., U.S. dollars). The weighting of each component is its market value divided by the total market value.

market exposure   For market-driven instruments, there is an amount at risk to default only when the contract is *in the money* (i.e., when the replacement cost of the contract exceeds the original value). This exposure/uncertainty is captured by calculating the netted mean and standard deviation of exposure(s).

market risk   Risk that arises from the fluctuating prices of investments as they are traded in the global markets. Market risk is highest for securities with above-average price volatility and lowest for stable securities such as Treasury bills.

market value   The price at which a security is trading and could presumably be purchased or sold (i.e., replacement cost).

mean   A statistical measure of central tendency. The sum of observation values is divided by the number of observations. It is the first moment of a distribution.

mean reversion   The statistical tendency in a time series to gravitate back toward a long-term historical level. This is on a much longer scale than a similar measure called *autocorrelation;* these two behaviors are mathematically independent of one another.

modern portfolio theory   Investment decision approach that permits an investor to classify, estimate, and control both the kind and the amount of expected risk and return.

modified duration   An indication of price sensitivity. It is equal to a security's Macaulay duration divided by 1 plus the yield.

Nasdaq   National Association of Securities Dealers Automated Quotations system, Nasdaq is a computerized system that provides brokers and dealers with price quotations for securities listed on the over-the-counter exchange.

net asset value (NAV)   The market value per share for mutual funds. NAV is calculated each day by aggregating the closing market value of assets and subtracting all liabilities, then dividing the result by the total number of shares outstanding.

net present value   Valuing a stream of future cash flows at appropriate (risk-adjusted) discount rates.

nonparametric   Potential market movements described by assumed scenarios, not by statistical parameters.

notional amount   The face amount of a transaction typically used as the basis for interest payment calculations. For swaps, this amount is not itself a cash flow. Credit exposure arises not against the notional but against the present value (market replacement cost) of in-the-money future terminal payment(s).

notional exposure   Refers to exposure in the amount of the predetermined dollar principal on which interest payments are based.

options   An option is the right, but not the obligation, to buy or sell a reference asset at a prespecified strike price on or before a prespecified future date. A European-style option can be exercised only at maturity, whereas an American-style option may be exercised any day before or on maturity.

out of the money   When an option has no intrinsic value (on a call option, when the price is below the strike; on a put option, when the price is above the strike).

parametric When a functional form for the distribution a set of data points is assumed. For example, when the normal distribution is used to characterize a set of returns.

performance risk Risk that a money manager may underperform his or her preestablished benchmark (e.g., S&P 500).

portfolio A collection of investments; these can be long (purchased) or short (sold) positions.

position The buyer of an asset is said to have a long position and the seller of an asset is said to have a short position.

put option The right, but not the obligation, to sell an asset at a prespecified price on or before a prespecified future date.

principal Face value of an obligation (such as a bond or a loan) that must be repaid at maturity, separate from interest.

relative market risk Risk measured relative to an index or benchmark.

relative return A measure of relative performance.

residual risk The risk in a position that is issue-specific.

risk Uncertainty about or exposure to loss or damage.

RiskGrade For a single position or portfolio, a ranking that measures the potential volatility of the position or portfolio relative to the volatility of a standard benchmark. The benchmark used is the average daily volatility of the market-capitalization-weighted average of international equity indices during the period from 1995 to 1999, which is defined to have a RiskGrade of 100. For example, if a position or portfolio has a RiskGrade of 200, the position or portfolio is twice as volatile as the benchmark.

RiskRanking A comparison of RiskGrade relative to an external benchmark such as peers or indices. For example, if your portfolio has a RiskRank of 32 percent relative to other sampled portfolios, it means that 68 percent of these portfolios are riskier than yours.

RiskImpact The RiskImpact for a single position is the percentage amount that the portfolio's RiskGrade will decrease upon removal of that position.

S&P 500 Index The Standard and Poor's 500 Index is a market-capitalization-weighted equity index of 500 U.S. stocks.

Sharpe ratio A return on risk ratio named after Nobel laureate and Stanford University professor William F. Sharpe. The Sharpe ratio is defined as annual return minus risk-free rate divided by standard deviation of return.

short If you sell an asset short, you are short the asset and will benefit if the price falls.

short position Opposite of long position—a bet that prices will fall. For example, a short position in a stock will benefit from the stock price falling.

skewness Characterizes the degree of asymmetry of the distribution around its mean. Positive skews indicate an asymmetric tail extending toward positive values (right-hand side). Negative skewness implies asymmetry toward negative values (left-hand side).

standard deviation A statistical measure that indicates the width of a distribution around the mean. A standard deviation is the square root of the second moment of a distribution.

stress testing A process of determining how much the value of a portfolio can fall under abnormal market conditions. Stress testing consists of generating worst-case scenarios (e.g., stock a market crash) and revaluing a portfolio under those scenarios.

strike price The stated price for which an underlying asset may be purchased (in case of a call) or sold (in the case of a put) by the option holder upon exercise of the option contract.

stock Ownership interest possessed by shareholders in a corporation (i.e., stocks as opposed to bonds).

systemic risk The risk of a portfolio after all unique risk has been diversified away. Systemic risks may arise from common driving factors (e.g., market and economic factors, natural disasters, war) and can influence the whole market's well-being. (Also known as *systematic risk*.)

tracking error In an indexing strategy, the difference between the performance of the benchmark and the replicating portfolio.

underlying An asset that may be bought or sold is referred to as the *underlying*.

unique risk Exposure to a particular company, sometimes referred to as *firm-specific risk*.

value-at-risk (VaR) A measure of the maximum potential change in value of a portfolio of financial instruments with a given probability over a preset horizon.

variance A statistical measure that indicates the width of a distribution around the mean. It is the second moment of a distribution. A related measure is the standard deviation, which is the square root of the variance.

volatility Risk as measured by the standard deviation of a security's price.

volatility clustering The tendency for unusully large market movements to occur in rapid succession.

Xloss   An abbreviated form for "loss in extreme markets." The XLoss for a single position or portfolio is the dollar value by which the position or portfolio's value could potentially fall during periods of high market volatility. *High-market-volatility periods* are defined as months in which market movements are in the ninety-fifth percentile or higher in terms of magnitude. The XLoss is calculated by using the expected value of the market moves during these high-market-volatility periods only.

yield   Return on an investor's capital investment.

Notes

Chapter 2. The Dilemma Facing Today's Investors

1. Michael Lewis, "Jonathan Lebed's Extracurricular Activities," *The New York Times Magazine*, February 25, 2001, p. 26.
2. U.S. Securities and Exchange Commission, Litigation Release No. 16671, August 31, 2000, *Securities and Exchange Commission v. Mark S. Jakob*, Civil Action No. EDCV-00-687 VAP (Mcx) (C.D. Cal.), www.sec.gov/litigation/litreleases/lr16671.htm.
3. Table data from Internal Revenue Service publication No. 590, Individual Retirement Arrangements (IRAs), Appendix E, Table 1, December 12, 1999.
4. Charts and data are from Social Security Administration, SSA Publication No. 05-0055, August 2000, ICN-462560.
5. From: Investment Company Institute, *2001 Mutual Fund Fact Books*, www.ici.org.
6. Ibid.
7. Quoted from *The Wall Street Journal*'s WSJ.com Online Investing, "Trading Stocks Online," by Dave Pettit, Dow Jones & Co., 2001.
8. Investors often use this term to express a tenfold increase on initial investments.
9. Edward Chancellor, *Devil Take the Hindmost: A History of Financial Speculation*, Farrar, Straus & Giroux, New York, 1999, p. 386.

Chapter 3. What Is Risk?

1. Ethan Berman and Alvin Lee, *401(k) CheckUp—Best Practices in the Measurement and Disclosure of Risk in 401(k) Plans*, first edition, February 2001, RiskMetrics Group, New York. Available from www.401k.riskmetrics.com/techdocs/401kBestPractices.pdf.
2. Definition of risk comes from Aswath Damodoran, in his book, *Applied Corporate Finance: A User's Manual*, John Wiley & Sons, New York 1999, p. 35.
3. "Folks Who Like to Buy a Stock and Forget It Face a Rude Awakening," *The Wall Street Journal*, February 7, 2001, p. A12.
4. Note that a RiskGrade of 100 corresponds to an annualized return standard devi-

ation of 20 percent, which is approximately the market-cap-weighted average volatility of international equity markets during normal market conditions from 1995 to 1999.

5. Richard Cookson, "The Party's Over," *The Economist,* Corporate Finance survey, January 27–February 2, 2000, p. 14.

6. RiskGrade estimates are based on exponential weighting of historical data, which makes them more adaptive to current market conditions than plain standard deviation. The RiskGrades approach is based on a study by J.P. Morgan that demonstrates that exponential weighting improves forecasting.

7. Burton G. Malkiel, *A Random Walk Down Wall Street,* W.W. Norton and Company, New York, 2000, p. 231.

8. Ibid., p. 233.

9. Brokerages like Fidelity Investments have started to offer specialized mutual funds focused on theme-based compilations, (e.g., PC-related stocks).

10. Roger G. Ibbotson and Gary P. Brinson, *Global Investing,* p. 45.

11. RiskMetrics Technical Document offers a more detailed description of the empirical tests that give support to this methodology. This document may be downloaded from www.riskmetrics.com.

Chapter 4. Return Is Only Half the Equation

1. Visual illusion and text excerpted from "Aspects of Investor Psychology," *Journal of Portfolio Management,* vol. 24, no. 4, 1998, by Daniel Kahneman, Ph.D., Eugene Higgins, and Mark W. Riepe.

2. Bernstein Research, "Household Risk-Taking: Facts and Psychology," *The Future of Money Management in America,* p. 81.

3. Source: Phoenix Investment Partners/Financial Research Corporation (FRC), "Investment Behavior and Its Impact on Long-Term Investment Success," December 2000, p. 67.

4. Source: Phoenix Investment Partners, Ltd./Financial Research Corporation. Chart assumes a minimum investment of $10,000 using three-year average returns of 10.92 percent for funds and 8.70 percent for investors. Dollar amount shown represents the 2.22 percentage-point gap between fund returns and investor returns over those time periods. Flows in and out of funds were used to determine actual investor average returns provided by long-term mutual funds in each Morningstar investment category during the 1990s. Subsequent three-year return figures were totaled and averaged to produce an unweighted category return for the holding period. These unweighted figures, called *fund returns,* can be viewed as a proxy for an investor who had dollar cost–averaged with a fund. Figures for the actual net flows into funds (new investor deposits minus investor redemptions) throughout the period were weighted. These flow-weighted returns are a general proxy for the returns the average individual investor received.

5. From *Investors Behaving Badly: An Analysis of Investor Trading Patterns in Mutual*

Funds, © 2001 by Gavin Quill, Senior Vice President of Financial Research Corporation.

6. Mutual fund *redemption rates* are defined as total dollars redeemed from a mutual fund in a given year as a percent of an investor's starting assets in that fund.

7. For more information on the Investors Behaving Badly study, refer to Phoenix Investment Partners, Ltd., or the Financial Research Corporation's website at www.frcnet.com. RiskMetrics would like to thank Phoenix Investment Partners, Ltd., and Financial Research Corporation for sharing their research to help us highlight to *investors* the importance of maintaining a diversified portfolio that is within their tolerance for risk and adopt a long-term-strategy.

8. For example, the Fidelity family of funds is expected to generate in the order of $380 million in the year 2000.

9. Brad M. Barber, Terrance Odean, and Lu Zheng, "The Behavior of Mutual Fund Investors," September 2000, unpublished working paper, p. 5.

10. Some would even consider the overall performance admirable given the high episodes of volatility during the year. By way of comparison, the S&P 500 Index was down 10.1 percent in 2000.

11. Chicago-based Morningstar, Inc., is a global investment research firm that provides financial data, research, online advice, consulting services, and investment solutions for individuals, financial advisors, institutions, and the media worldwide. Morningstar is a trusted source of investment information and analysis for stocks, mutual funds, exchange-traded funds, closed-end funds, and variable annuities and tracks nearly 100,000 securities worldwide. For more information, visit www.morningstar.com or call 1-800-735-0700.

12. Mercer Bullard, "From Worst to First: Jacob Internet Moves to Cutting Edge of Disclosure", January 26, 2001, www.thestreet.com/funds/mercerbullard/1278201.html (5 May 2002). Mercer Bullard is founder of Fund Democracy (an information resource for mutual fund shareholders) and an advocate for shareholders' rights. He is a former assistant chief counsel in the SEC's Division of Investment Management.

13. Jacob voluntarily amended his prospectus to prominently display Jacob Internet's 79 percent performance in 2000 (the only Internet fund to do so); incorporated strong cautionary language in the prospectus's discussion of risk factors; and pulled the brochure off the fund's website for revisions.

14. Karen Damato, "Stars Alone Don't Illuminate Performance Picture," *The Wall Street Journal,* March 22, 2002, p. C1.

15. "SEC proposes amendments to improve mutual fund ad disclosure for investors," SEC press release, www.sec.gov/news/press/2002-66.htm.

Chapter 5. Buy, Hold, or Sell?

1. Benjamin Graham, *The Intelligent Investor,* p. 4.

2. Ibid., p. 4.

3. James Glassman and Kevin Hassett argue in their *Dow 36,000: The New Strategy for*

Profiting from the Coming Rise in the Stock Market that traditional valuation models need to be reassessed. Needless to say, such words proved to be additional fuel for the fire.

4. Jeremy J. Siegel, *Stocks for the Long Run*, 2d ed., Irwin Professional, Burr Ridge, IL, 1998, p. 28.
5. "Betting On the Market," January 27, 1997. New content ©2002 PBS/WGBH, at www.pbs.org/wgbh/pages/frontline/shows/betting/pros/lynch.html.
6. The data and analysis is based on Professor Jeremy J. Siegel's *Stocks for the Long Run*.
7. Jeremy J. Siegel, *Stocks for the Long Run*, p. 26.
8. Victor Niederhoffer, *The Education of a Speculator*, John Wiley & Sons, New York, 1997, p. 176.
9. General Electric is the sole survivor among the original 12 Dow Jones Industrial stocks.
10. Benjamin Graham, *The Intelligent Investor*, Harper Business, NY, 1973, p. 96.
11. Ibid., p. 95.
12. David Gardner and Tom Gardner, *The Motley Fool Investment Guide*, p. 26.
13. John C. Bogle, *John Bogle on Investing*, p. 58.
14. Peter Lynch, *Beating the Street*, p. 36.
15. John C. Bogle, *John Bogle on Investing*, p. 30.
16. Victor Niederhoffer, *The Education of a Speculator*, p. 301.
17. "Folks Who Like to Buy a Stock and Forget It Face Rude Awakening," *The Wall Street Journal*, February 7, 2001.
18. Benjamin Graham, *The Intelligent Investor*, p. 106.
19. Gary Jacobson and John Hillkirk published a book titled *Xerox: American Samurai* in 1986 chronicling Xerox's success against Japanese competition.
20. Benjamin Graham, *The Intelligent Investor*, p. 106.
21. Robert Metz and George Stasen, *"It's a Sure Thing,"* p. 181.
22. Ibid., p. 177.
23. Ibid., p. 183.
24. Gerald M. Loeb, *The Battle for Investment Survival*, Simon & Schuster, New York, 1965, p. 52.
25. "Personal Finance," *The Wall Street Journal*, January 29, 2001. Based on efficient market theory, the odds of the market rising or declining at any point in time is 50 percent. Accurately predicting each inflection 10 consecutive times can be expressed as ½ to the 10th power.
26. Source: Morningstar Principia Pro.

Chapter 6. Asset Allocation

1. Alec Ellinger, *The Art of Investment*, p. 79.
2. Roger G. Ibbotson and Gary P. Brinson, *Global Investing*, p. 58. This discussion draws from work by Gary P. Brinson, Brian D. Singer, and Gilbert L. Beebower,

"Determinants of Portfolio Performance II: An Update," *Financial Analysts Journal* 47, no. 3, 1991, pp. 40–48.

3. Alec Ellinger, *The Art of Investment*, p. 79.

4. 401(k) CheckUp: Best Practices in the Measurement and Disclosure of Risk in 401(k) Plans is a freely available to all; a copy can be downloaded at www.401k .riskmetrics.com/index.html.

5. Charles Schwab, *Charles Schwab's Guide to Financial Independence*, p. 72.

Chapter 7. Diversification

1. Jonathan Clemens, "Learning Lessons from Market Losses," *The Wall Street Journal*, December 5, 2000, p. C1.

2. This exercise of jelly beans is simply a reflection of the law of large numbers introduced by statistician Jakob Bernoulli in the seventeenth century. According to Peter Bernstein in *Against the Gods: The Remarkable Story of Risk*, the law of large numbers suggests that "the average of a large number of throws will be more likely than the average of a small number of throws to differ from the true mean by less than some stated amount." As Bernstein points out, the law of large numbers should clearly be distinguished from the law of averages.

3. Empirical studies have shown that under extreme market conditions, correlation among stocks tends to rise. Recently, this type of behavior was most prevalent during the global financial crisis in 1998. A study by RiskMetrics (Fingers, Malz) concludes that this is in fact the case. (Jongwoo Kim and Christopher C. Finger, "A Stress Test to Incorporate Breakdown," *Journal of Risk*, vol. 2, no. 3, spring 2000, pp. 5–19.)

4. Peter L. Bernstein, *Against the Gods*, pp. 252–253.

5. Studies that have focused on more recent periods suggest that the optimal number is close to 50. In a working paper titled "Have Individual Stocks Become More Volatile," the group of John Campbell, Martin Lettau, Burton Malkiel, and Yexiao Xu conclude that in the period between 1986 and 1997, a portfolio of more than 50 randomly selected stocks was in fact more appropriate than 20 in capturing full diversification benefits. "The increase in idiosyncratic volatility over time has increased the number of randomly selected stocks needed to achieve complete portfolio diversification." A slew of reasons are offered to explain why "idiosyncratic" or individual stock volatility has increased since the mid-1980s. Whether this trend will continue or revert to more "normal" levels is difficult to determine. Irrespective of how volatility shifts in the near term, the underlying message is that complete diversification requires more than a handful of stocks. The number may be greater than 50, but 50 still significantly reduces nonsystematic risk. Readers should note that the difference in risk between holding 50 stocks in the latest period (1986–1997) versus holding 50 stocks in the the other two periods examined (1963–1973 and 1974–1985) was less than 10 percent in standard deviation terms.

6. This analysis can easily be extended to a global portfolio. The results are strik-

ingly similar in that diversification benefits slow after the fiftieth stock. Introducing international assets can further cut the total risk of a portfolio, but perhaps not to the extent once believed. A team of analysts at Merrill Lynch has recently concluded that correlation among global markets has increased recently, reducing some of the benefits of holding global assets as a hedge. (Jonathan Fuerbringer, "Hedging Your Bets? Look Homeward Investor!" *The New York Times,* February 4, 2001, p. 5.)

7. This analysis stems from research by Modigliani and Pogue, which is referenced in Burton Malkiel's *A Random Walk Down Wall Street.* However, we have supplemented our analysis with RiskGrades instead of the traditional measure of risk, standard deviation.

8. Peter Lynch, in Peter J. Tanous, *Investment Gurus,* p. 116.

Chapter 8. Risk Tolerance

1. Burton G. Malkiel, *A Random Walk Down Wall Street,* p. 200.
2. David F. Swensen, *Pioneering Portfolio Management,* p. 54.
3. Paraphrase of Peter Bernstein comes from his book, *Capital Ideas.*
4. Lee Clifford, "Getting Over the Hump Before You're Over the Hill," *Fortune,* August 14, 2000, p. 26.
5. Ibid., p. 28–29.
6. The RiskGrade on a U.S. Treasury 30-year bond was about twice that of the 10-year note in January 2001.
7. Rex Sinquefield, from Peter J. Tanous's *Investment Gurus.*
8. David F. Swensen, *Pioneering Portfolio Management,* p. 107.
9. Gerald M. Loeb, *The Battle for Investment Survival,* John Wiley & Sons, NY, 1996, p. 130.
10. Ibid., p. 17.
11. David F. Swensen, *Pioneering Portfolio Management,* p. 60.
12. What separates this rigorous statistical approach from a more basic exercise is that the predictability of future returns can be more accurately captured. This is because simulations use historic patterns as an indication of prospective returns.
13. As the risk-free rate continually fluctuates, we have taken a short-term average. However, this could be reset to reflect what each individual could currently receive in the market. At time of writing, the risk-free short-term rate was closer to 4.5 percent.

Chapter 9. Developing Your Portfolio's True Picture of Risk

1. From Morgan Stanley Capital International (www.msi.com). The Global Industry Classification Standard (GICS) was developed by and is the exclusive property and a service mark of Morgan Stanley Capital International Inc. (MSCI) and Standard &

Poor's, a division of The McGraw-Hill Companies, Inc. (S&P) and is licensed for use by [licensee]. Neither MSCI, S&P, nor any other party involved in making or compiling the GICS or any GICS classifications makes any expressed or implied warranties or representations with respect to such standard or classification (or the results to be obtained by the use thereof), and all such parties hereby expressly disclaim all warranties of originality, accuracy, completeness, merchantability, or fitness for a particular purpose with respect to any such standard or classification. Without limiting any of the foregoing, in no event shall MSCI, S&P, any of their affiliates, or any third party involved in making or compiling the GICS or any GICS classifications have any liability for any direct, indirect, special, punitive, consequential or any other damages (including lost profits) even if notified of the possibility of such damages.

Chapter 11. The Final Frontier

1. Berkshire Hathaway 2001 Annual Report.

Index